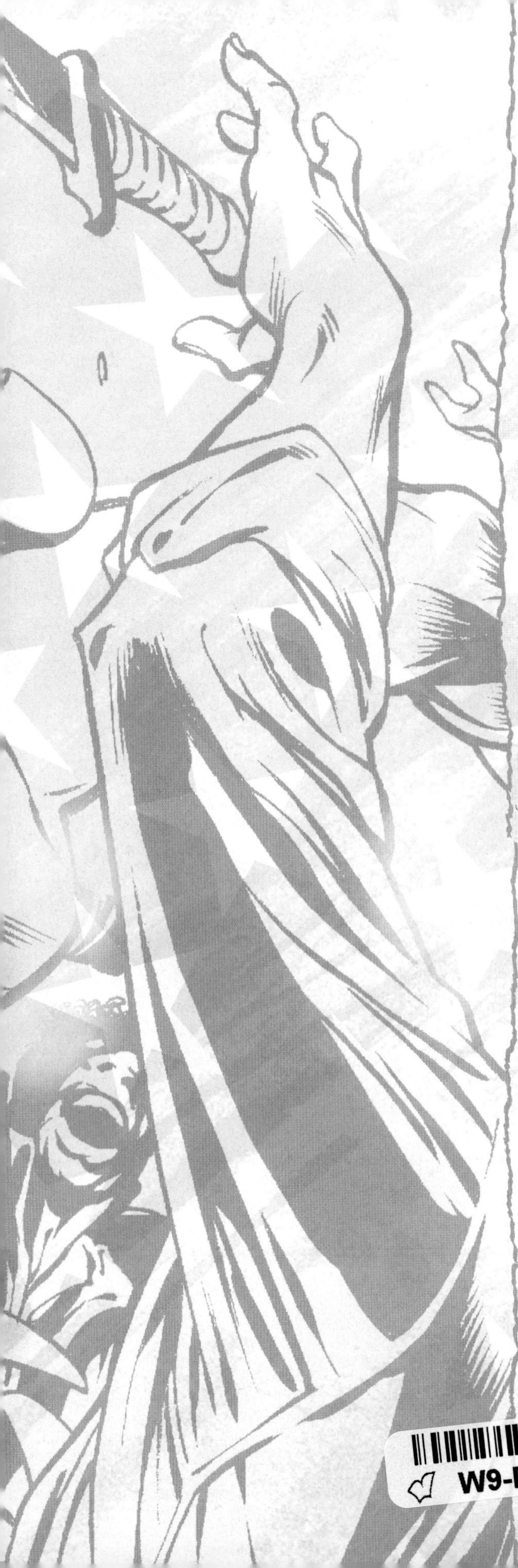

WRITER
ED BRUBAKER

PENCILER
ALAN DAVIS

INKER
MARK FARMER

COLORIST
LAURA MARTIN
WITH **LARRY MOLINAR** (#7)

LETTERER
VC'S JOE CARAMAGNA

COVER ART
ALAN DAVIS,
MARK FARMER &
LAURA MARTIN

ASSISTANT EDITOR
JOHN DENNING

ASSOCIATE EDITOR
LAUREN SANKOVITCH

EDITOR
TOM BREVOORT

CAPTAIN AMERICA CREATED BY
JOE SIMON & JACK KIRBY

COLLECTION EDITOR
JENNIFER GRÜNWALD
ASSISTANT EDITORS
ALEX STARBUCK & NELSON RIBEIRO
EDITOR, SPECIAL PROJECTS
MARK D. BEAZLEY
SENIOR EDITOR, SPECIAL PROJECTS
JEFF YOUNGQUIST
SENIOR VICE PRESIDENT OF SALES
DAVID GABRIEL
SVP OF BRAND PLANNING & COMMUNICATIONS
MICHAEL PASCIULLO
BOOK DESIGN
JEFF POWELL

EDITOR IN CHIEF
AXEL ALONSO
CREATIVE OFFICER
JOE QUESADA
PUBLISHER
DAN BUCKLEY
EXECUTIVE PRODUCER
ALAN FINE

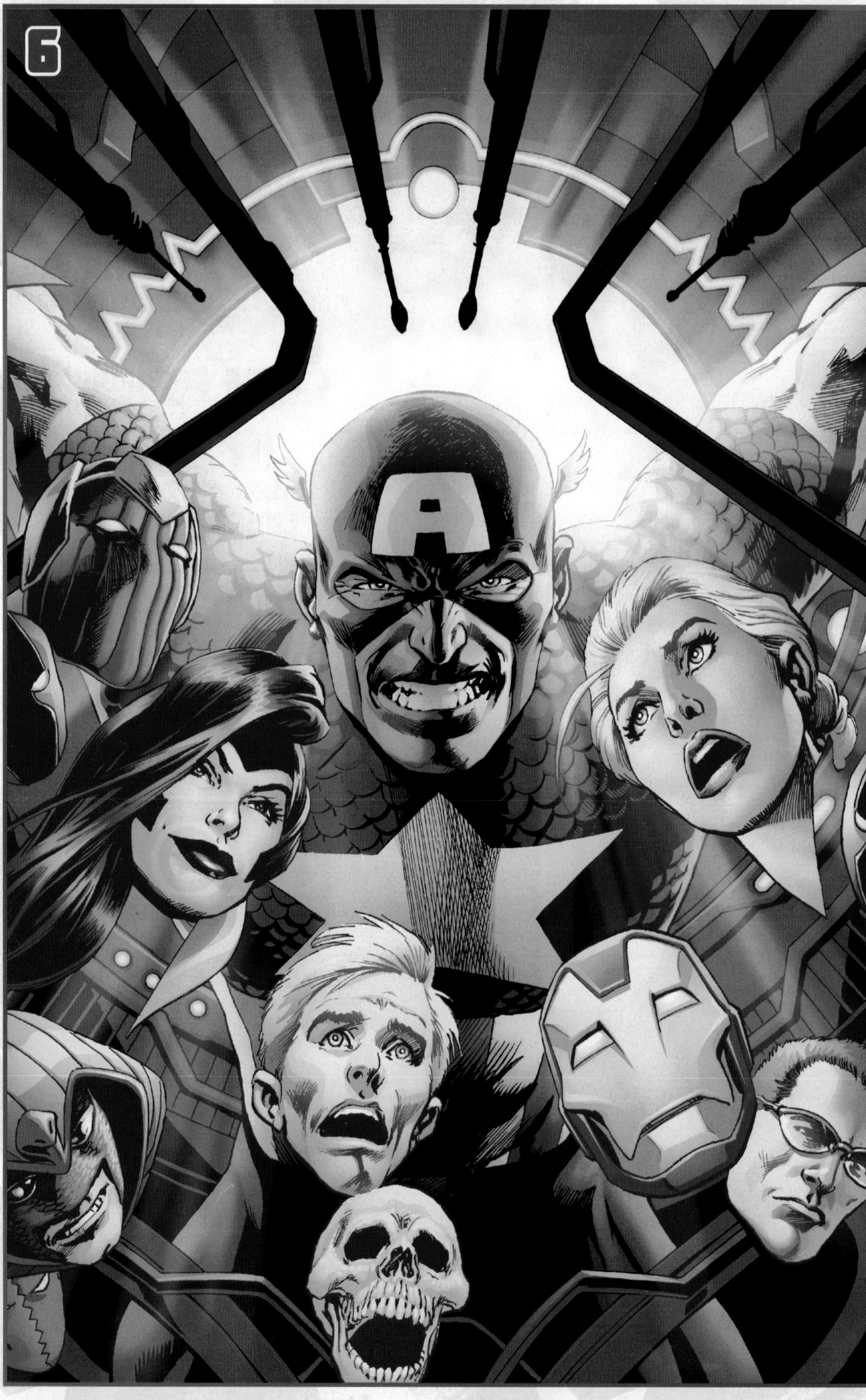
6

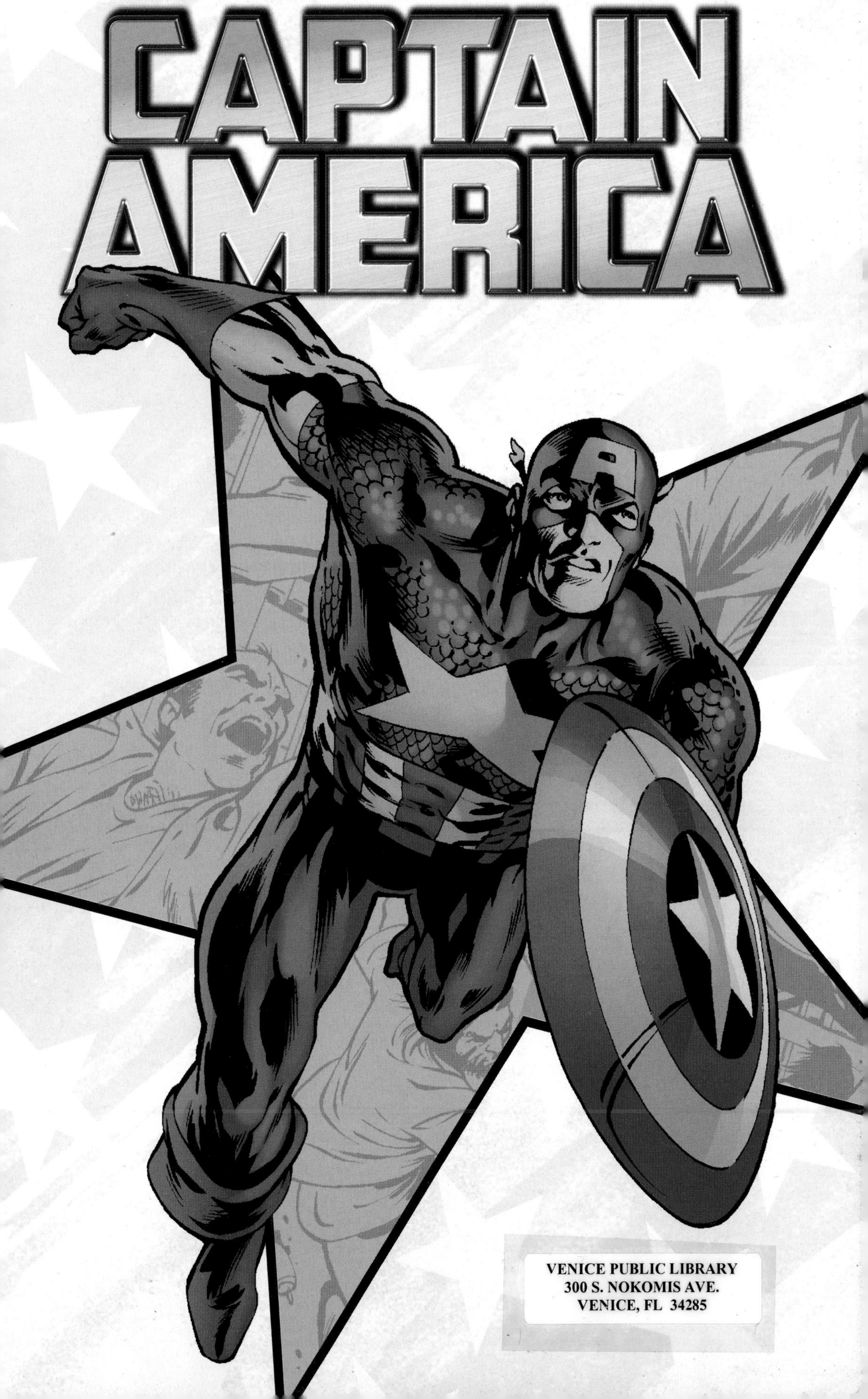
CAPTAIN
AMERICA

IN 1944, WHILE PURSUING MEMBERS OF THE TERRORIST ORGANIZATION HYDRA, AN ALLIED OPERATIVE KNOWN AS CODENAME BRAVO WAS LOST IN AN EXTRA-DIMENSIONAL DREAM WORLD, THE LAND OF NOWHERE. IN THE PRESENT, BRAVO HAS RETURNED HOME AND IS IN LEAGUE WITH A NEWER AND DEADLIER BRANCH OF HYDRA, LED BY HIS WIFE, THE QUEEN HYDRA. AFTER CAPTAIN AMERICA FOILED THEIR PLAN TO REMOLD THE ENTIRE WORLD USING THE LAND OF NOWHERE, BRAVO WAS INCARCERATED WHILE THE QUEEN REMAINED AT LARGE, BIDING HER TIME WITH HER BURGEONING TERROR CELL. DESPITE HIS VICTORY OVER BRAVO, STEVE ROGERS WASN'T RESTING EASY. IN FACT, HIS DREAMS ALMOST SEEMED...REAL.

CAPTAIN AMERICA

CAPTAIN AMERICA BY ED BRUBAKER VOL. 2. Contains material originally published in magazine form as CAPTAIN AMERICA #6-10. First printing 2012. Hardcover ISBN# 978-0-7851-5710-6. Softcover ISBN# 978-0-7851-5711-3. Published by MARVEL WORLDWIDE, INC., a subsidiary of MARVEL ENTERTAINMENT, LLC. OFFICE OF PUBLICATION: 135 West 50th Street, New York, NY 10020. Copyright © 2011 and 2012 Marvel Characters, Inc. All rights reserved. Hardcover: $19.99 per copy in the U.S. and $21.99 in Canada (GST #R127032852). Softcover: $16.99 per copy in the U.S. and $18.99 in Canada (GST #R127032852). Canadian Agreement #40668537. All characters featured in this issue and the distinctive names and likenesses thereof, and all related indicia are trademarks of Marvel Characters, Inc. No similarity between any of the names, characters, persons, and/or institutions in this magazine with those of any living or dead person or institution is intended, and any such similarity which may exist is purely coincidental. **Printed in the U.S.A.** ALAN FINE, EVP - Office of the President, Marvel Worldwide, Inc. and EVP & CMO Marvel Characters B.V.; DAN BUCKLEY, Publisher & President - Print, Animation & Digital Divisions; JOE QUESADA, Chief Creative Officer; TOM BREVOORT, SVP of Publishing; DAVID BOGART, SVP of Operations & Procurement, Publishing; RUWAN JAYATILLEKE, SVP & Associate Publisher, Publishing; C.B. CEBULSKI, SVP of Creator & Content Development; DAVID GABRIEL, SVP of Publishing Sales & Circulation; MICHAEL PASCIULLO, SVP of Brand Planning & Communications; JIM O'KEEFE, VP of Operations & Logistics; DAN CARR, Executive Director of Publishing Technology; SUSAN CRESPI, Editorial Operations Manager; ALEX MORALES, Publishing Operations Manager; STAN LEE, Chairman Emeritus. For information regarding advertising in Marvel Comics or on Marvel.com, please contact John Dokes, SVP Integrated Sales and Marketing, at jdokes@marvel.com. For Marvel subscription inquiries, please call 800-217-9158. **Manufactured between 3/26/2012 and 11/28/2012 (hardcover), and 3/26/2012 and 11/26/2012 (softcover), by R.R. DONNELLEY, INC., SALEM, VA, USA.**

10 9 8 7 6 5 4 3 2 1

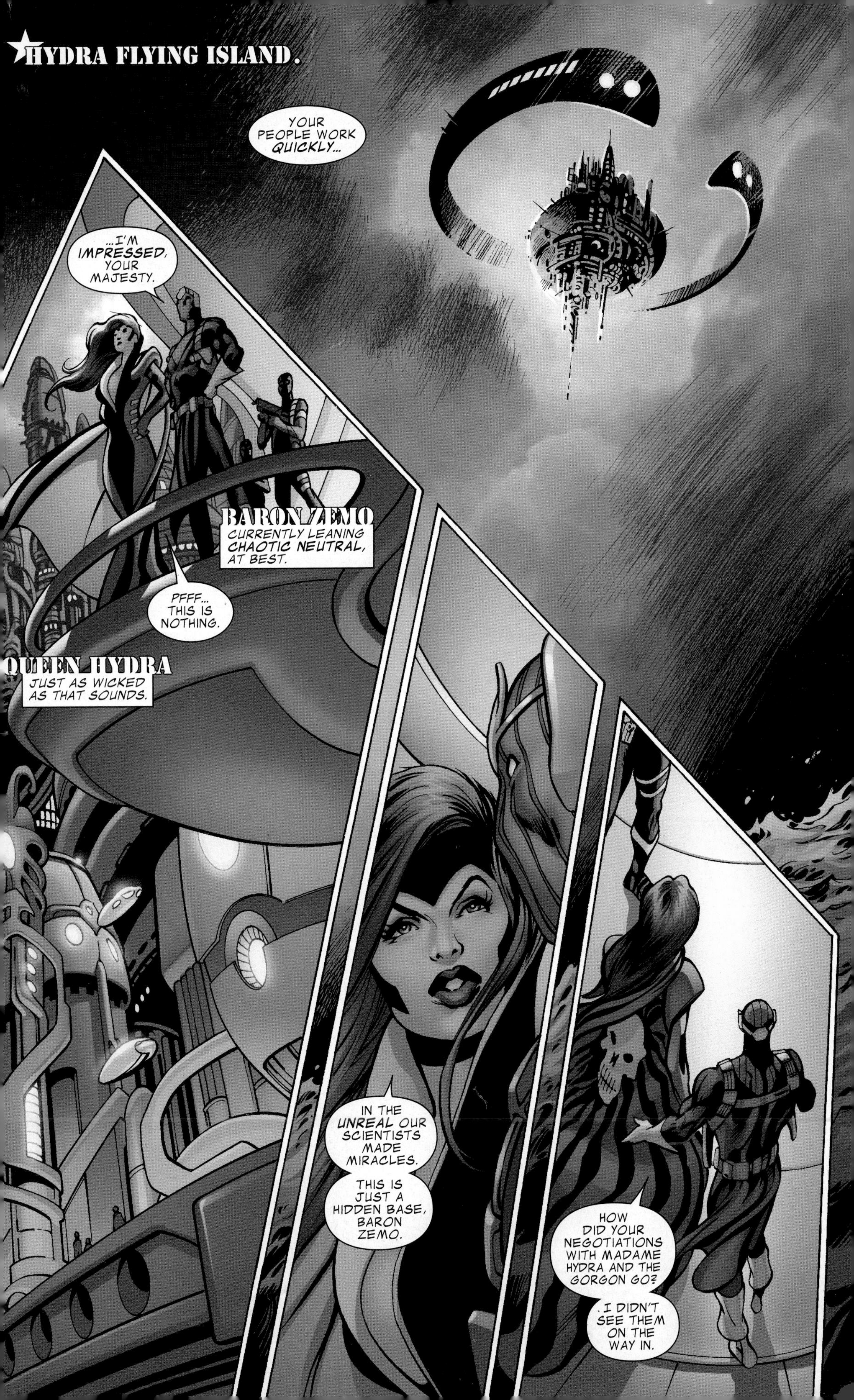
HYDRA FLYING ISLAND.
YOUR PEOPLE WORK QUICKLY...
...I'M IMPRESSED, YOUR MAJESTY.
BARON ZEMO CURRENTLY LEANING CHAOTIC NEUTRAL, AT BEST.
PFFF... THIS IS NOTHING.
QUEEN HYDRA JUST AS WICKED AS THAT SOUNDS.
IN THE UNREAL OUR SCIENTISTS MADE MIRACLES.
THIS IS JUST A HIDDEN BASE, BARON ZEMO.
HOW DID YOUR NEGOTIATIONS WITH MADAME HYDRA AND THE GORGON GO?
I DIDN'T SEE THEM ON THE WAY IN.

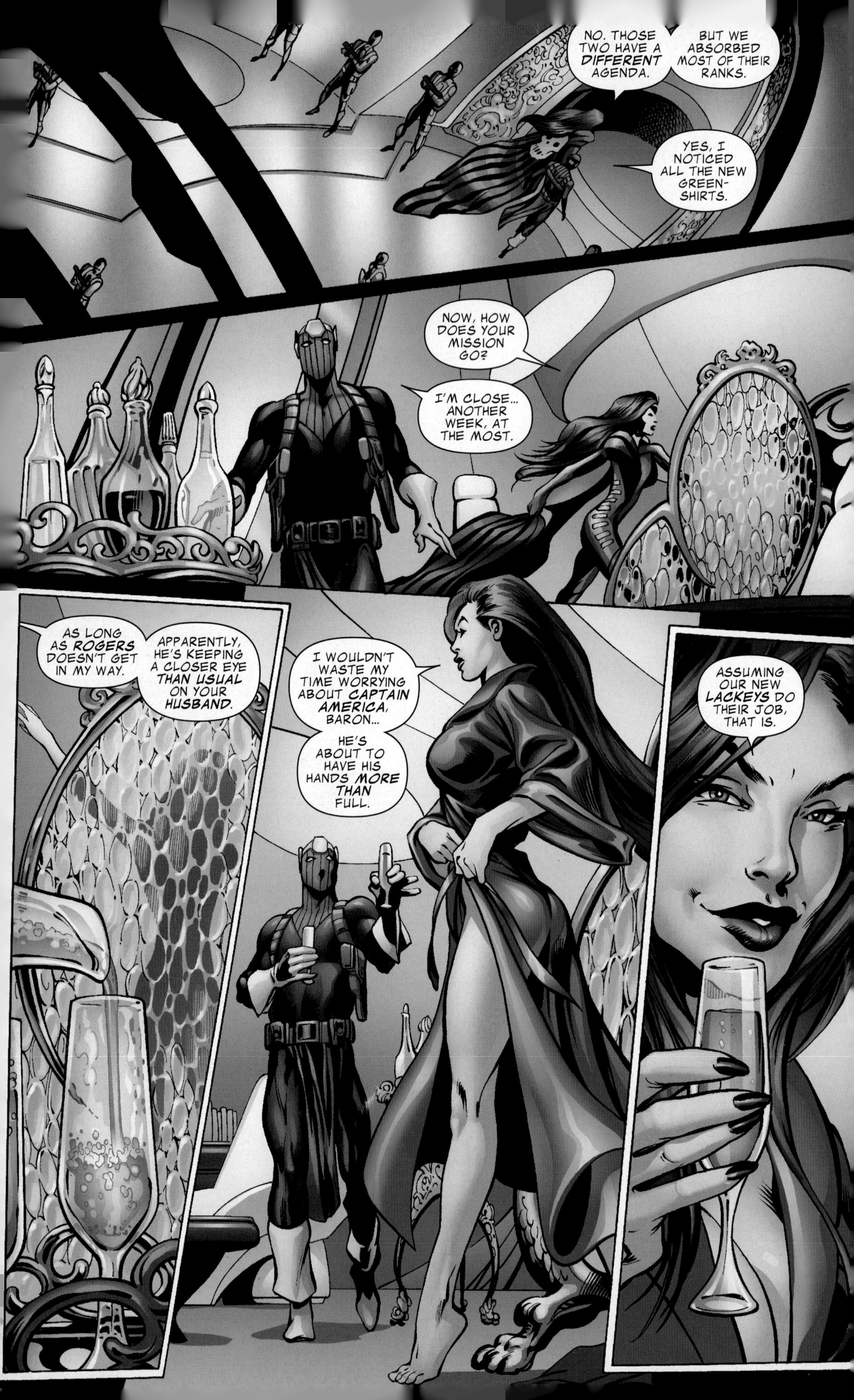
NO. THOSE TWO HAVE A DIFFERENT AGENDA.
BUT WE ABSORBED MOST OF THEIR RANKS.
YES, I NOTICED ALL THE NEW GREEN-SHIRTS.
NOW, HOW DOES YOUR MISSION GO?
I'M CLOSE... ANOTHER WEEK, AT THE MOST.
AS LONG AS ROGERS DOESN'T GET IN MY WAY.
APPARENTLY, HE'S KEEPING A CLOSER EYE THAN USUAL ON YOUR HUSBAND.
I WOULDN'T WASTE MY TIME WORRYING ABOUT CAPTAIN AMERICA, BARON...
HE'S ABOUT TO HAVE HIS HANDS MORE THAN FULL.
ASSUMING OUR NEW LACKEYS DO THEIR JOB, THAT IS.

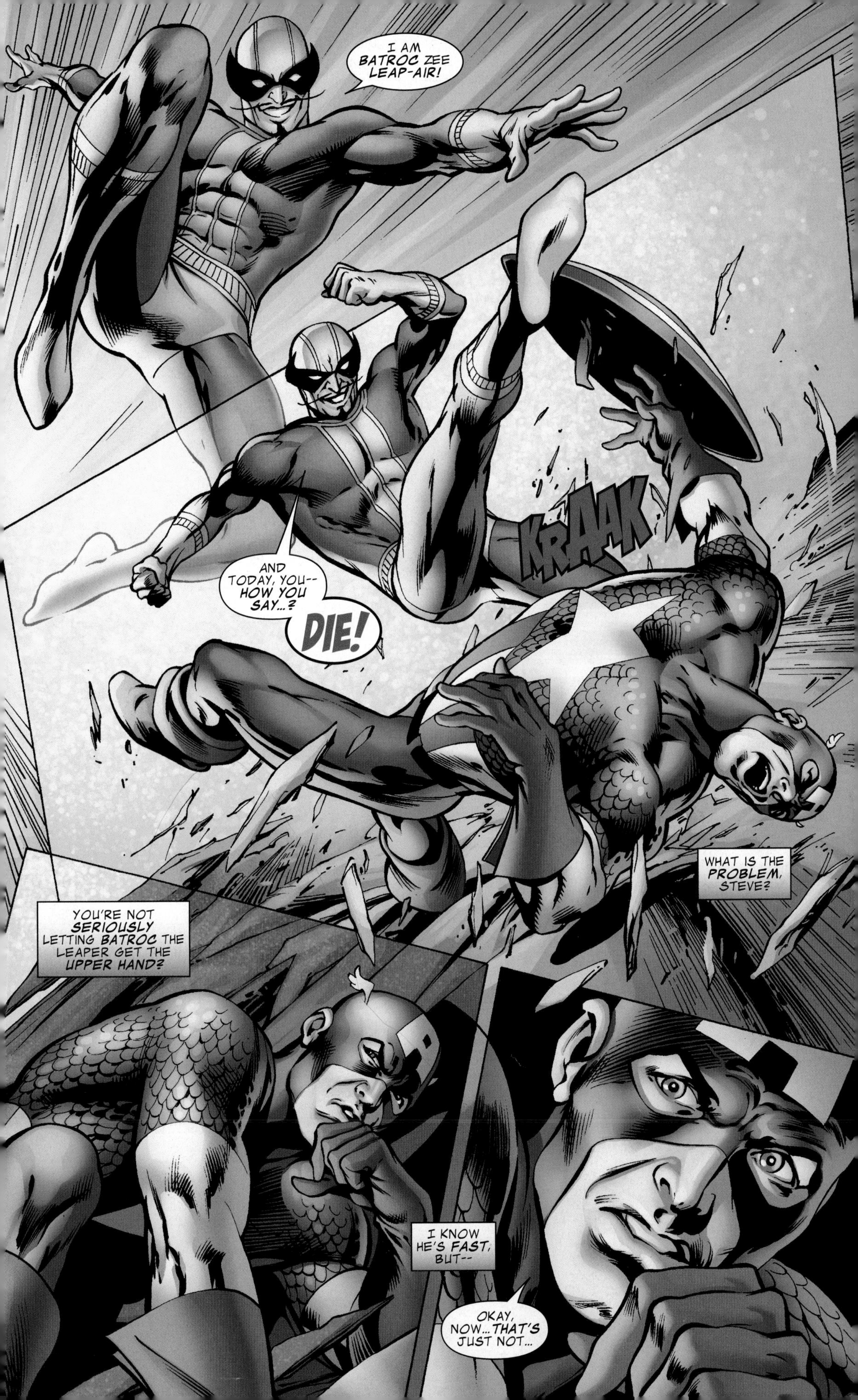
I AM BATROC ZEE LEAP-AIR!
AND TODAY, YOU-- HOW YOU SAY...? DIE!
KRAAK
YOU'RE NOT SERIOUSLY LETTING BATROC THE LEAPER GET THE UPPER HAND?
WHAT IS THE PROBLEM, STEVE?
I KNOW HE'S FAST, BUT--
OKAY, NOW...THAT'S JUST NOT...

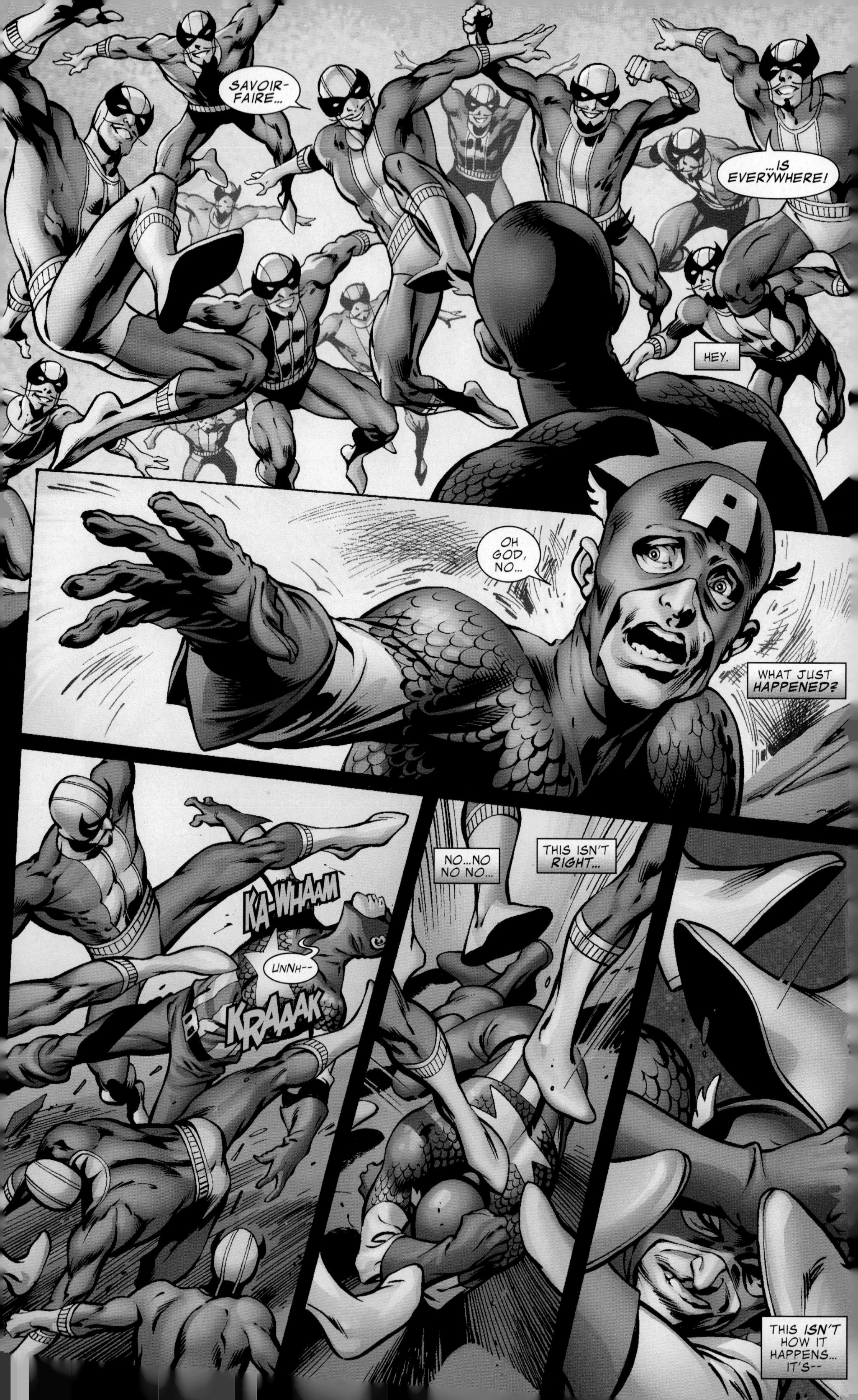
SAVOIR-FAIRE...
...IS EVERYWHERE!
HEY.
OH GOD, NO...
WHAT JUST HAPPENED?
KA-WHAAM
UNNH--
KRAAAK
NO...NO NO NO...
THIS ISN'T RIGHT...
THIS ISN'T HOW IT HAPPENS... IT'S--

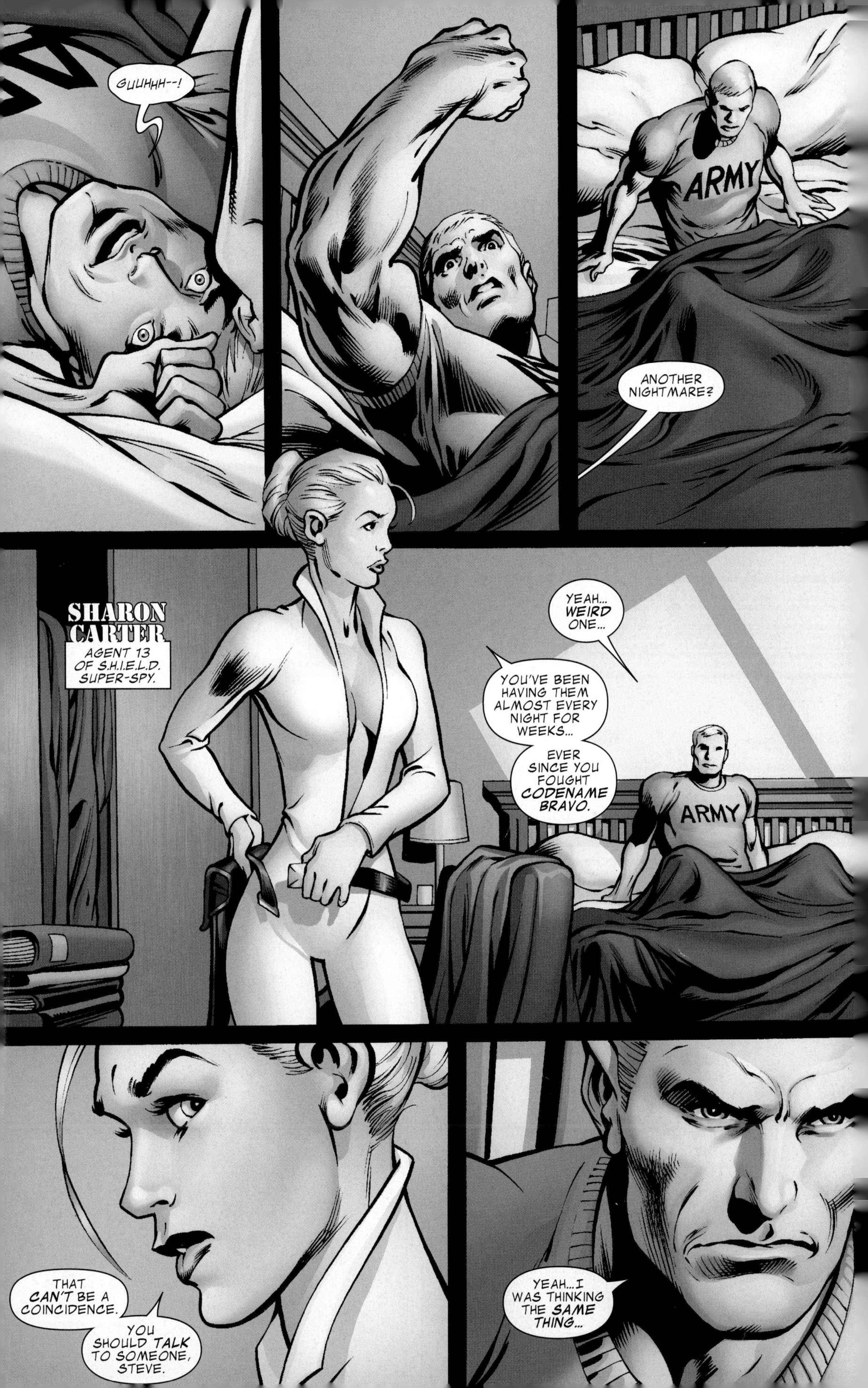
GUUHHH--!
ANOTHER NIGHTMARE?
SHARON CARTER
AGENT 13 OF S.H.I.E.L.D. SUPER-SPY.
YEAH... WEIRD ONE...
YOU'VE BEEN HAVING THEM ALMOST EVERY NIGHT FOR WEEKS...
EVER SINCE YOU FOUGHT CODENAME BRAVO.
ARMY
THAT CAN'T BE A COINCIDENCE.
YOU SHOULD TALK TO SOMEONE, STEVE.
YEAH...I WAS THINKING THE SAME THING...

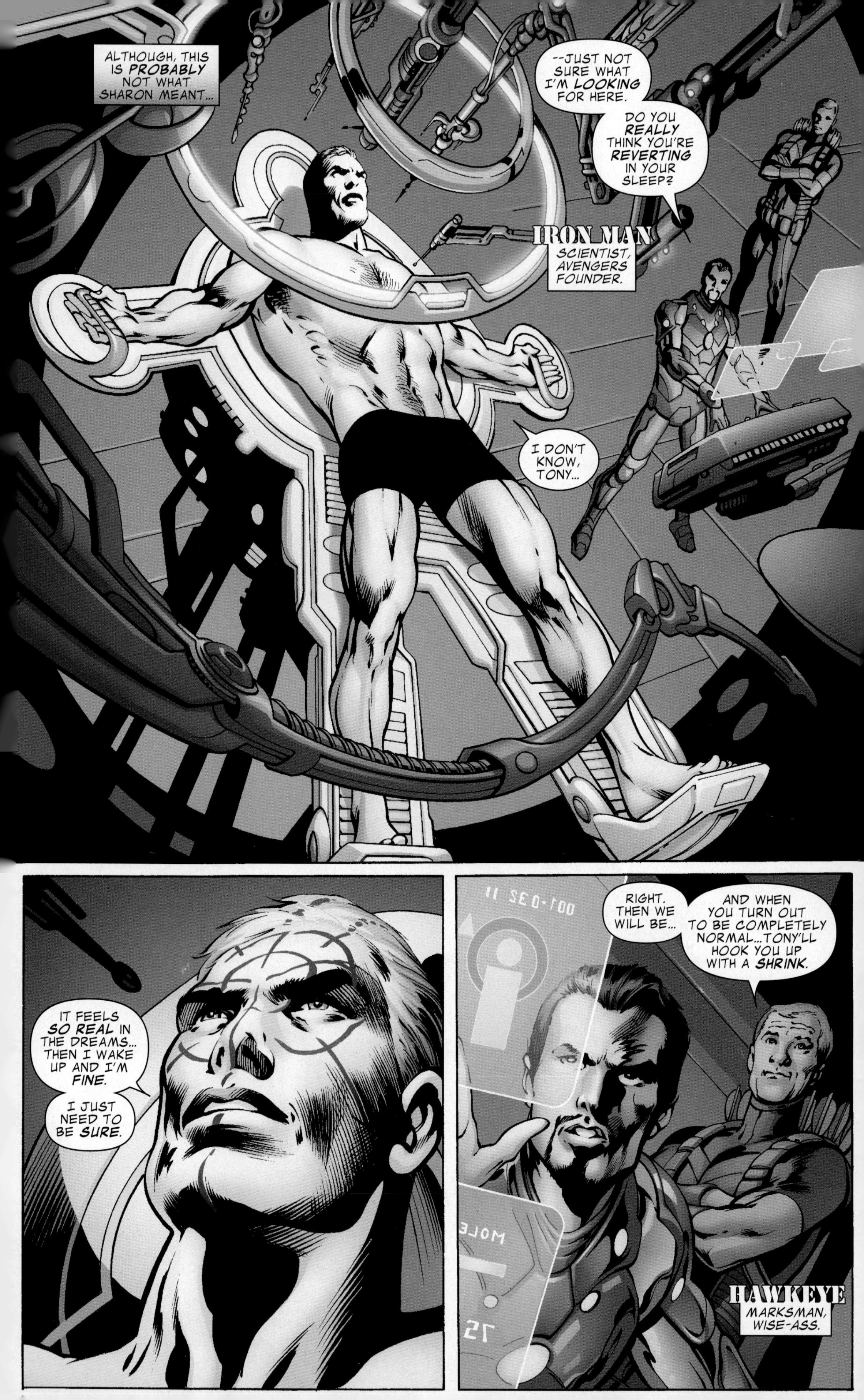

ALTHOUGH, THIS IS PROBABLY NOT WHAT SHARON MEANT...
--JUST NOT SURE WHAT I'M LOOKING FOR HERE.
DO YOU REALLY THINK YOU'RE REVERTING IN YOUR SLEEP?
IRON MAN
SCIENTIST, AVENGERS FOUNDER.
I DON'T KNOW, TONY...
IT FEELS SO REAL IN THE DREAMS... THEN I WAKE UP AND I'M FINE.
I JUST NEED TO BE SURE.
RIGHT. THEN WE WILL BE...
AND WHEN YOU TURN OUT TO BE COMPLETELY NORMAL...TONY'LL HOOK YOU UP WITH A SHRINK.
HAWKEYE
MARKSMAN, WISE-ASS.

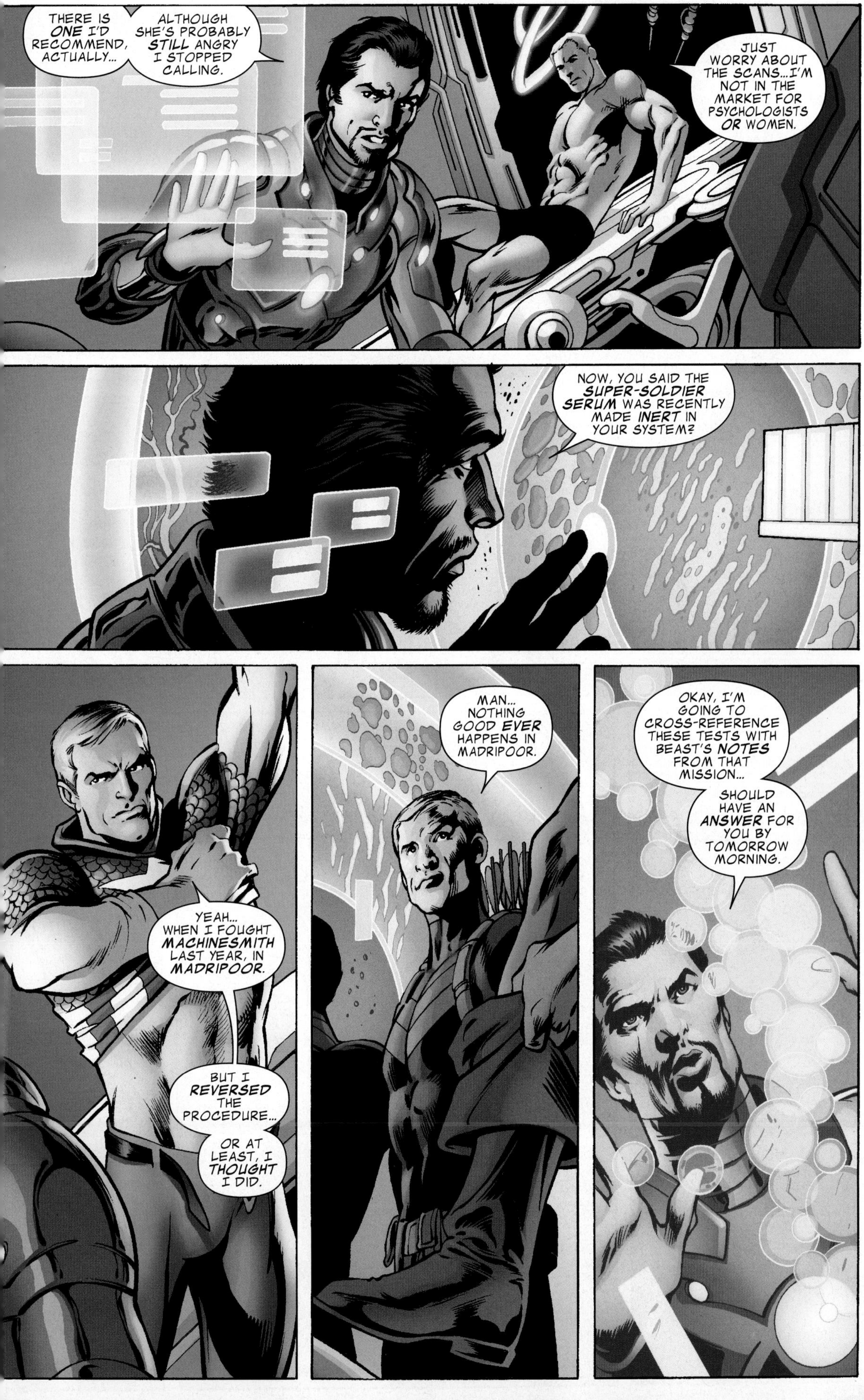
THERE IS ONE I'D RECOMMEND, ACTUALLY...
ALTHOUGH SHE'S PROBABLY STILL ANGRY I STOPPED CALLING.
JUST WORRY ABOUT THE SCANS...I'M NOT IN THE MARKET FOR PSYCHOLOGISTS OR WOMEN.
NOW, YOU SAID THE SUPER-SOLDIER SERUM WAS RECENTLY MADE INERT IN YOUR SYSTEM?
YEAH... WHEN I FOUGHT MACHINESMITH LAST YEAR, IN MADRIPOOR.
BUT I REVERSED THE PROCEDURE...
OR AT LEAST, I THOUGHT I DID.
MAN... NOTHING GOOD EVER HAPPENS IN MADRIPOOR.
OKAY, I'M GOING TO CROSS-REFERENCE THESE TESTS WITH BEAST'S NOTES FROM THAT MISSION...
SHOULD HAVE AN ANSWER FOR YOU BY TOMORROW MORNING.

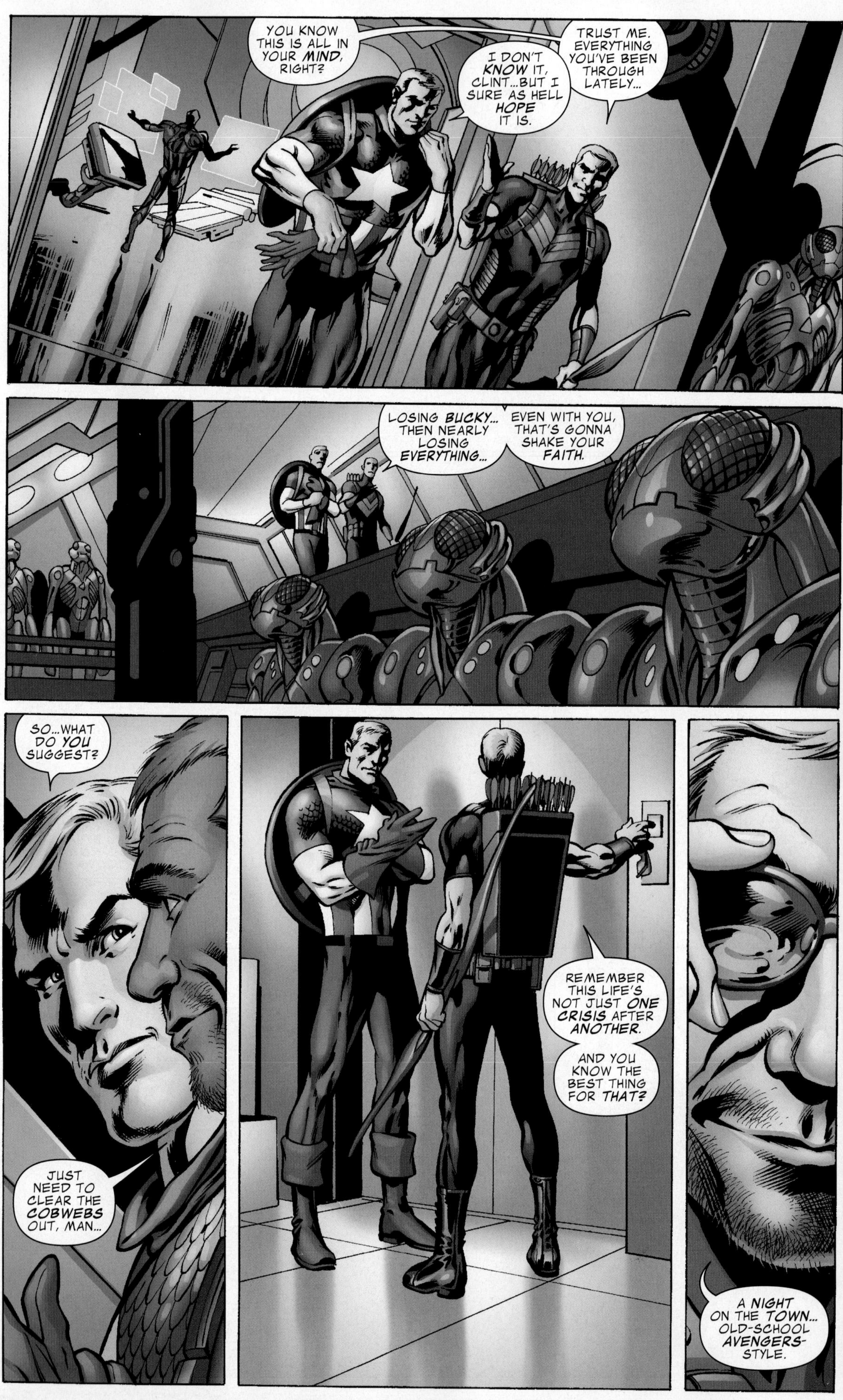

YOU KNOW THIS IS ALL IN YOUR MIND, RIGHT?
I DON'T KNOW IT, CLINT...BUT I SURE AS HELL HOPE IT IS.
TRUST ME. EVERYTHING YOU'VE BEEN THROUGH LATELY...
LOSING BUCKY... THEN NEARLY LOSING EVERYTHING...
EVEN WITH YOU, THAT'S GONNA SHAKE YOUR FAITH.
SO...WHAT DO YOU SUGGEST?
JUST NEED TO CLEAR THE COBWEBS OUT, MAN...
REMEMBER THIS LIFE'S NOT JUST ONE CRISIS AFTER ANOTHER.
AND YOU KNOW THE BEST THING FOR THAT?
A NIGHT ON THE TOWN... OLD-SCHOOL AVENGERS-STYLE.

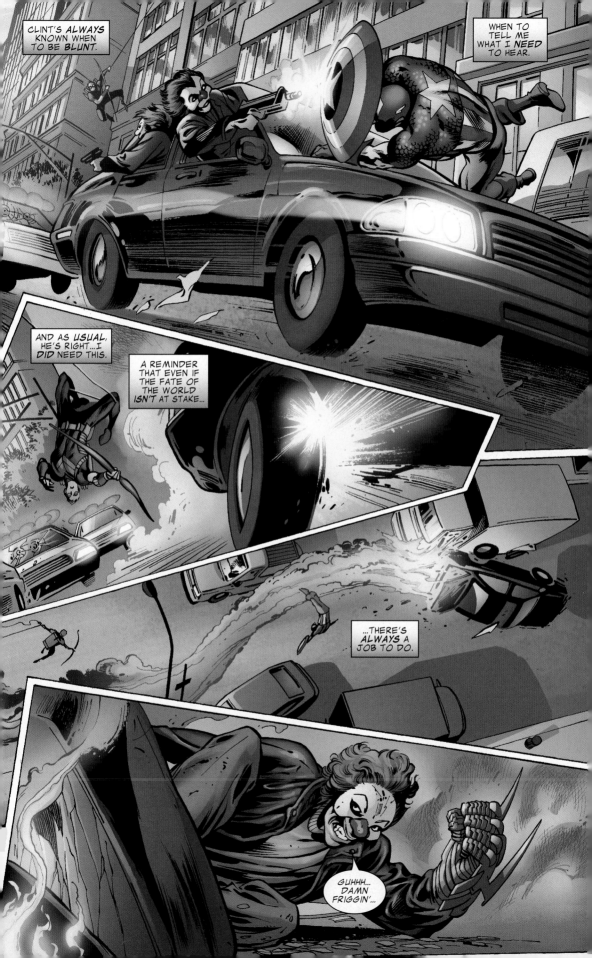

CLINT'S *ALWAYS* KNOWN WHEN TO BE *BLUNT*.

WHEN TO *TELL* ME WHAT I *NEED* TO *HEAR*.

AND AS *USUAL*, HE'S RIGHT...I *DID* NEED THIS.

A REMINDER THAT EVEN IF THE FATE OF THE WORLD ISN'T AT STAKE...

...THERE'S *ALWAYS* A JOB TO DO.

GUHHH... *DAMN* FRIGGIN'...

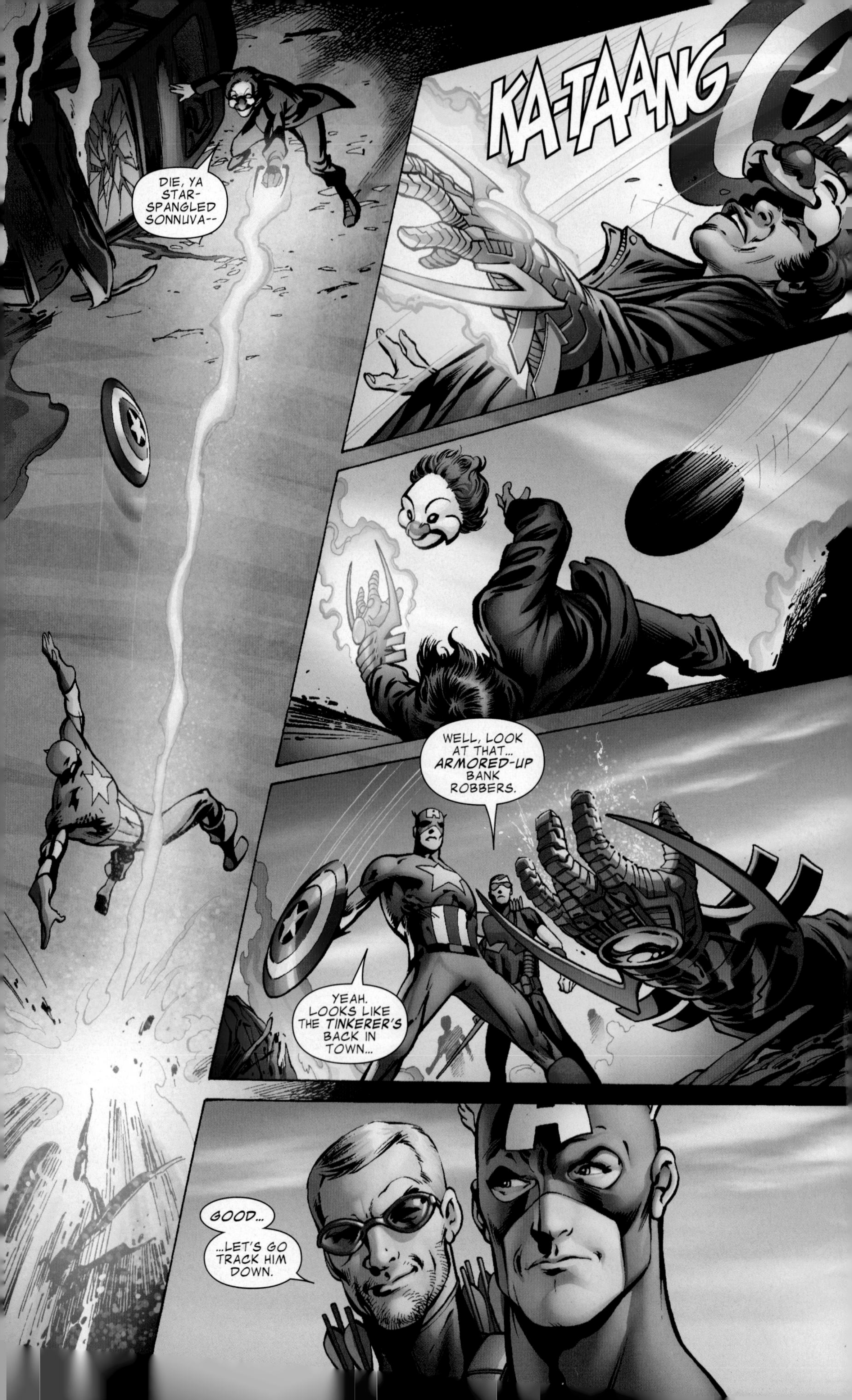
DIE, YA STAR-SPANGLED SONNUVA--
KA-TAANG
WELL, LOOK AT THAT... ARMORED-UP BANK ROBBERS.
YEAH. LOOKS LIKE THE TINKERER'S BACK IN TOWN...
GOOD...
...LET'S GO TRACK HIM DOWN.

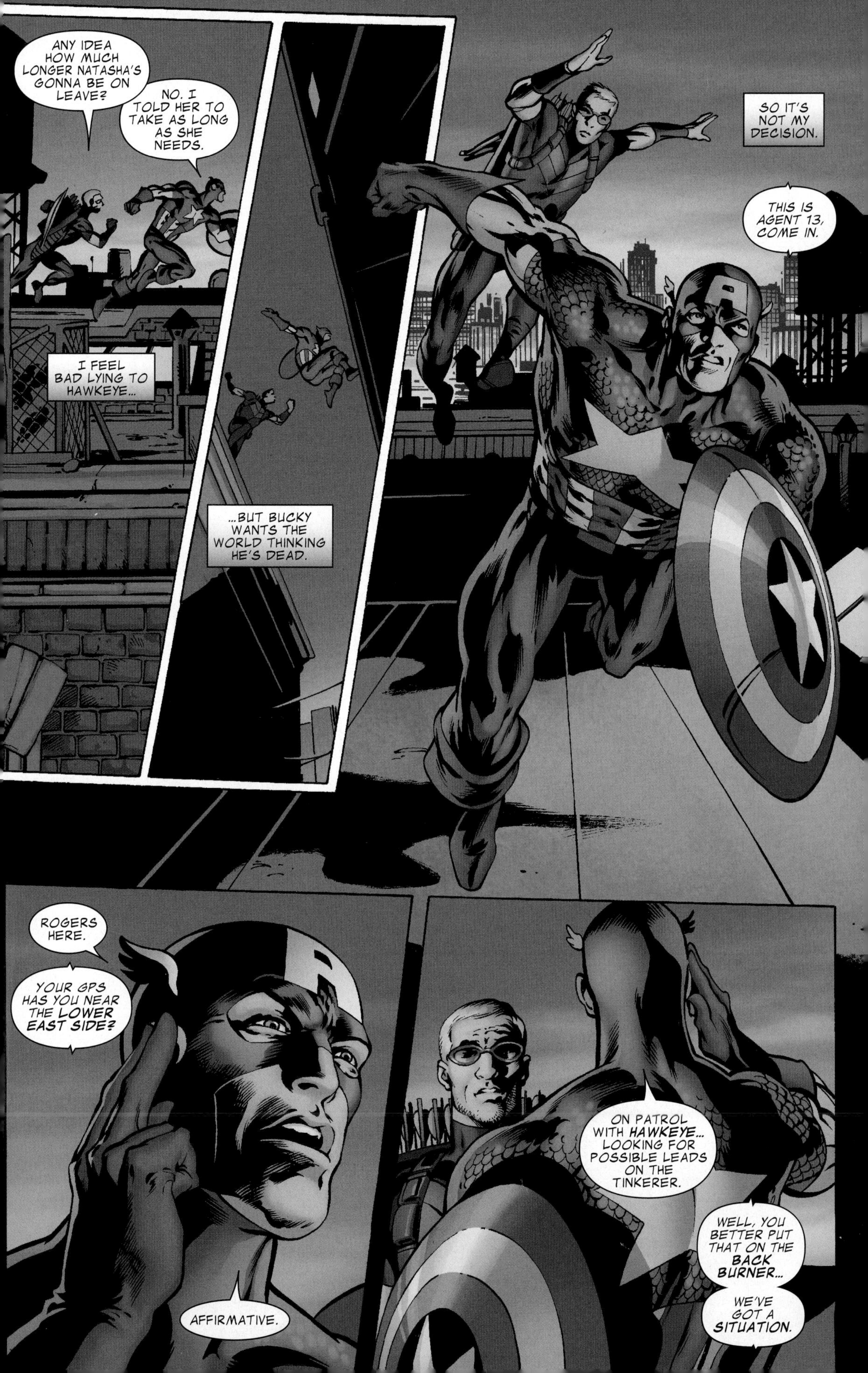
ANY IDEA HOW MUCH LONGER NATASHA'S GONNA BE ON LEAVE?
NO. I TOLD HER TO TAKE AS LONG AS SHE NEEDS.
I FEEL BAD LYING TO HAWKEYE...
...BUT BUCKY WANTS THE WORLD THINKING HE'S DEAD.
SO IT'S NOT MY DECISION.
THIS IS AGENT 13, COME IN.
ROGERS HERE.
YOUR GPS HAS YOU NEAR THE LOWER EAST SIDE?
AFFIRMATIVE.
ON PATROL WITH HAWKEYE... LOOKING FOR POSSIBLE LEADS ON THE TINKERER.
WELL, YOU BETTER PUT THAT ON THE BACK BURNER...
WE'VE GOT A SITUATION.

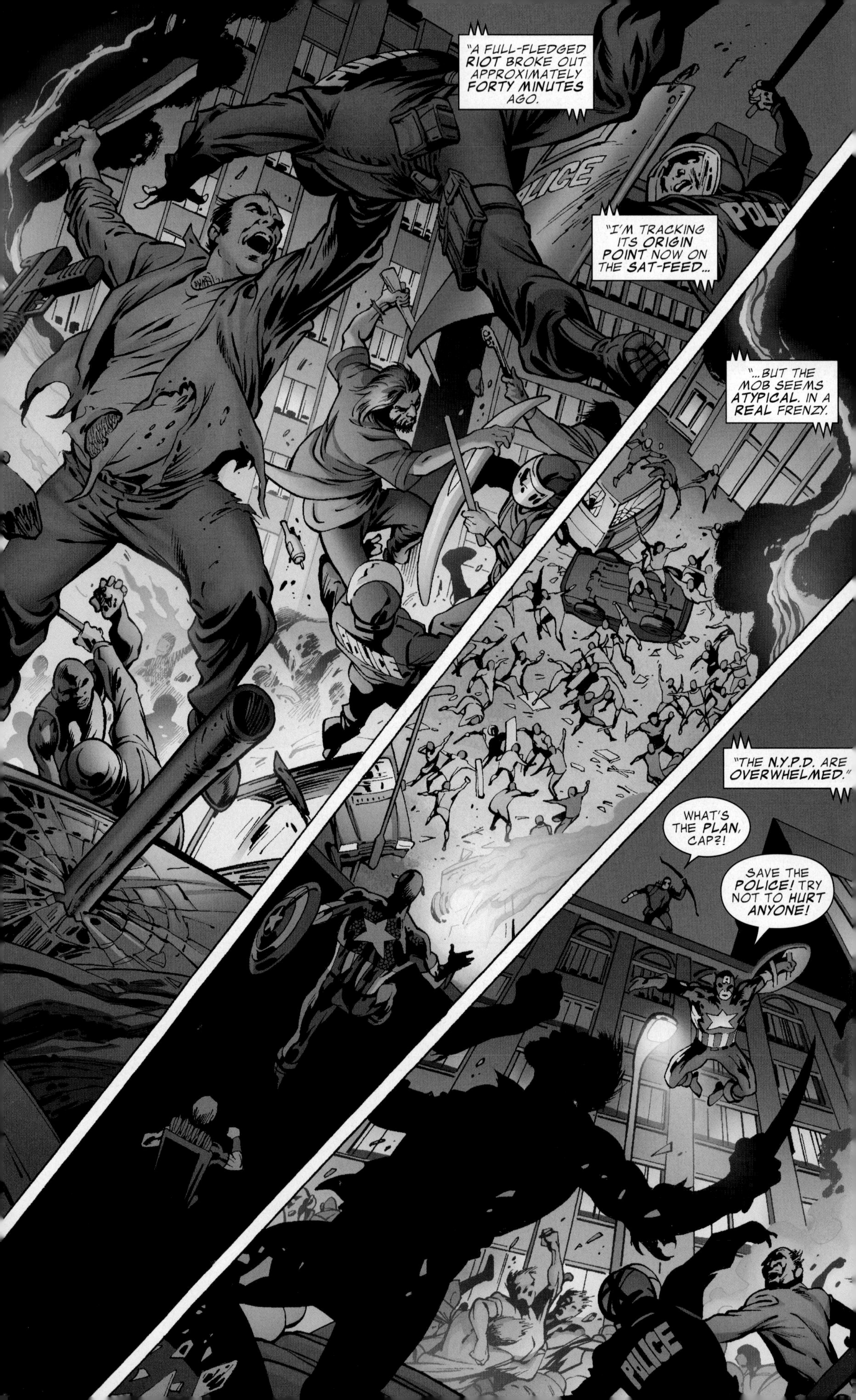
"A FULL-FLEDGED RIOT BROKE OUT APPROXIMATELY FORTY MINUTES AGO.
"I'M TRACKING ITS ORIGIN POINT NOW ON THE SAT-FEED...
"...BUT THE MOB SEEMS ATYPICAL. IN A REAL FRENZY.
"THE N.Y.P.D. ARE OVERWHELMED."
WHAT'S THE PLAN, CAP?!
SAVE THE POLICE! TRY NOT TO HURT ANYONE!

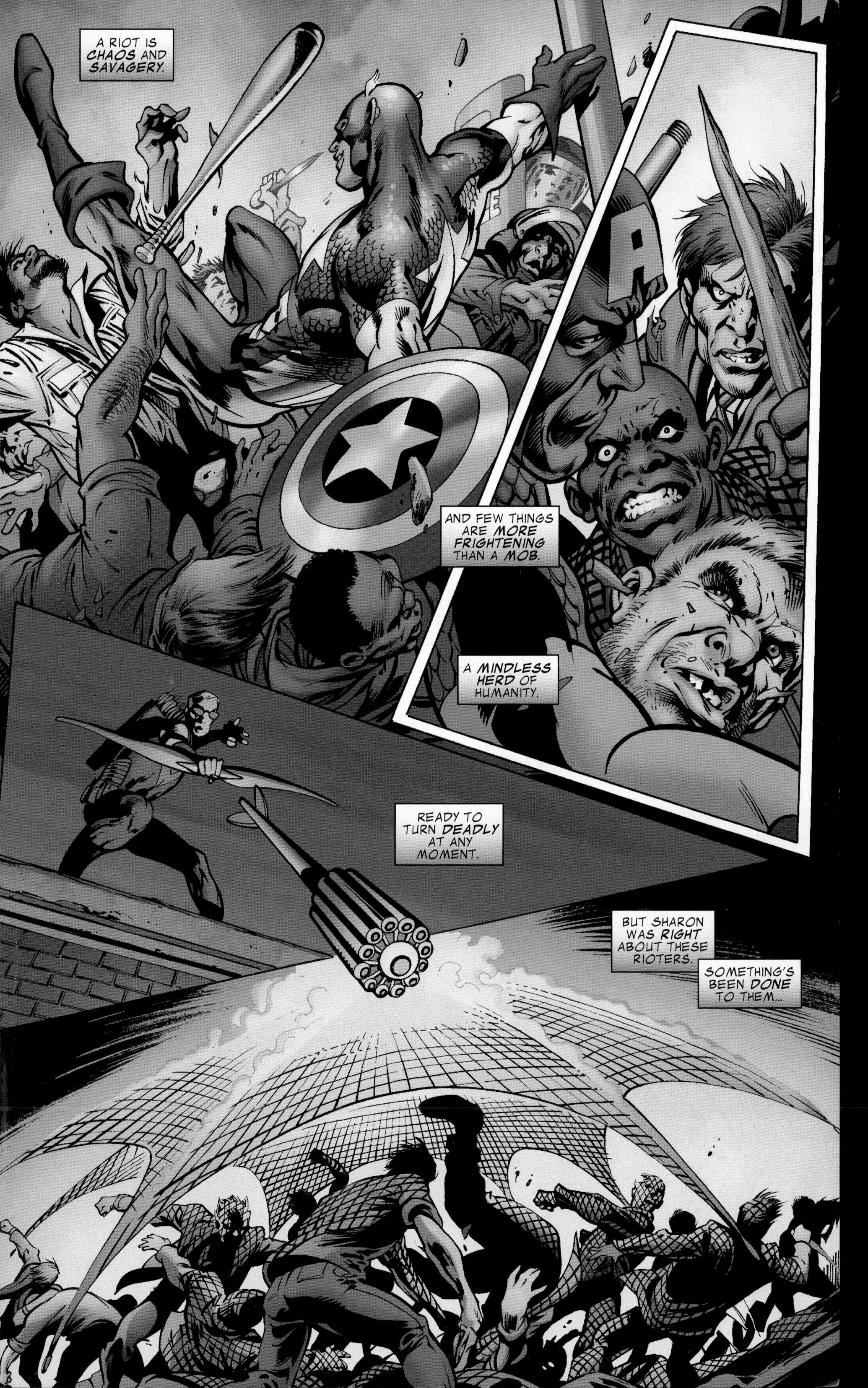
A RIOT IS CHAOS AND SAVAGERY.
AND FEW THINGS ARE MORE FRIGHTENING THAN A MOB.
A MINDLESS HERD OF HUMANITY.
READY TO TURN DEADLY AT ANY MOMENT.
BUT SHARON WAS RIGHT ABOUT THESE RIOTERS.
SOMETHING'S BEEN DONE TO THEM...

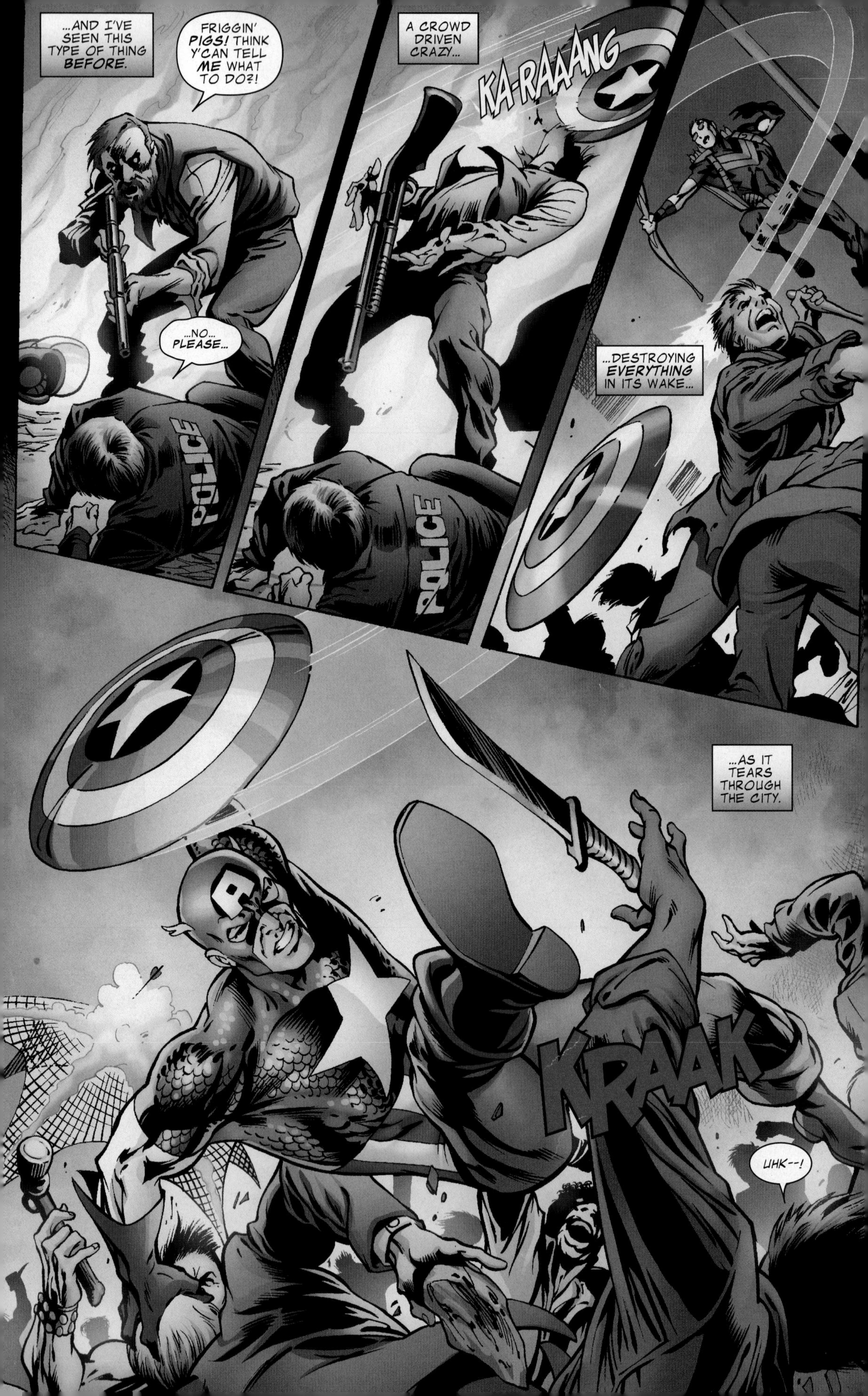

...AND I'VE SEEN THIS TYPE OF THING BEFORE.
FRIGGIN' PIGS! THINK Y'CAN TELL ME WHAT TO DO?!
...NO... PLEASE...
POLICE
A CROWD DRIVEN CRAZY...
KA-RAAANG
POLICE
...DESTROYING EVERYTHING IN ITS WAKE...
...AS IT TEARS THROUGH THE CITY.
KRAAK
UHK--!

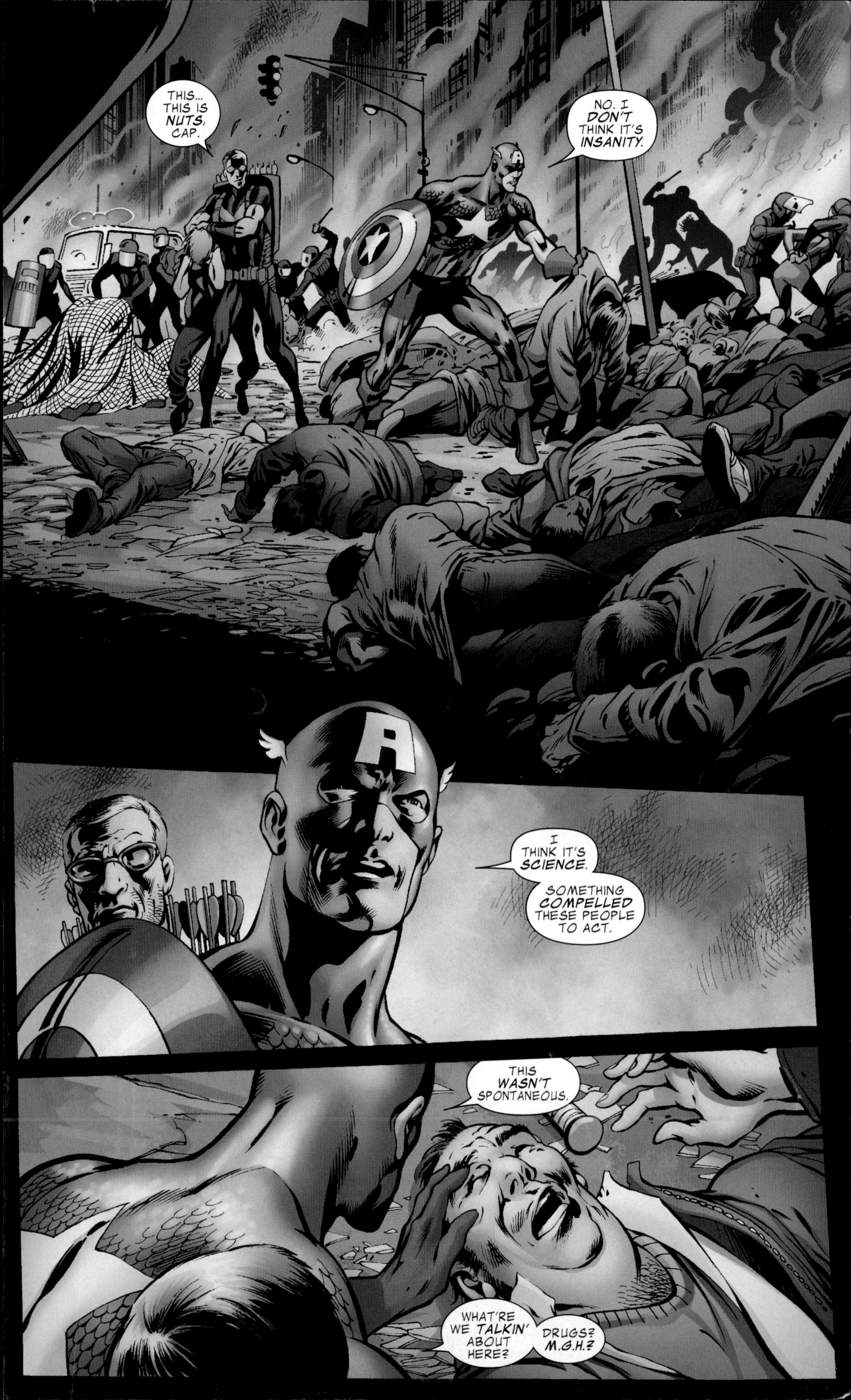
THIS... THIS IS NUTS, CAP.
NO. I DON'T THINK IT'S INSANITY.
I THINK IT'S SCIENCE.
SOMETHING COMPELLED THESE PEOPLE TO ACT.
THIS WASN'T SPONTANEOUS.
WHAT'RE WE TALKIN' ABOUT HERE?
DRUGS? M.G.H.?

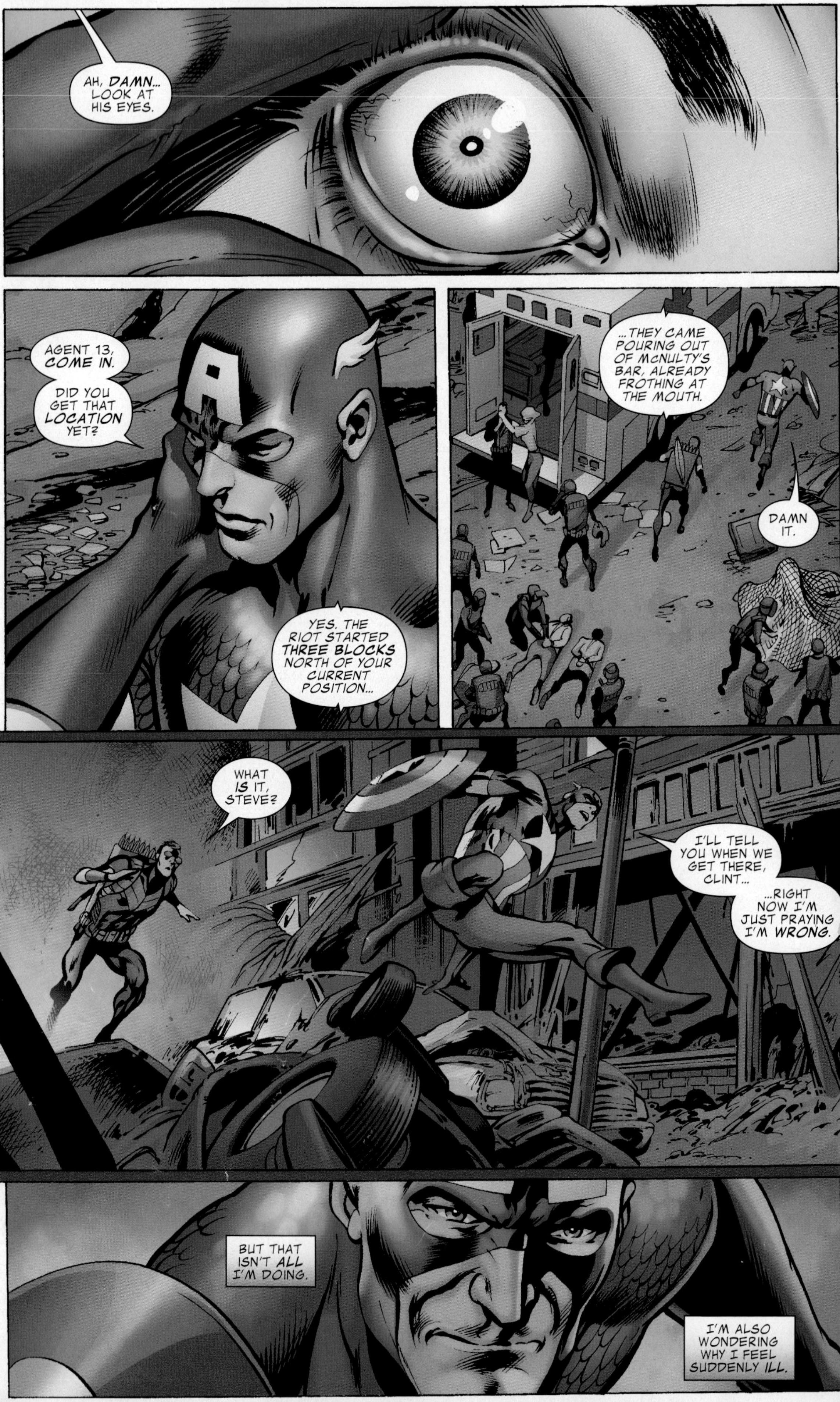
AH, DAMN... LOOK AT HIS EYES.
AGENT 13, COME IN.
DID YOU GET THAT LOCATION YET?
YES. THE RIOT STARTED THREE BLOCKS NORTH OF YOUR CURRENT POSITION...
...THEY CAME POURING OUT OF McNULTY'S BAR, ALREADY FROTHING AT THE MOUTH.
DAMN IT.
WHAT IS IT, STEVE?
I'LL TELL YOU WHEN WE GET THERE, CLINT...
...RIGHT NOW I'M JUST PRAYING I'M WRONG.
BUT THAT ISN'T ALL I'M DOING.
I'M ALSO WONDERING WHY I FEEL SUDDENLY ILL.

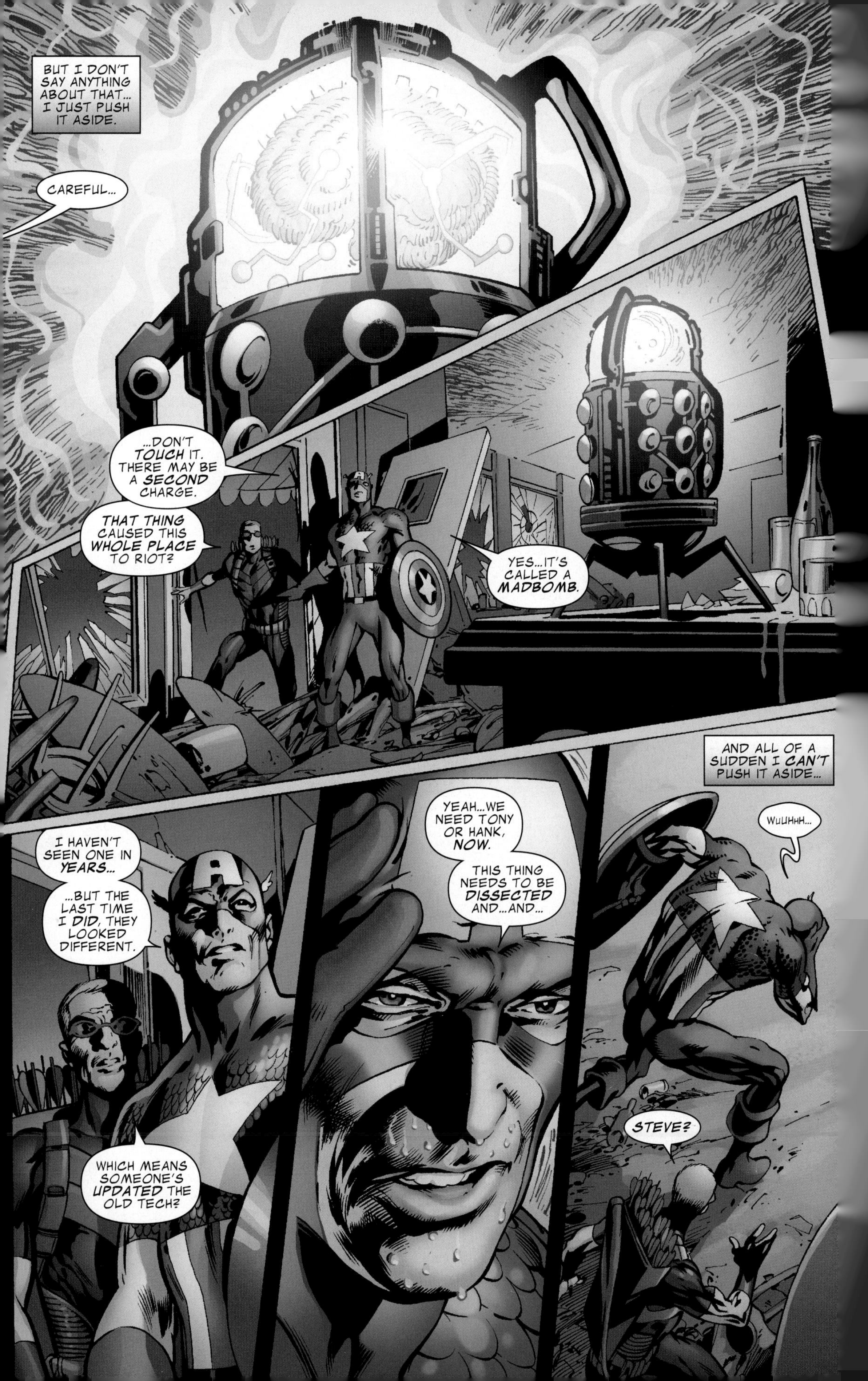
BUT I DON'T SAY ANYTHING ABOUT THAT... I JUST PUSH IT ASIDE.
CAREFUL...
...DON'T TOUCH IT. THERE MAY BE A SECOND CHARGE.
THAT THING CAUSED THIS WHOLE PLACE TO RIOT?
YES...IT'S CALLED A MADBOMB.
I HAVEN'T SEEN ONE IN YEARS...
...BUT THE LAST TIME I DID, THEY LOOKED DIFFERENT.
WHICH MEANS SOMEONE'S UPDATED THE OLD TECH?
YEAH...WE NEED TONY OR HANK, NOW.
THIS THING NEEDS TO BE DISSECTED AND...AND...
AND ALL OF A SUDDEN I CAN'T PUSH IT ASIDE...
WUUHHH...
STEVE?

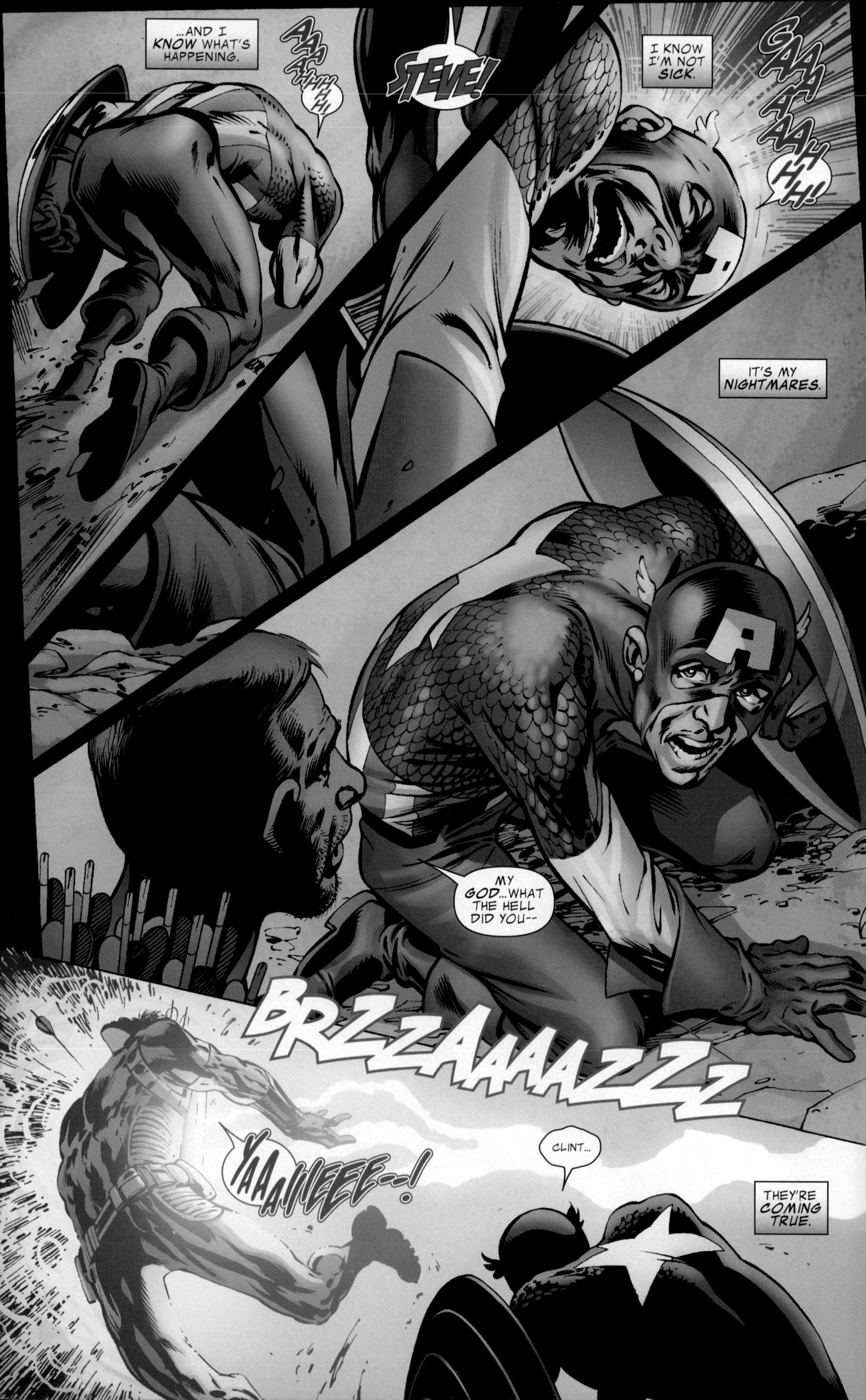
...AND I KNOW WHAT'S HAPPENING.
AAAAHHH!
STEVE!
I KNOW I'M NOT SICK.
GAAAAAAHHH!
IT'S MY NIGHTMARES.
MY GOD...WHAT THE HELL DID YOU--
BRZZAAAAAZZZ
YAAAIIEEEE--!
CLINT...
THEY'RE COMING TRUE.

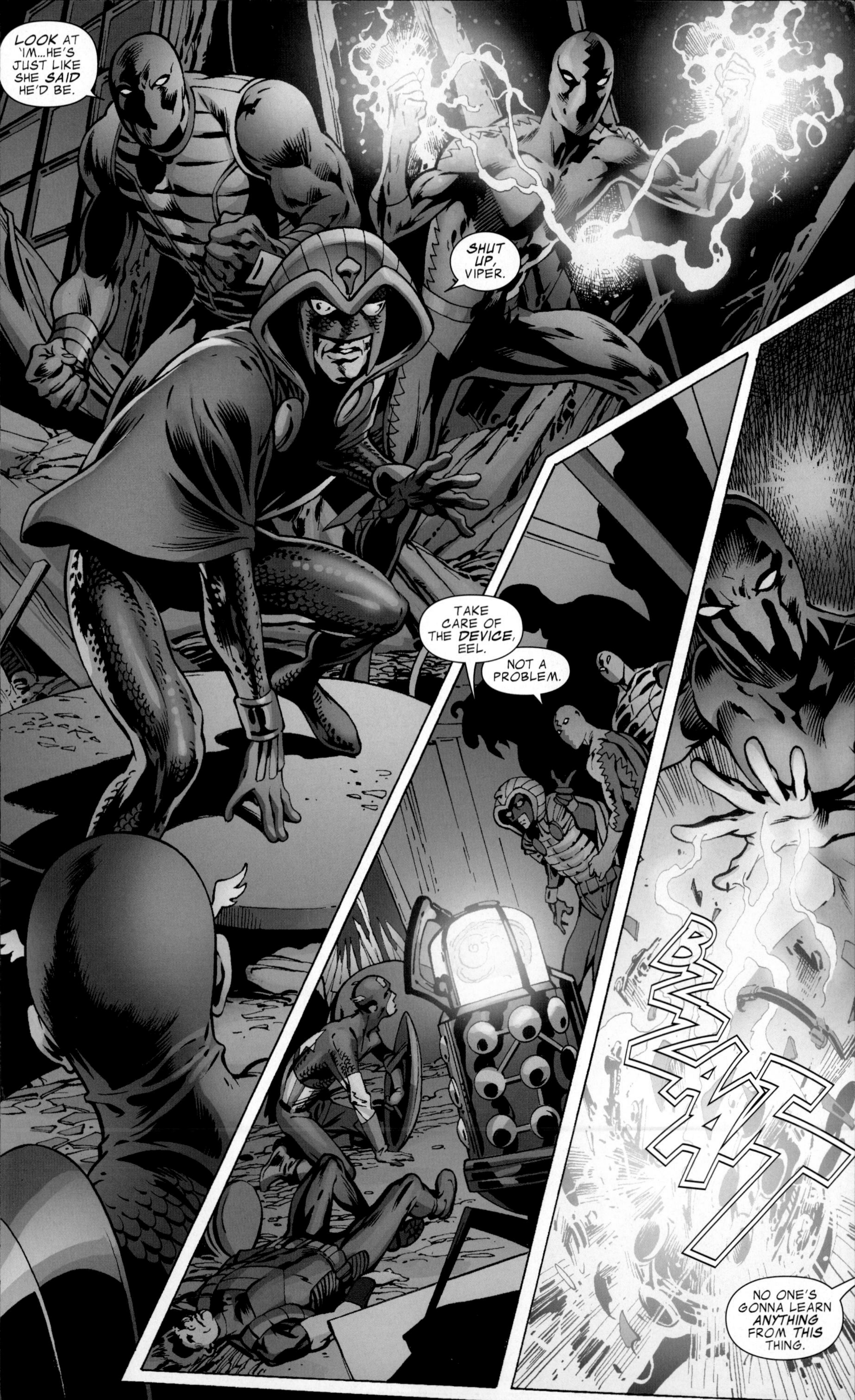
LOOK AT 'IM...HE'S JUST LIKE SHE SAID HE'D BE.
SHUT UP, VIPER.
TAKE CARE OF THE DEVICE, EEL.
NOT A PROBLEM.
BWZZAT
NO ONE'S GONNA LEARN ANYTHING FROM THIS THING.

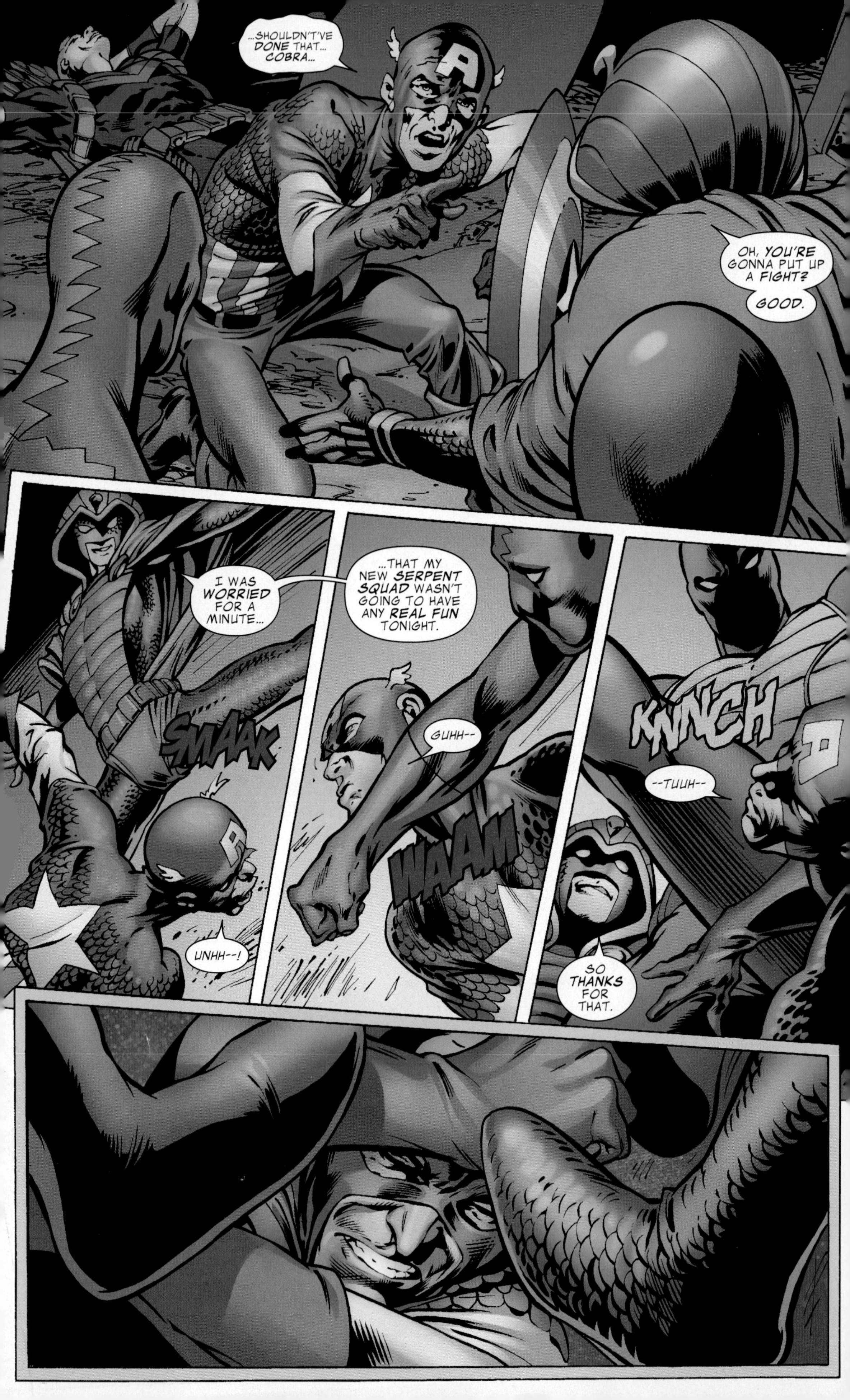
...SHOULDN'T'VE DONE THAT... COBRA...
OH, YOU'RE GONNA PUT UP A FIGHT?
GOOD.
I WAS WORRIED FOR A MINUTE...
SMAAK
UNHH--!
...THAT MY NEW SERPENT SQUAD WASN'T GOING TO HAVE ANY REAL FUN TONIGHT.
GUHH--
WAAM
KNNCH
--TUUH--
SO THANKS FOR THAT.

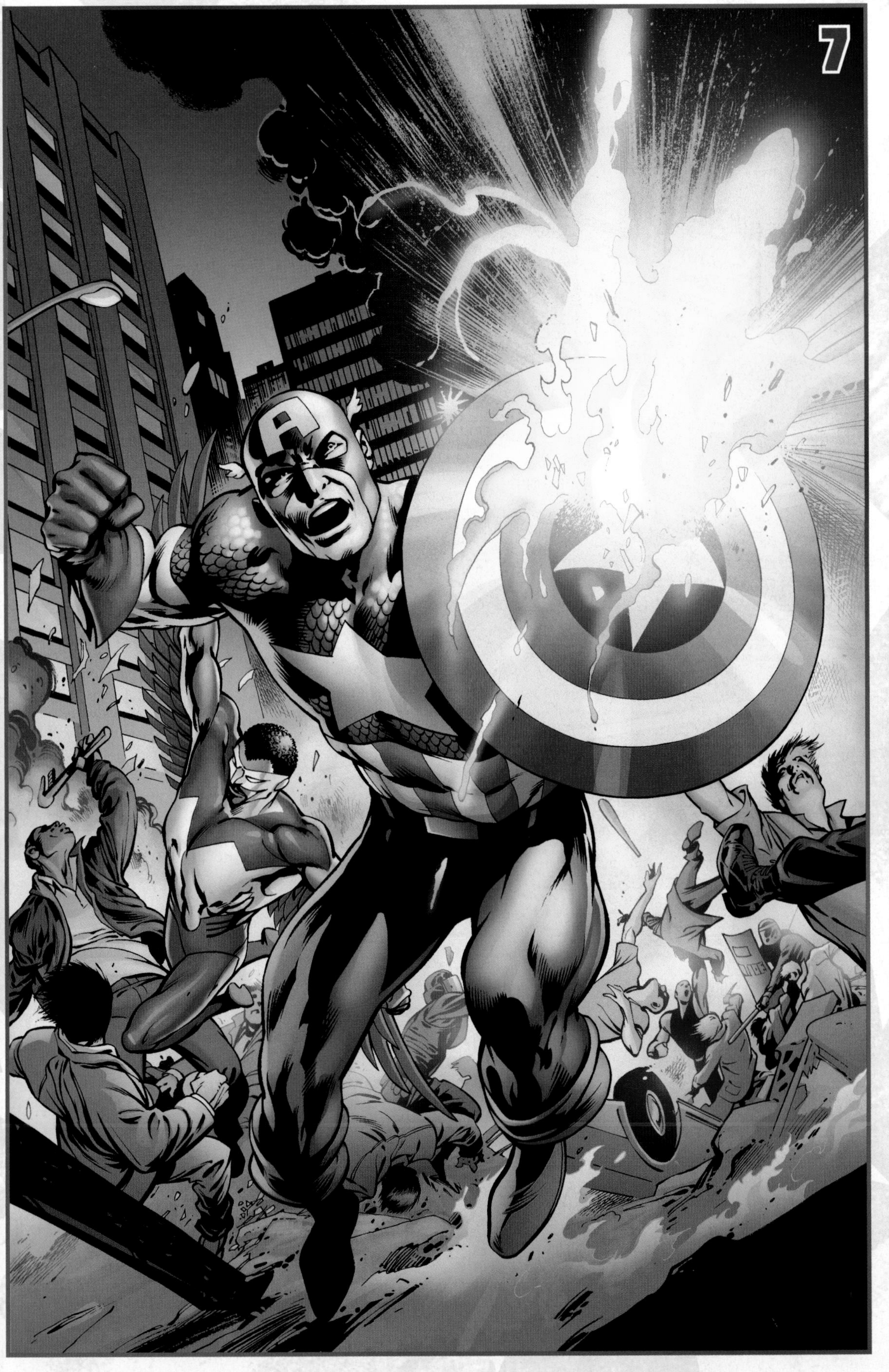
7

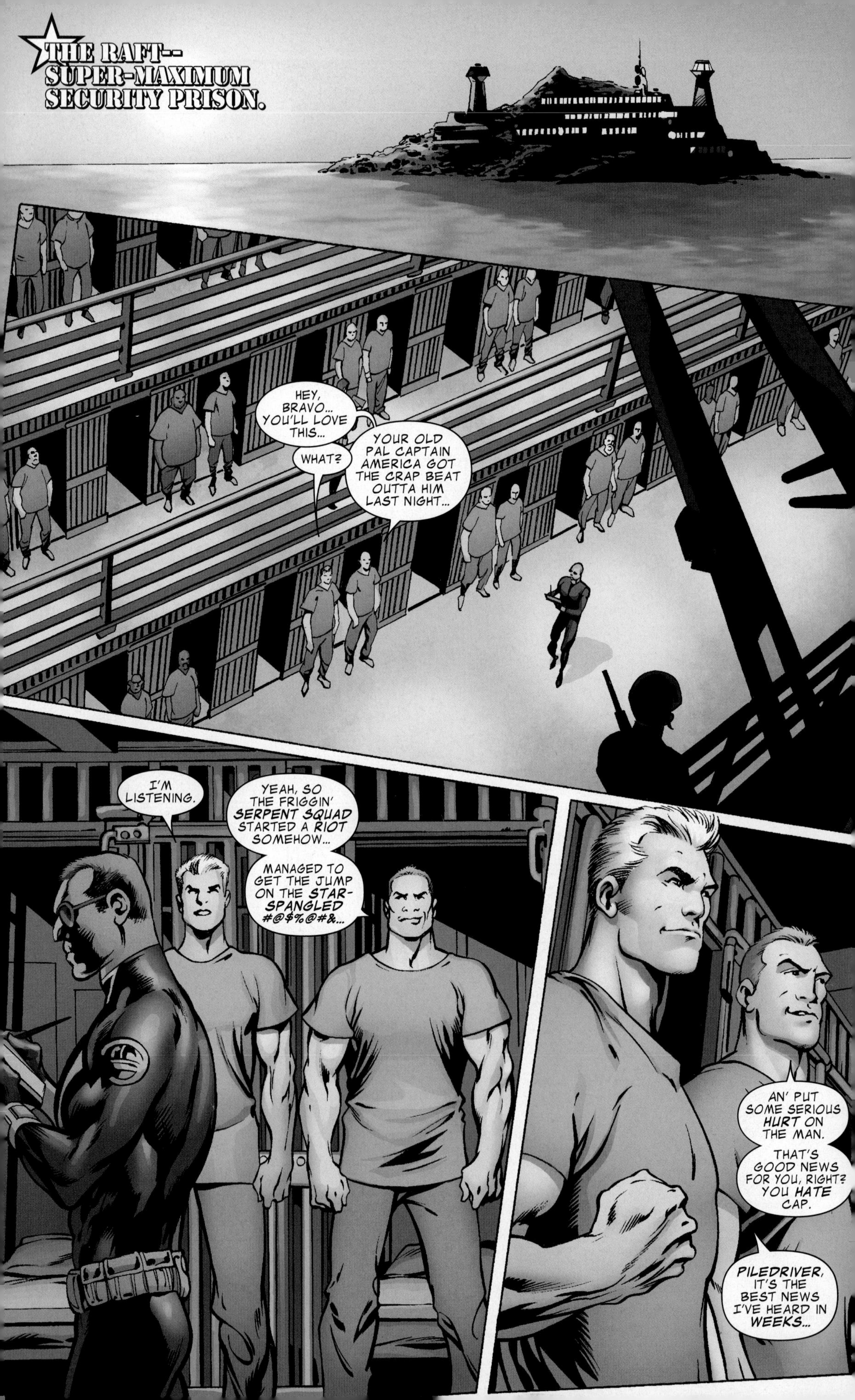
THE RAFT-- SUPER-MAXIMUM SECURITY PRISON.
HEY, BRAVO... YOU'LL LOVE THIS...
WHAT?
YOUR OLD PAL CAPTAIN AMERICA GOT THE CRAP BEAT OUTTA HIM LAST NIGHT...
I'M LISTENING.
YEAH, SO THE FRIGGIN' SERPENT SQUAD STARTED A RIOT SOMEHOW...
MANAGED TO GET THE JUMP ON THE STAR-SPANGLED #@$%@#&...
AN' PUT SOME SERIOUS HURT ON THE MAN.
THAT'S GOOD NEWS FOR YOU, RIGHT? YOU HATE CAP.
PILEDRIVER, IT'S THE BEST NEWS I'VE HEARD IN WEEKS...

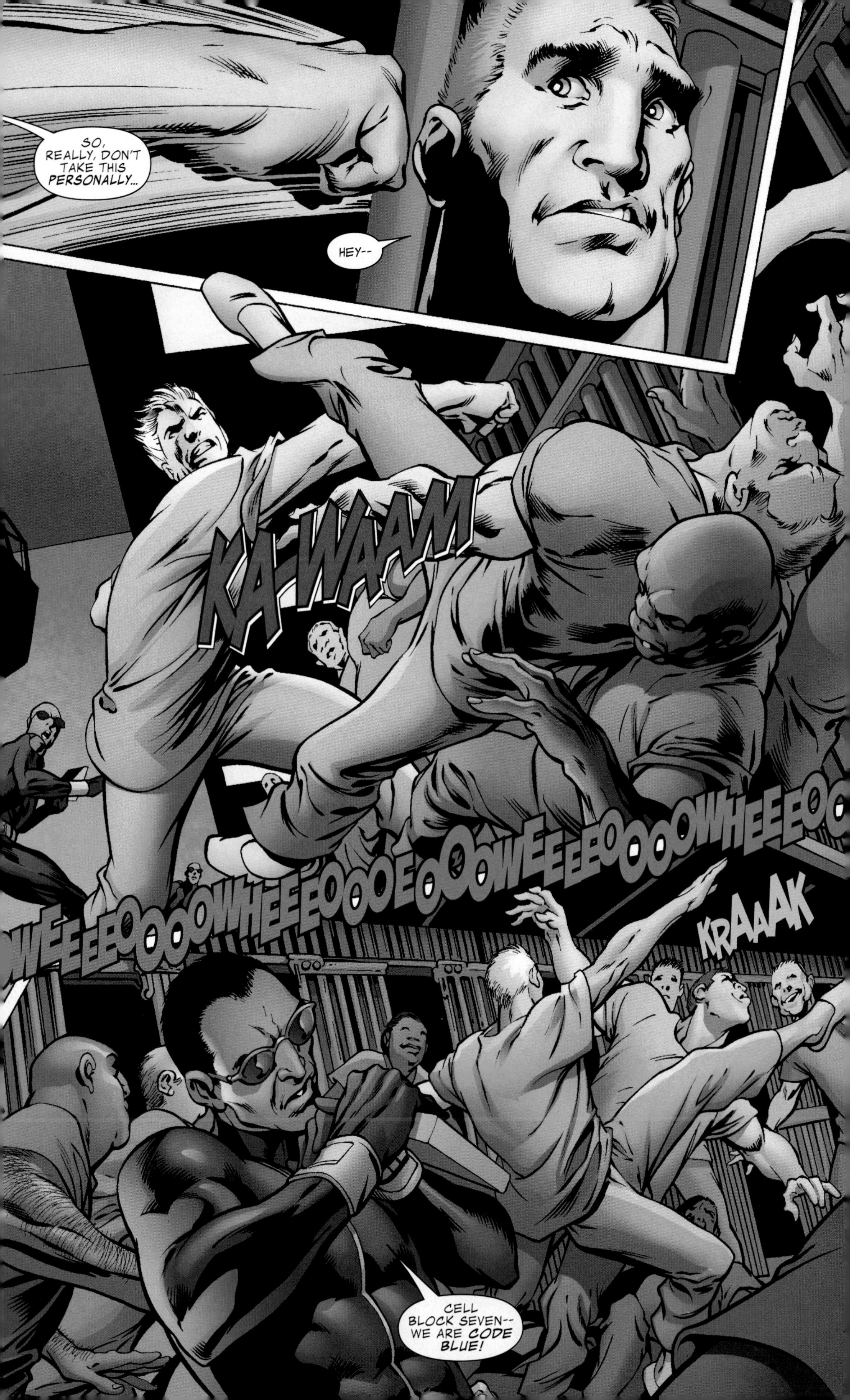
SO, REALLY, DON'T TAKE THIS PERSONALLY...
HEY--
KA-WAAM
KRAAAK
CELL BLOCK SEVEN-- WE ARE CODE BLUE!

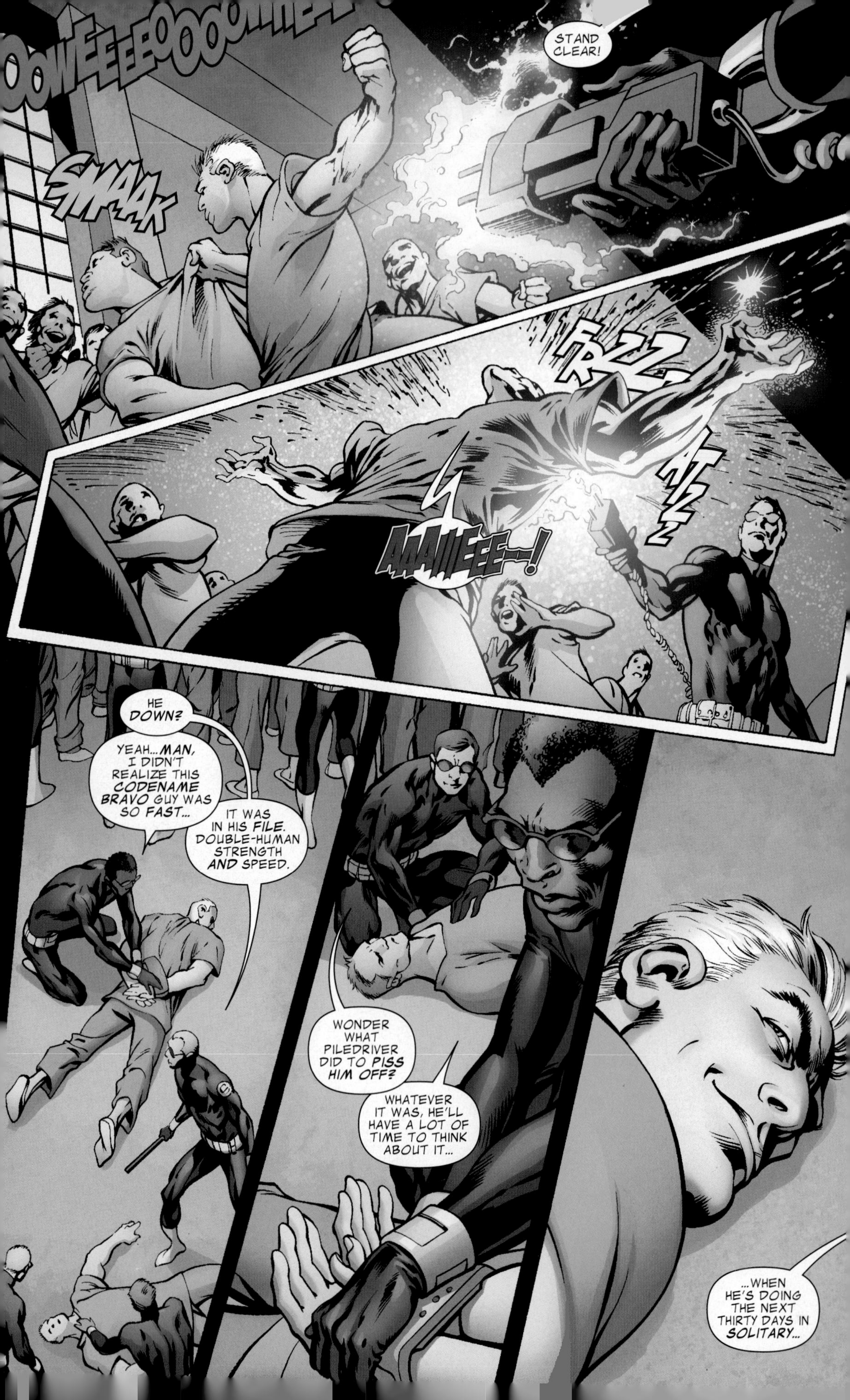
OOWEEEEOOOOWHEE
STAND CLEAR!
SMAAK
FRZZZZZZ
AAAIIIEEE--!
HE DOWN?
YEAH...MAN, I DIDN'T REALIZE THIS CODENAME BRAVO GUY WAS SO FAST...
IT WAS IN HIS FILE. DOUBLE-HUMAN STRENGTH AND SPEED.
WONDER WHAT PILEDRIVER DID TO PISS HIM OFF?
WHATEVER IT WAS, HE'LL HAVE A LOT OF TIME TO THINK ABOUT IT...
...WHEN HE'S DOING THE NEXT THIRTY DAYS IN SOLITARY...

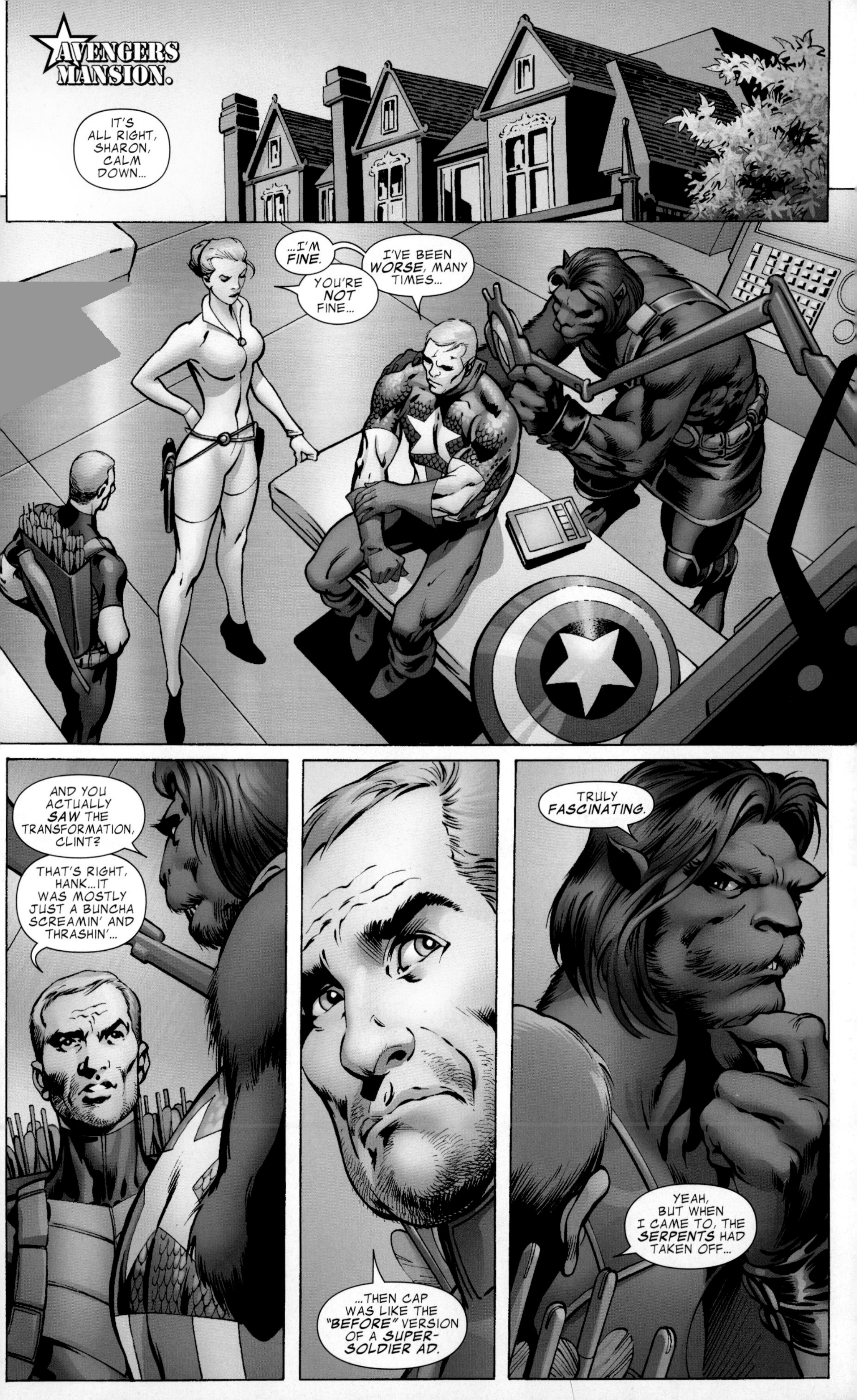
AVENGERS MANSION.
IT'S ALL RIGHT, SHARON, CALM DOWN...
...I'M FINE.
YOU'RE NOT FINE...
I'VE BEEN WORSE, MANY TIMES...
AND YOU ACTUALLY SAW THE TRANSFORMATION, CLINT?
THAT'S RIGHT, HANK...IT WAS MOSTLY JUST A BUNCHA SCREAMIN' AND THRASHIN'...
...THEN CAP WAS LIKE THE "BEFORE" VERSION OF A SUPER-SOLDIER AD.
TRULY FASCINATING.
YEAH, BUT WHEN I CAME TO, THE SERPENTS HAD TAKEN OFF...

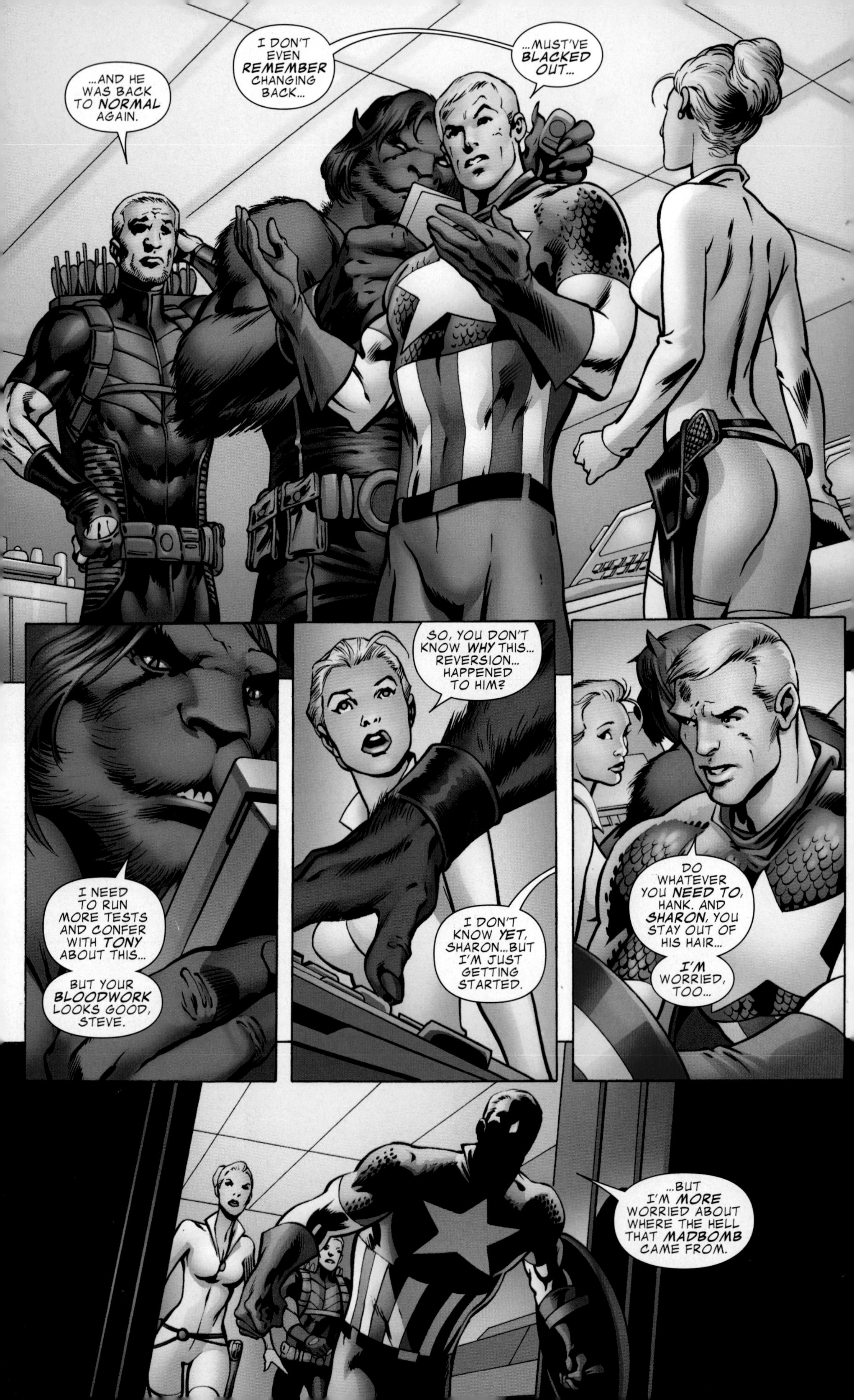
...AND HE WAS BACK TO NORMAL AGAIN.
I DON'T EVEN REMEMBER CHANGING BACK...
...MUST'VE BLACKED OUT...
I NEED TO RUN MORE TESTS AND CONFER WITH TONY ABOUT THIS...
BUT YOUR BLOODWORK LOOKS GOOD, STEVE.
SO, YOU DON'T KNOW WHY THIS... REVERSION... HAPPENED TO HIM?
I DON'T KNOW YET, SHARON...BUT I'M JUST GETTING STARTED.
DO WHATEVER YOU NEED TO, HANK. AND SHARON, YOU STAY OUT OF HIS HAIR...
I'M WORRIED, TOO...
...BUT I'M MORE WORRIED ABOUT WHERE THE HELL THAT MADBOMB CAME FROM.

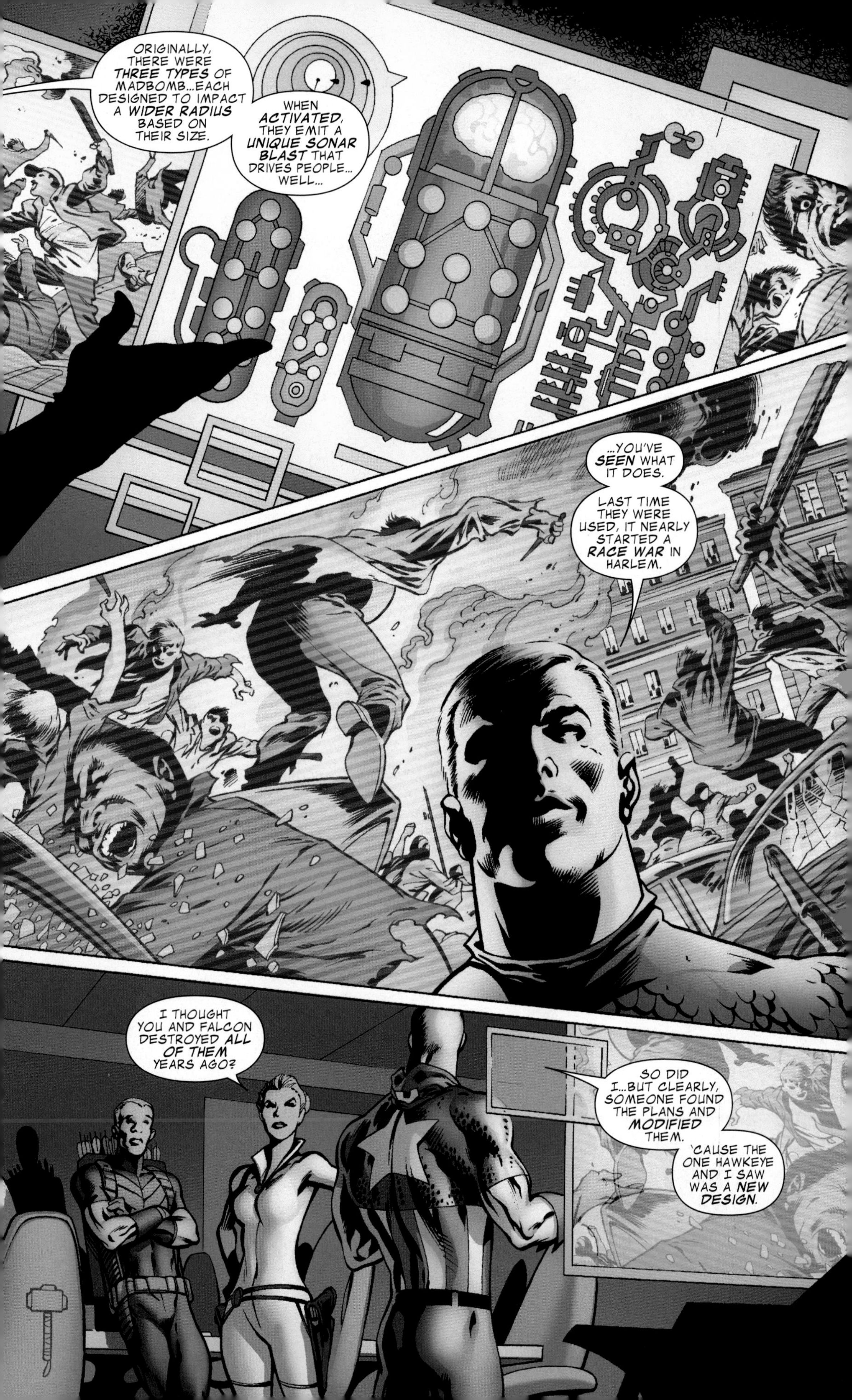
ORIGINALLY, THERE WERE THREE TYPES OF MADBOMB...EACH DESIGNED TO IMPACT A WIDER RADIUS BASED ON THEIR SIZE.
WHEN ACTIVATED, THEY EMIT A UNIQUE SONAR BLAST THAT DRIVES PEOPLE... WELL...
...YOU'VE SEEN WHAT IT DOES.
LAST TIME THEY WERE USED, IT NEARLY STARTED A RACE WAR IN HARLEM.
I THOUGHT YOU AND FALCON DESTROYED ALL OF THEM YEARS AGO?
SO DID I...BUT CLEARLY, SOMEONE FOUND THE PLANS AND MODIFIED THEM.
'CAUSE THE ONE HAWKEYE AND I SAW WAS A NEW DESIGN.

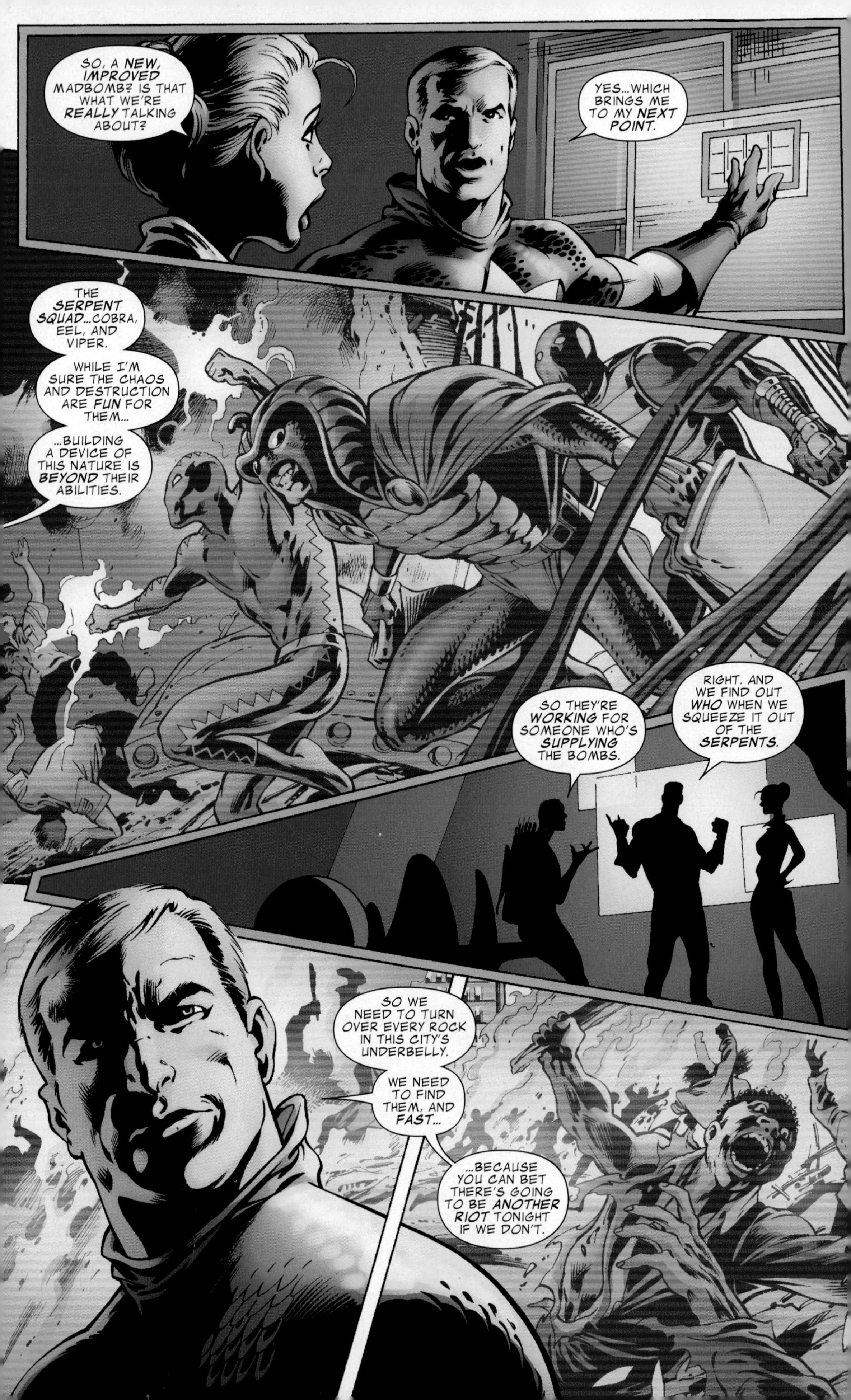

SO, A NEW, IMPROVED MADBOMB? IS THAT WHAT WE'RE REALLY TALKING ABOUT?
YES...WHICH BRINGS ME TO MY NEXT POINT.
THE SERPENT SQUAD...COBRA, EEL, AND VIPER.
WHILE I'M SURE THE CHAOS AND DESTRUCTION ARE FUN FOR THEM...
...BUILDING A DEVICE OF THIS NATURE IS BEYOND THEIR ABILITIES.
SO THEY'RE WORKING FOR SOMEONE WHO'S SUPPLYING THE BOMBS.
RIGHT. AND WE FIND OUT WHO WHEN WE SQUEEZE IT OUT OF THE SERPENTS.
SO WE NEED TO TURN OVER EVERY ROCK IN THIS CITY'S UNDERBELLY.
WE NEED TO FIND THEM, AND FAST...
...BECAUSE YOU CAN BET THERE'S GOING TO BE ANOTHER RIOT TONIGHT IF WE DON'T.

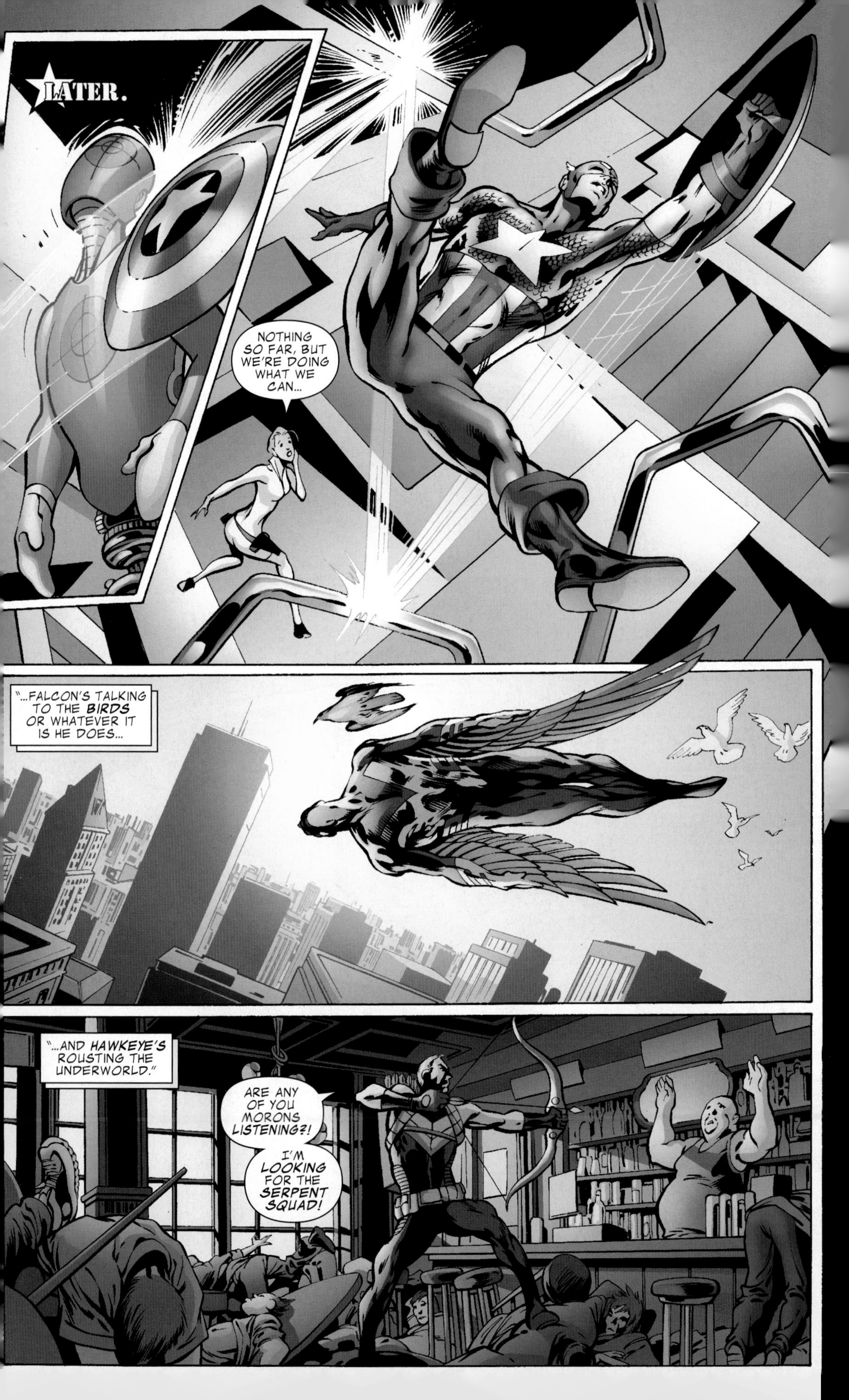
LATER.
NOTHING SO FAR, BUT WE'RE DOING WHAT WE CAN...
"...FALCON'S TALKING TO THE BIRDS OR WHATEVER IT IS HE DOES...
"...AND HAWKEYE'S ROUSTING THE UNDERWORLD."
ARE ANY OF YOU MORONS LISTENING?!
I'M LOOKING FOR THE SERPENT SQUAD!

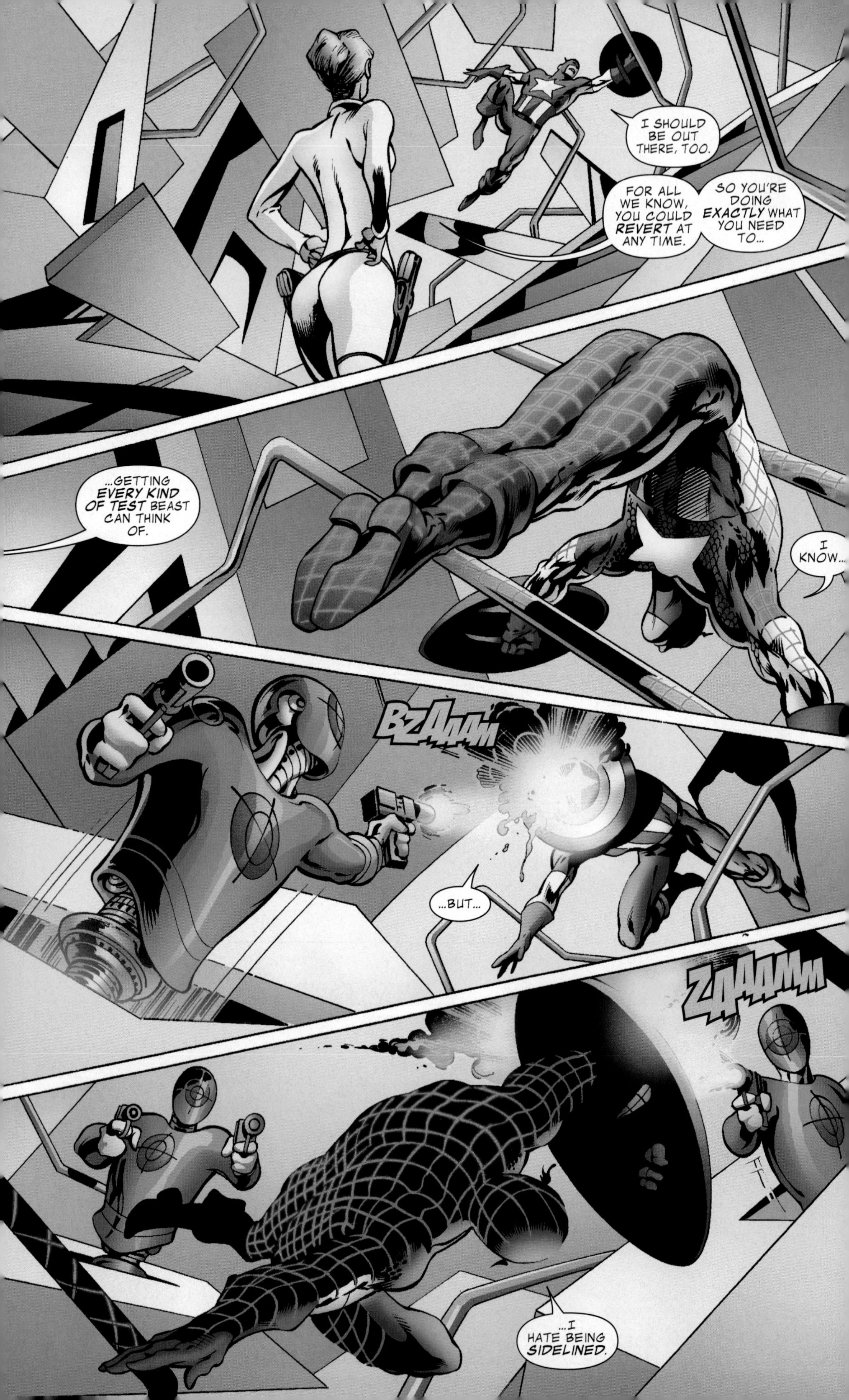
I SHOULD BE OUT THERE, TOO.
SO YOU'RE DOING EXACTLY WHAT YOU NEED TO...
FOR ALL WE KNOW, YOU COULD REVERT AT ANY TIME.
...GETTING EVERY KIND OF TEST BEAST CAN THINK OF.
I KNOW...
BZAAAM
...BUT...
ZAAAMM
...I HATE BEING SIDELINED.

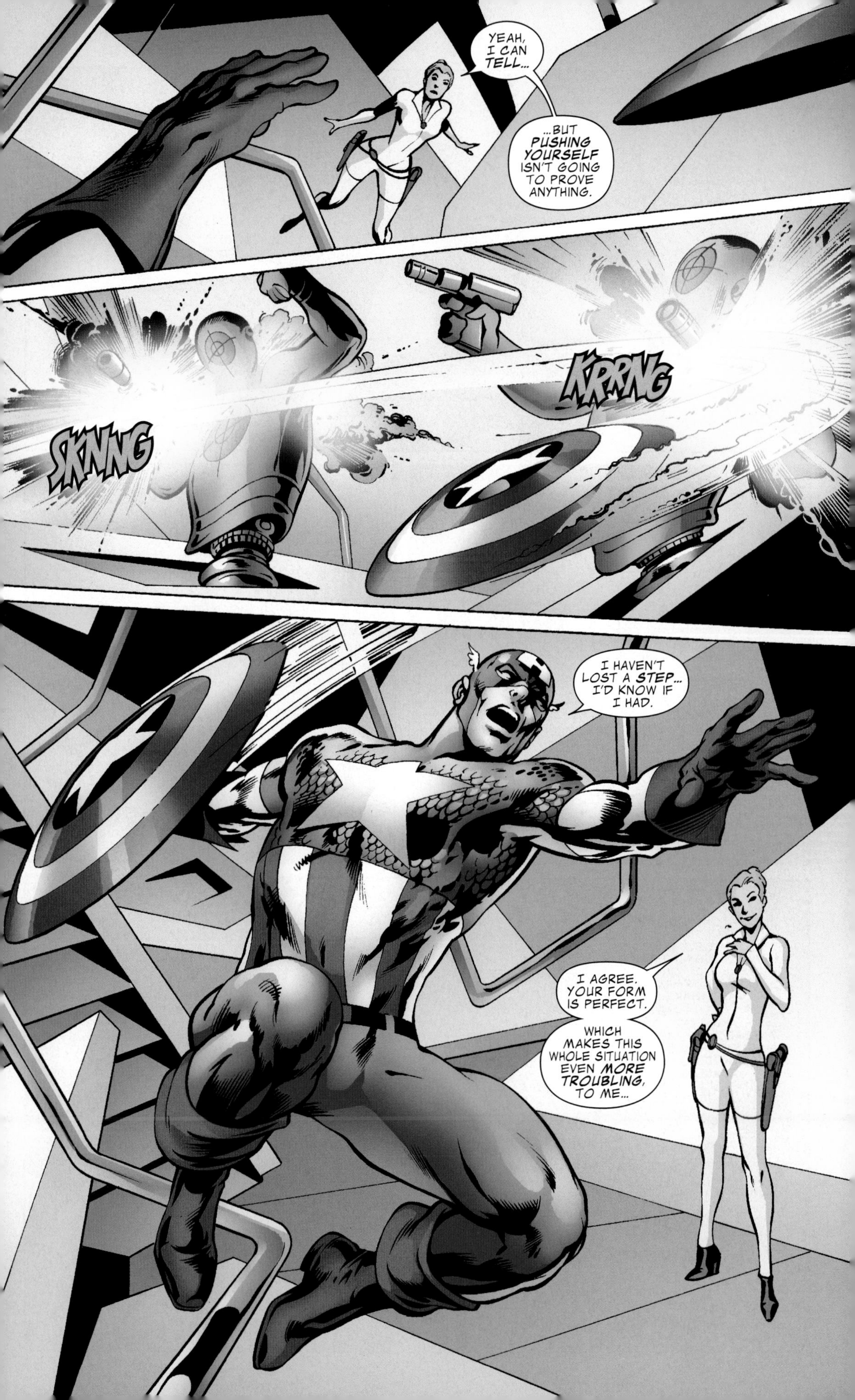
YEAH, I CAN TELL...
...BUT PUSHING YOURSELF ISN'T GOING TO PROVE ANYTHING.
KRRNG
SKNNG
I HAVEN'T LOST A STEP... I'D KNOW IF I HAD.
I AGREE. YOUR FORM IS PERFECT.
WHICH MAKES THIS WHOLE SITUATION EVEN MORE TROUBLING, TO ME...

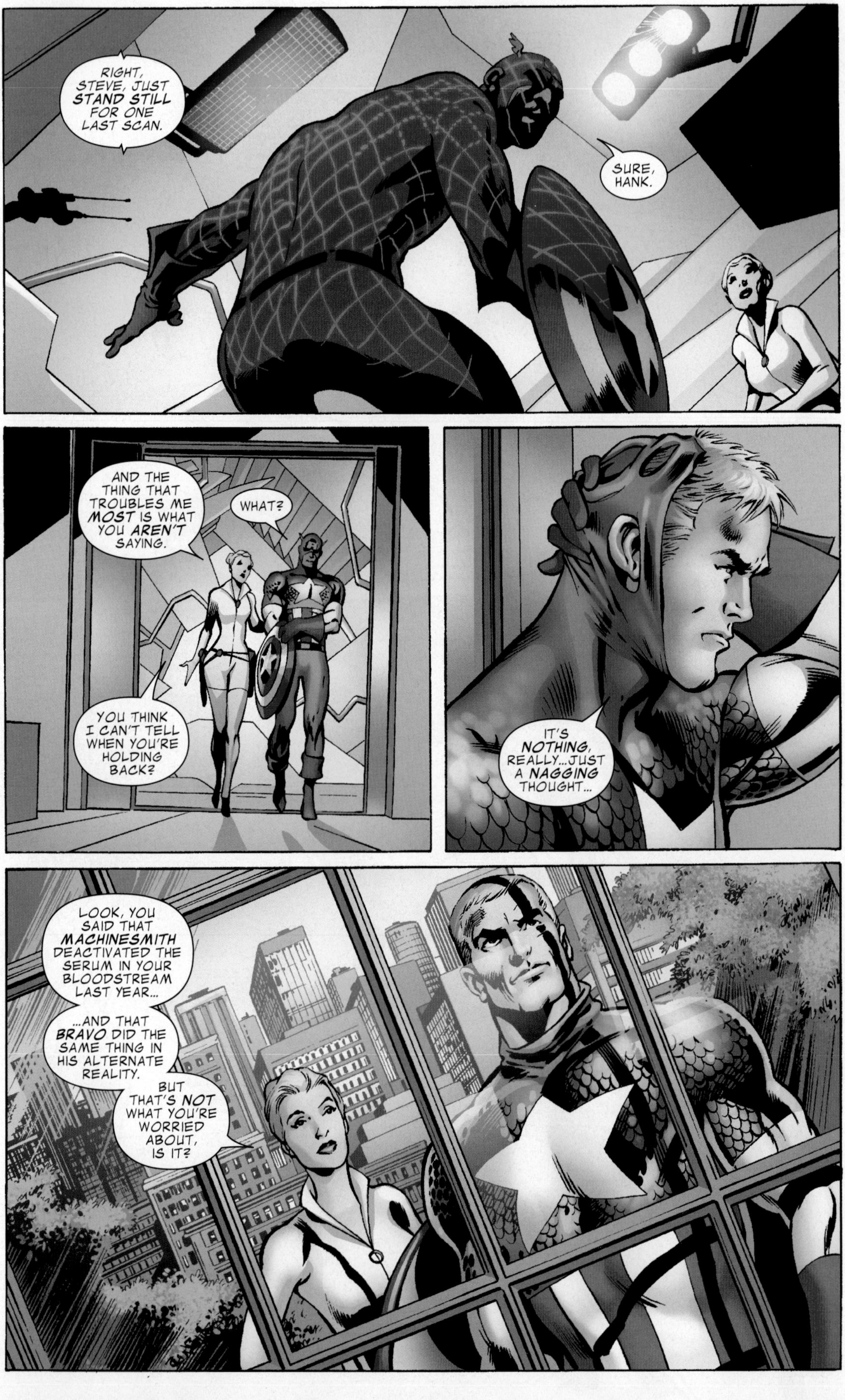

RIGHT, STEVE, JUST **STAND STILL** FOR ONE LAST SCAN.
SURE, HANK.
AND THE THING THAT TROUBLES ME **MOST** IS WHAT YOU **AREN'T** SAYING.
WHAT?
YOU THINK I CAN'T TELL WHEN YOU'RE HOLDING BACK?
IT'S **NOTHING**, REALLY...JUST A **NAGGING** THOUGHT...
LOOK, YOU SAID THAT **MACHINESMITH** DEACTIVATED THE SERUM IN YOUR BLOODSTREAM LAST YEAR...
...AND THAT **BRAVO** DID THE SAME THING IN HIS ALTERNATE REALITY.
BUT THAT'S **NOT** WHAT YOU'RE WORRIED ABOUT, IS IT?

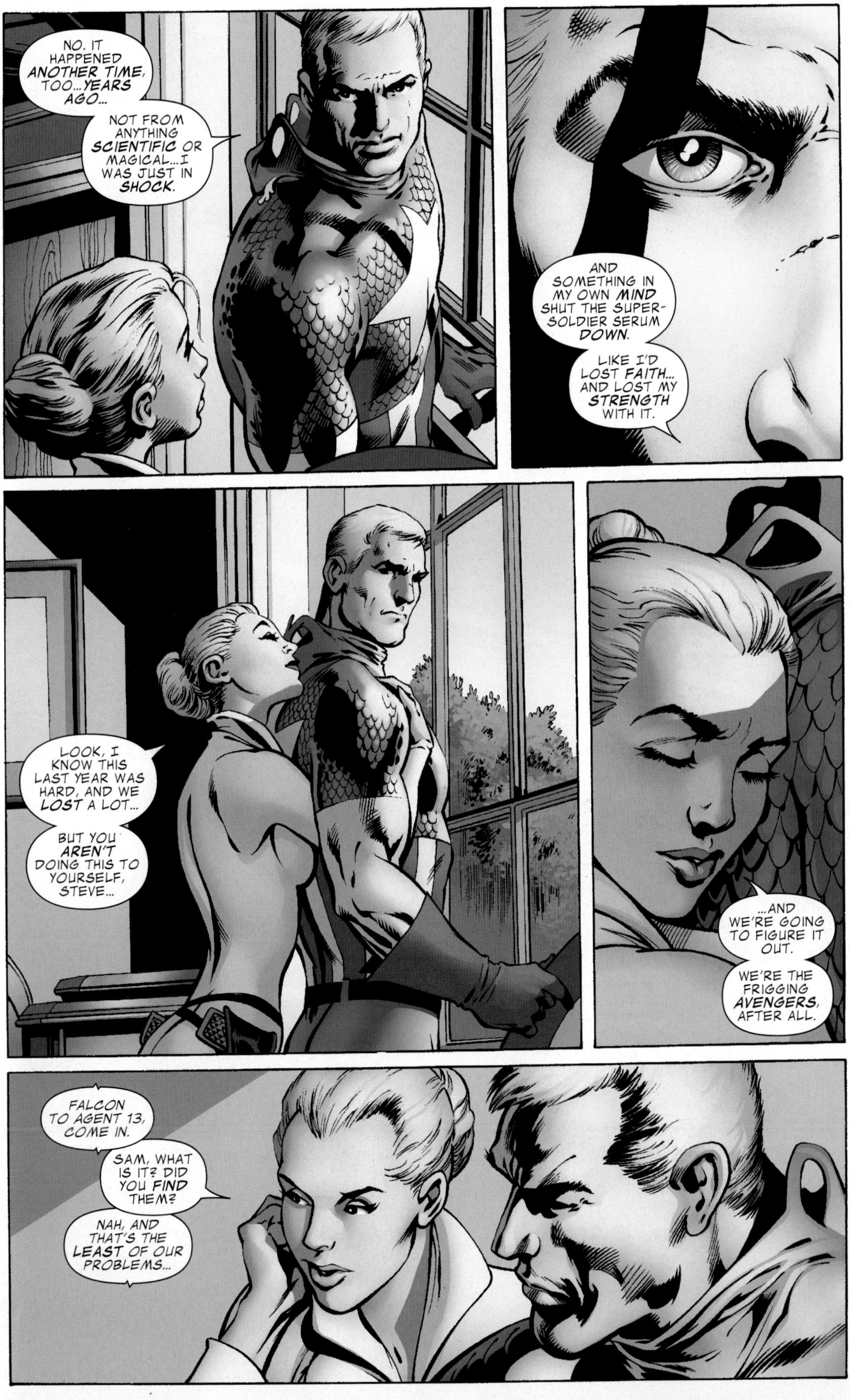
NO. IT HAPPENED ANOTHER TIME, TOO...YEARS AGO...
NOT FROM ANYTHING SCIENTIFIC OR MAGICAL...I WAS JUST IN SHOCK.
AND SOMETHING IN MY OWN MIND SHUT THE SUPER-SOLDIER SERUM DOWN.
LIKE I'D LOST FAITH... AND LOST MY STRENGTH WITH IT.
LOOK, I KNOW THIS LAST YEAR WAS HARD, AND WE LOST A LOT...
BUT YOU AREN'T DOING THIS TO YOURSELF, STEVE...
...AND WE'RE GOING TO FIGURE IT OUT.
WE'RE THE FRIGGING AVENGERS, AFTER ALL.
FALCON TO AGENT 13, COME IN.
SAM, WHAT IS IT? DID YOU FIND THEM?
NAH, AND THAT'S THE LEAST OF OUR PROBLEMS...

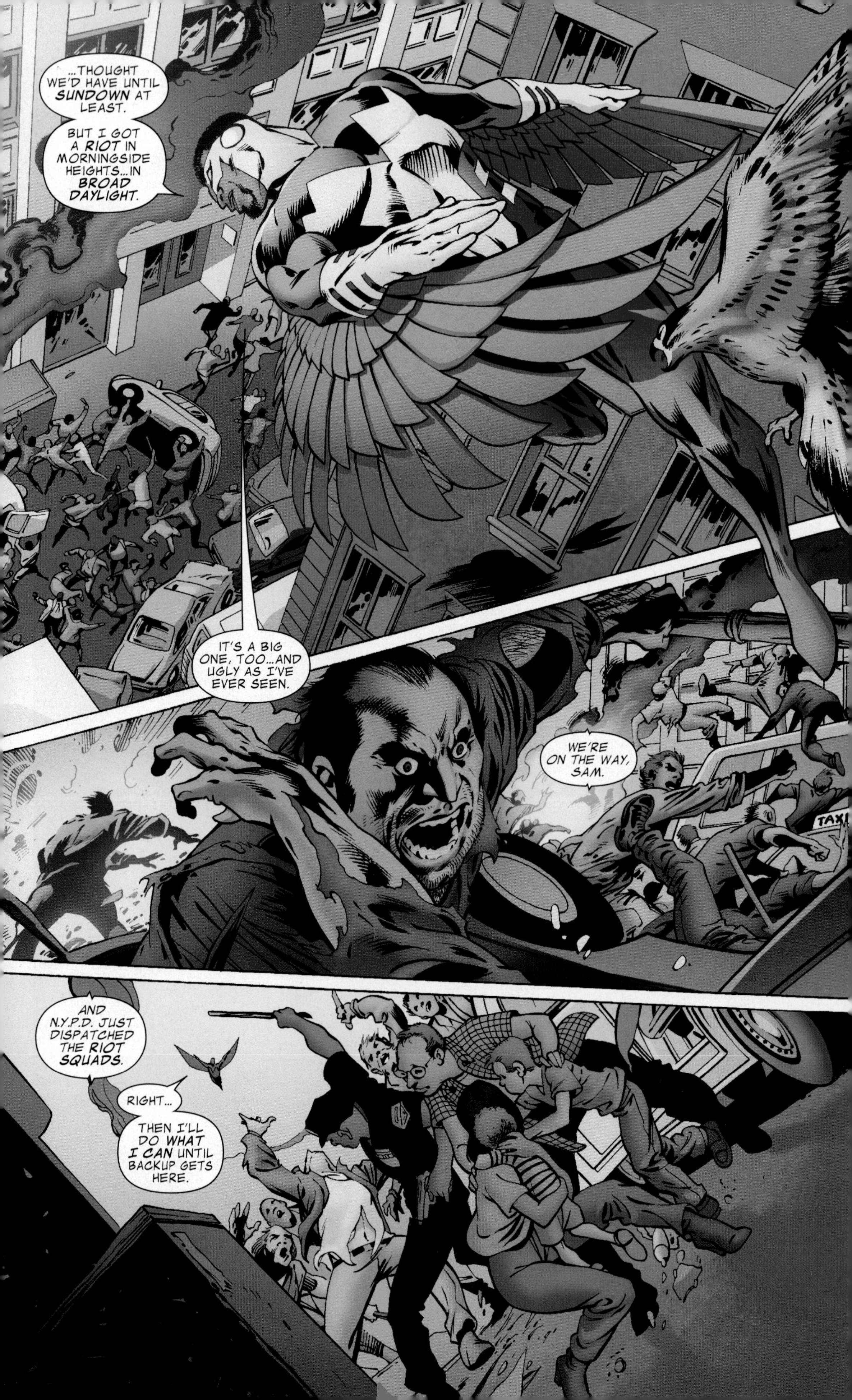
...THOUGHT WE'D HAVE UNTIL SUNDOWN AT LEAST.
BUT I GOT A RIOT IN MORNINGSIDE HEIGHTS...IN BROAD DAYLIGHT.
IT'S A BIG ONE, TOO...AND UGLY AS I'VE EVER SEEN.
WE'RE ON THE WAY, SAM.
TAXI
AND N.Y.P.D. JUST DISPATCHED THE RIOT SQUADS.
RIGHT...
THEN I'LL DO WHAT I CAN UNTIL BACKUP GETS HERE.

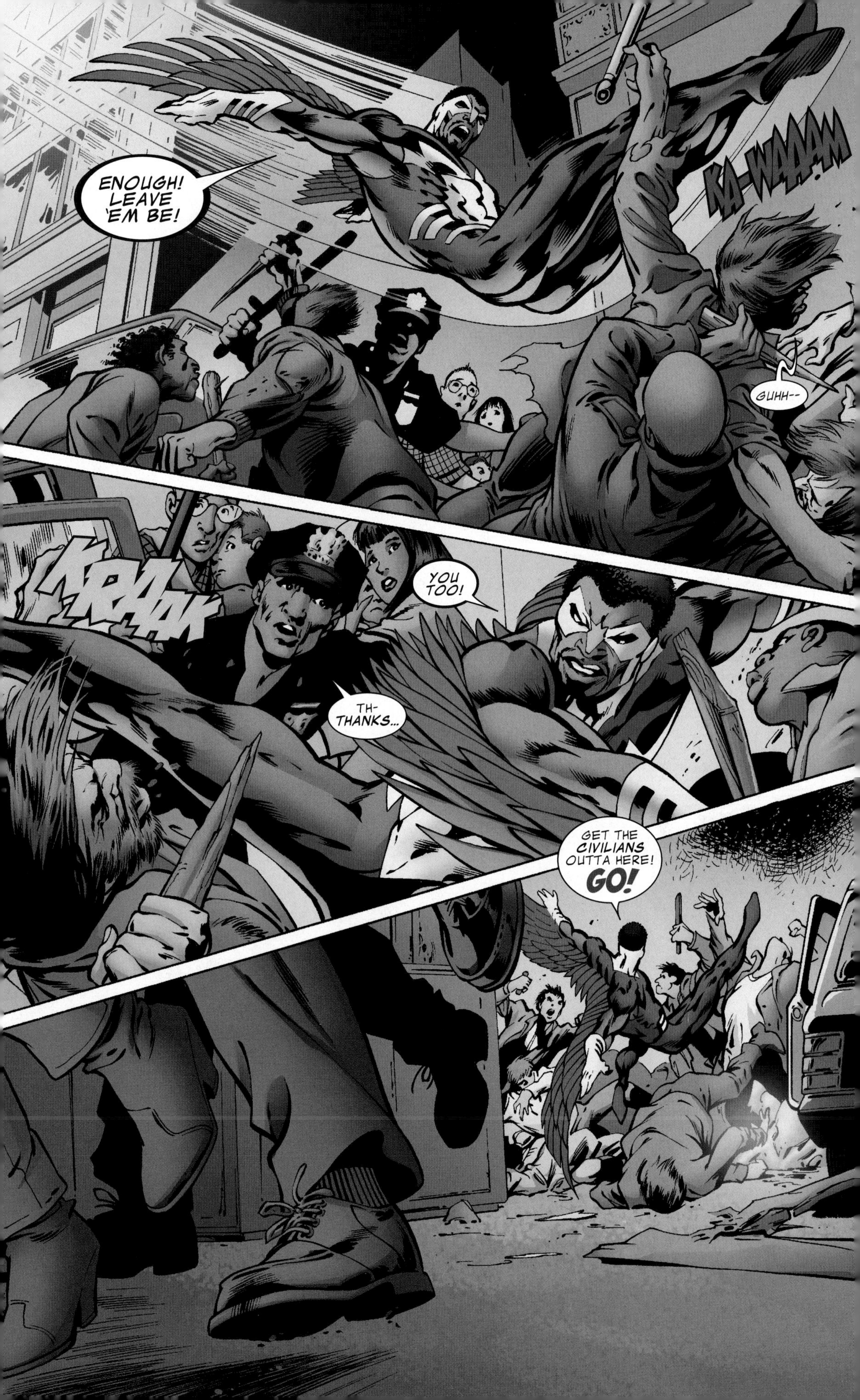
ENOUGH! LEAVE 'EM BE!
KA-WAAAM
GUHH--
KRAAAK
YOU TOO!
TH- THANKS...
GET THE CIVILIANS OUTTA HERE! GO!

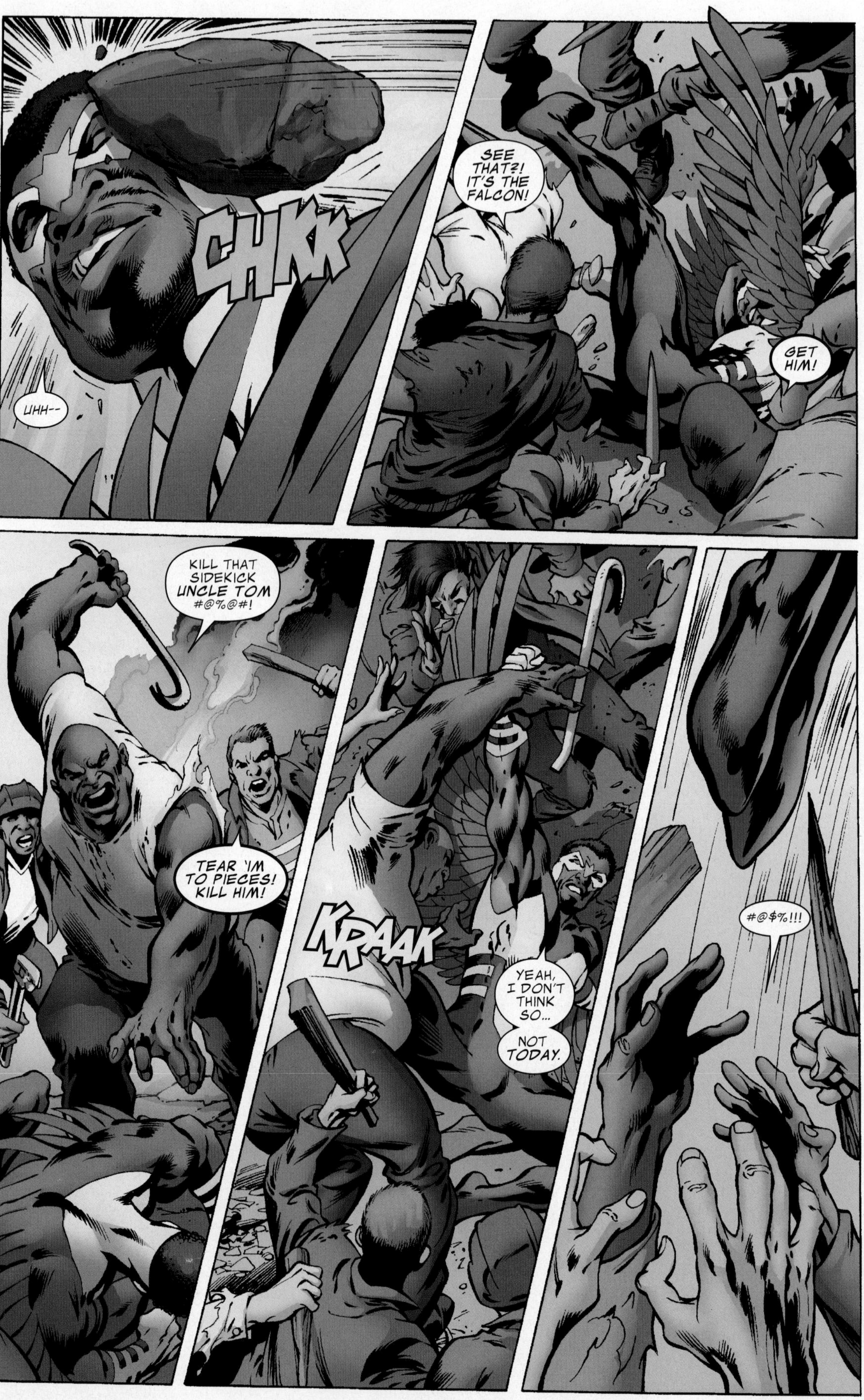
CHKK
UHH--
SEE THAT?! IT'S THE FALCON!
GET HIM!
KILL THAT SIDEKICK UNCLE TOM #@%@#!
TEAR 'IM TO PIECES! KILL HIM!
KRAAK
YEAH, I DON'T THINK SO...
NOT TODAY.
#@$%!!!

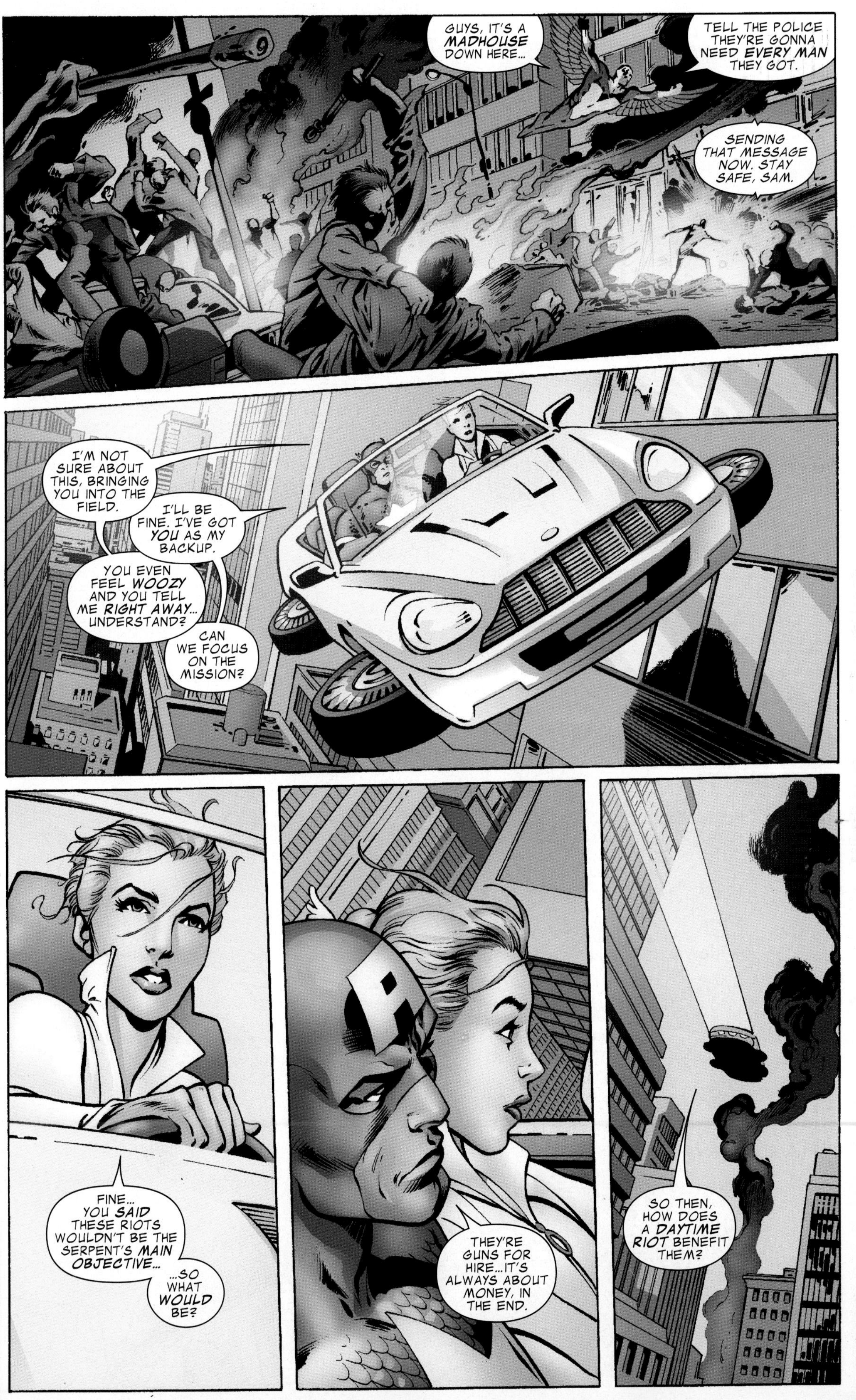
GUYS, IT'S A MADHOUSE DOWN HERE...
TELL THE POLICE THEY'RE GONNA NEED EVERY MAN THEY GOT.
SENDING THAT MESSAGE NOW. STAY SAFE, SAM.
I'M NOT SURE ABOUT THIS, BRINGING YOU INTO THE FIELD.
I'LL BE FINE. I'VE GOT YOU AS MY BACKUP.
YOU EVEN FEEL WOOZY AND YOU TELL ME RIGHT AWAY... UNDERSTAND?
CAN WE FOCUS ON THE MISSION?
FINE... YOU SAID THESE RIOTS WOULDN'T BE THE SERPENT'S MAIN OBJECTIVE...
...SO WHAT WOULD BE?
THEY'RE GUNS FOR HIRE... IT'S ALWAYS ABOUT MONEY, IN THE END.
SO THEN, HOW DOES A DAYTIME RIOT BENEFIT THEM?

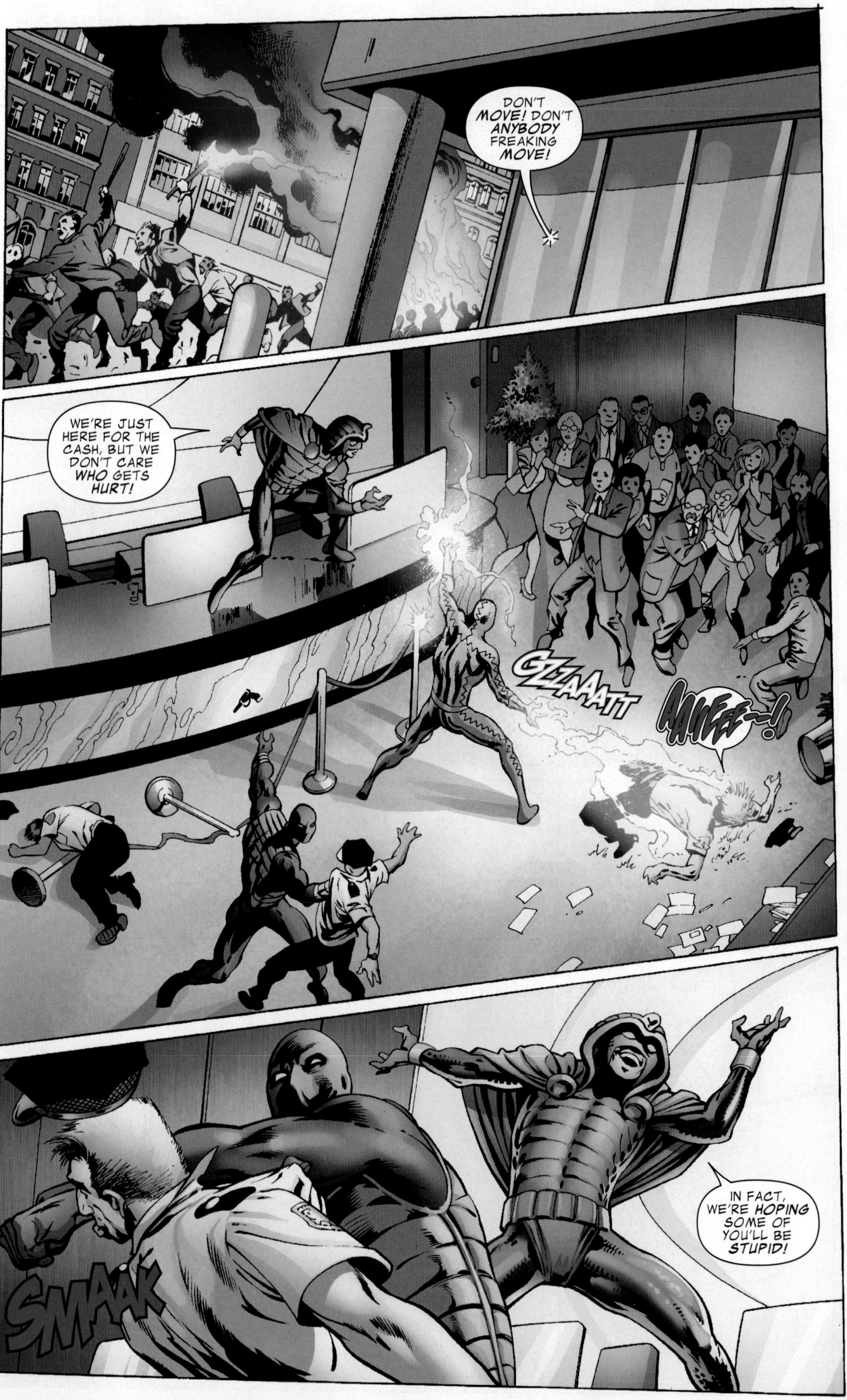
DON'T MOVE! DON'T ANYBODY FREAKING MOVE!
WE'RE JUST HERE FOR THE CASH, BUT WE DON'T CARE WHO GETS HURT!
GZZAAATT
AAIEEE--!
IN FACT, WE'RE HOPING SOME OF YOU'LL BE STUPID!
SMAAK

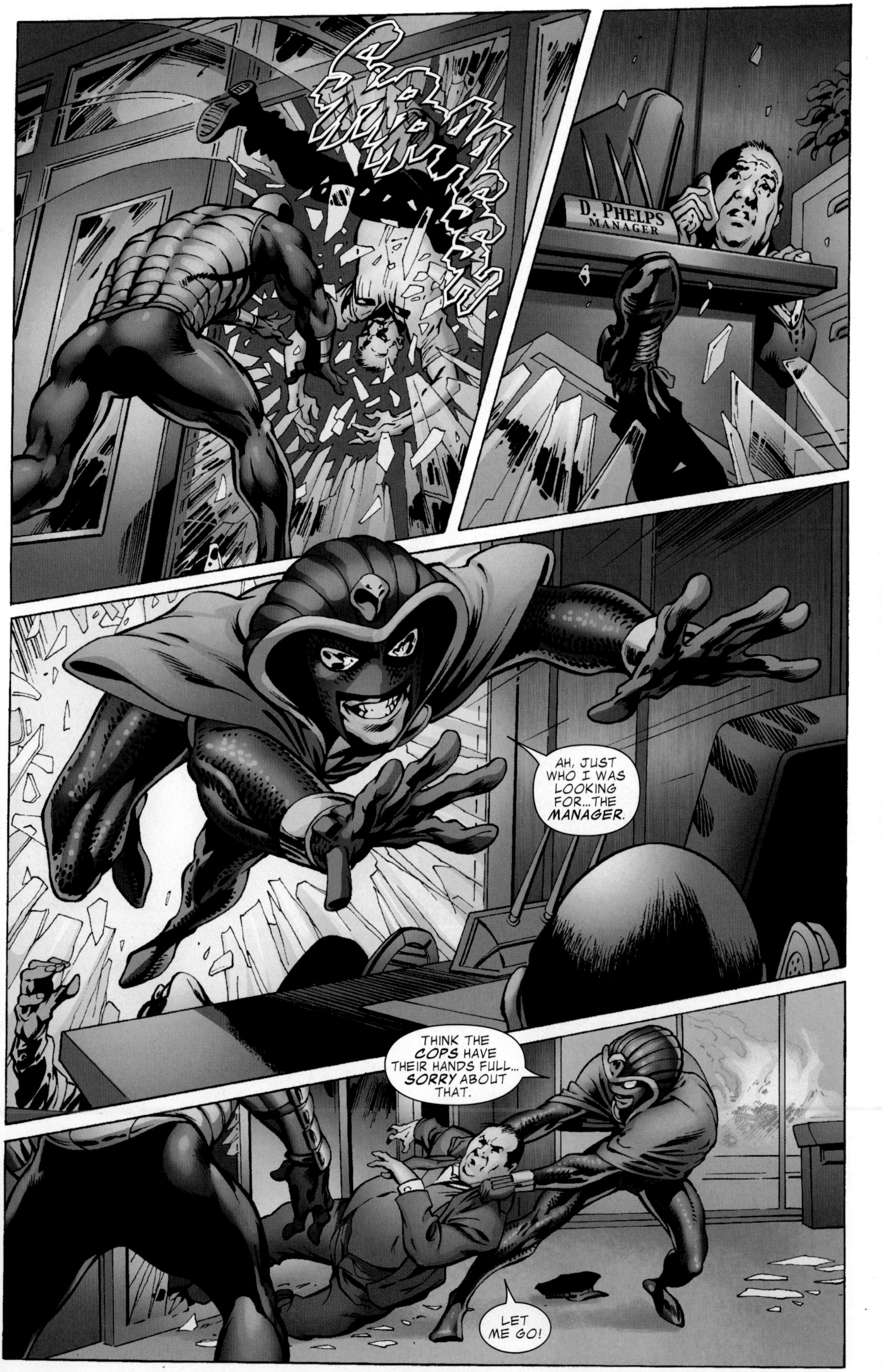
D. PHELPS
MANAGER
AH, JUST WHO I WAS LOOKING FOR...THE MANAGER.
THINK THE COPS HAVE THEIR HANDS FULL... SORRY ABOUT THAT.
LET ME GO!

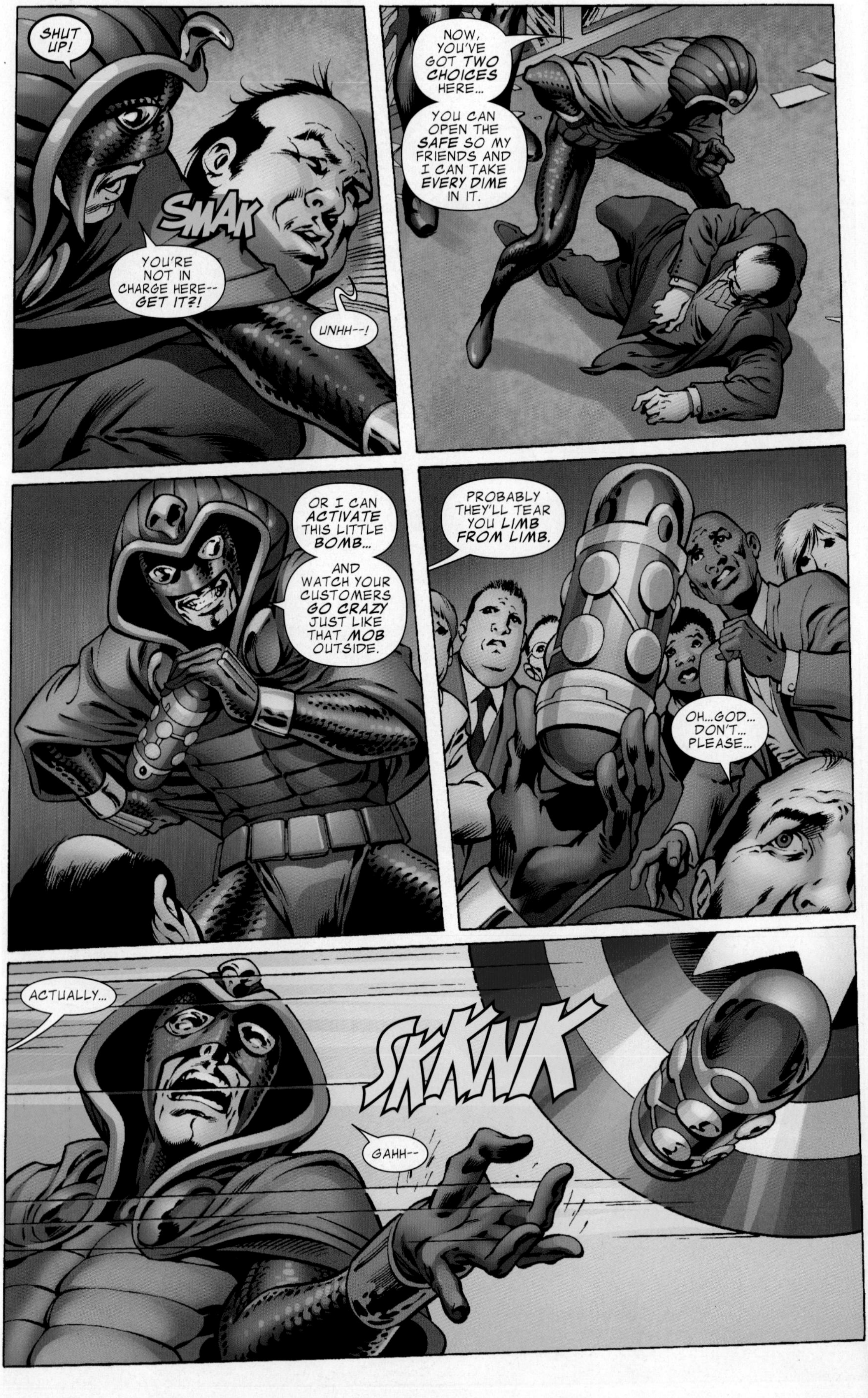

SHUT UP!
SMAK
YOU'RE NOT IN CHARGE HERE-- GET IT?!
UNHH--!
NOW, YOU'VE GOT TWO CHOICES HERE...
YOU CAN OPEN THE SAFE SO MY FRIENDS AND I CAN TAKE EVERY DIME IN IT.
OR I CAN ACTIVATE THIS LITTLE BOMB...
AND WATCH YOUR CUSTOMERS GO CRAZY JUST LIKE THAT MOB OUTSIDE.
PROBABLY THEY'LL TEAR YOU LIMB FROM LIMB.
OH...GOD... DON'T... PLEASE...
ACTUALLY...
SKKNK
GAHH--

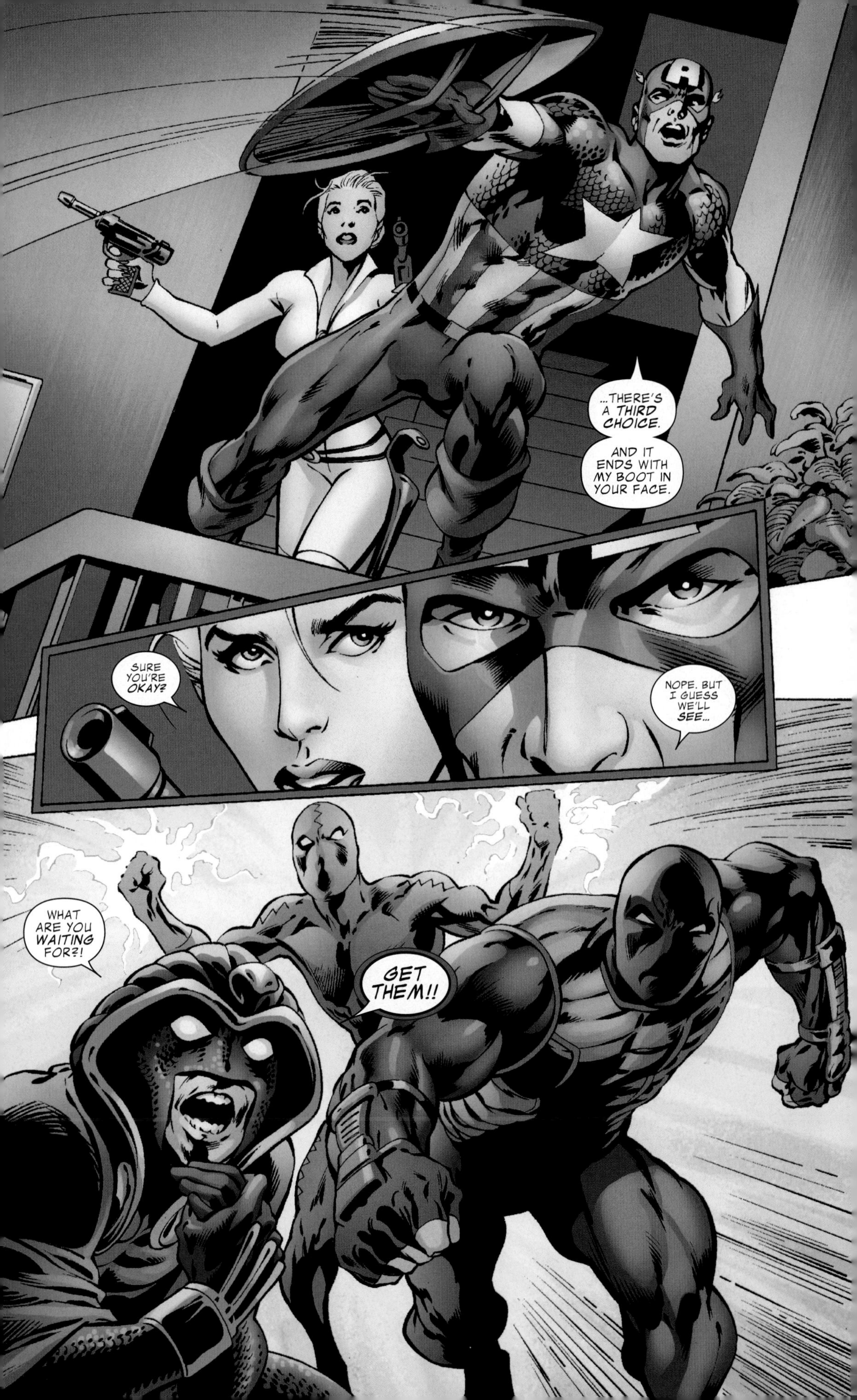
...THERE'S A THIRD CHOICE.
AND IT ENDS WITH MY BOOT IN YOUR FACE.
SURE YOU'RE OKAY?
NOPE. BUT I GUESS WE'LL SEE...
WHAT ARE YOU WAITING FOR?!
GET THEM!!

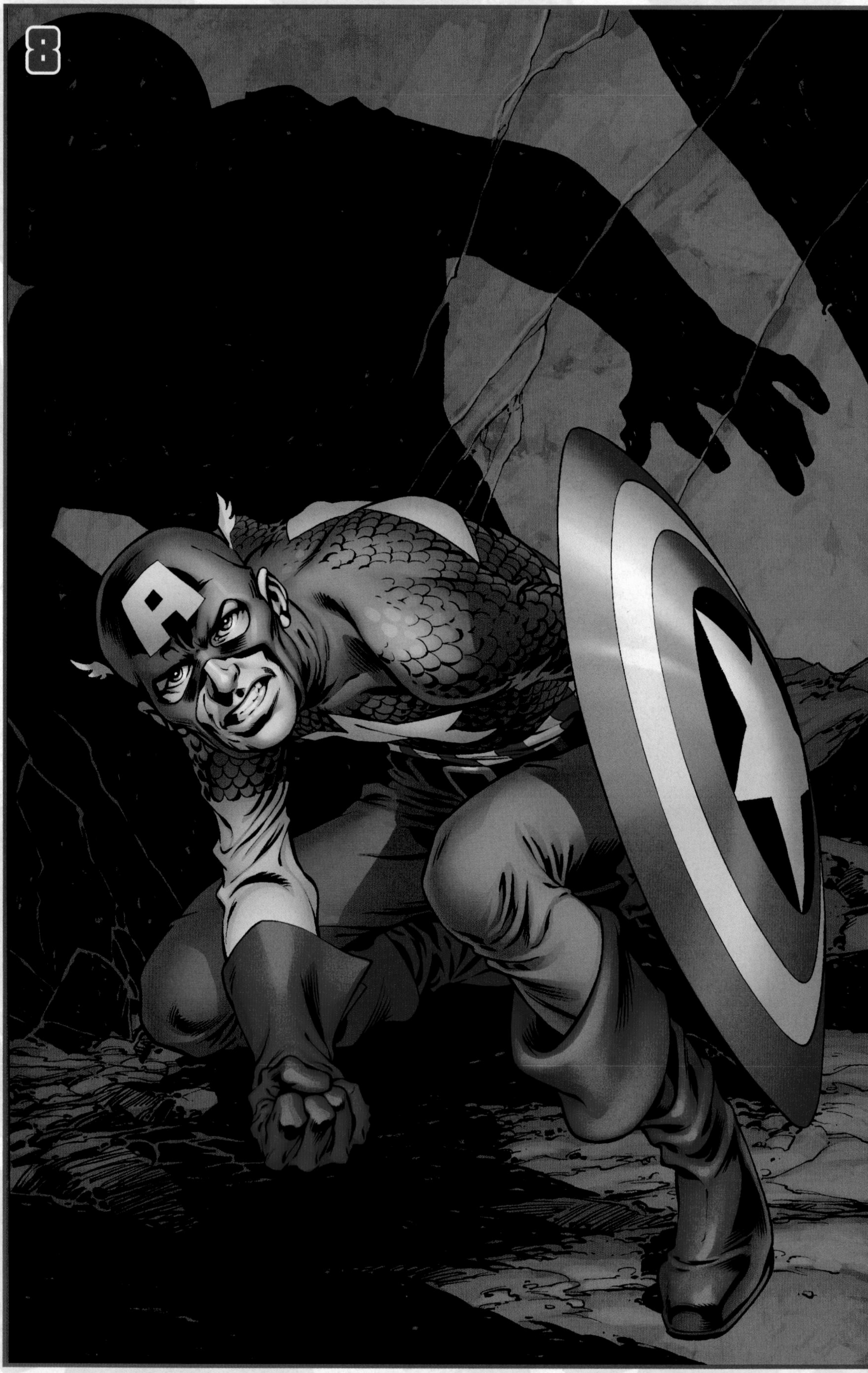
8

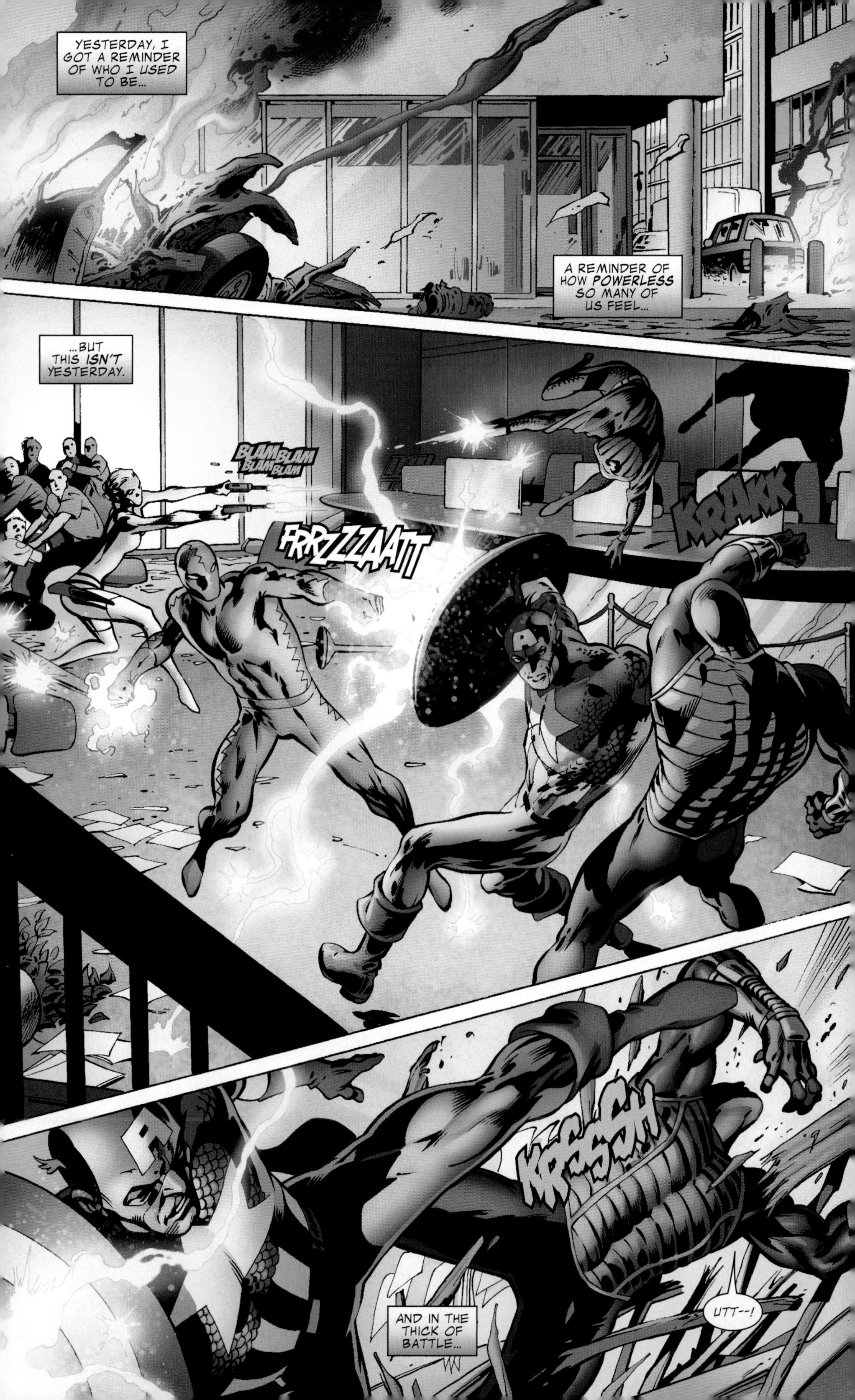
YESTERDAY, I GOT A REMINDER OF WHO I USED TO BE...
A REMINDER OF HOW POWERLESS SO MANY OF US FEEL...
...BUT THIS ISN'T YESTERDAY.
BLAM BLAM BLAM BLAM
FRRZZZAATT
KRAKK
KRSSH
AND IN THE THICK OF BATTLE...
UTT--!

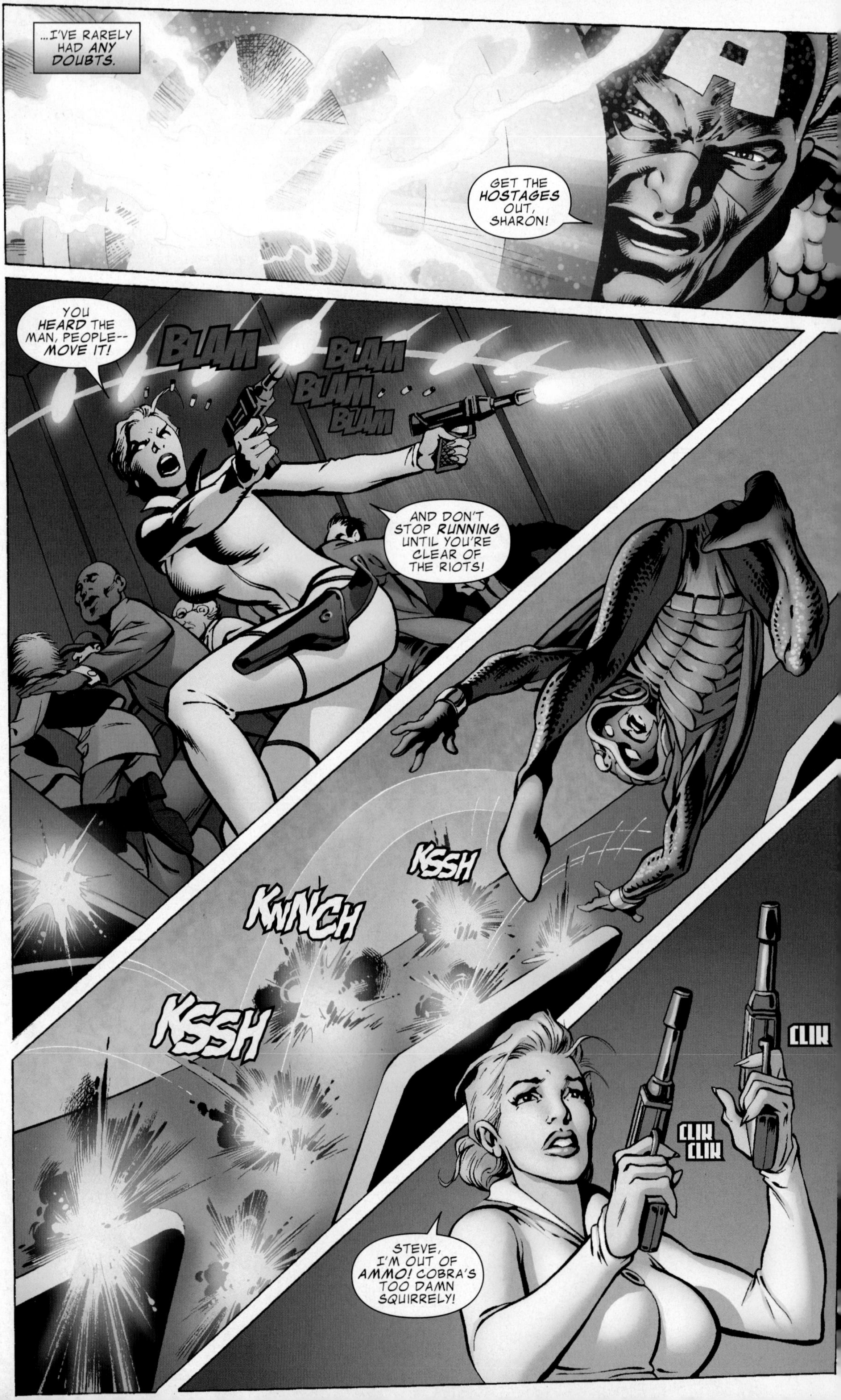

...I'VE RARELY HAD ANY DOUBTS.
GET THE HOSTAGES OUT, SHARON!
YOU HEARD THE MAN, PEOPLE-- MOVE IT!
BLAM
BLAM
BLAM
BLAM
AND DON'T STOP RUNNING UNTIL YOU'RE CLEAR OF THE RIOTS!
KSSH
KWNCH
KSSH
CLIK
CLIK CLIK
STEVE, I'M OUT OF AMMO! COBRA'S TOO DAMN SQUIRRELY!

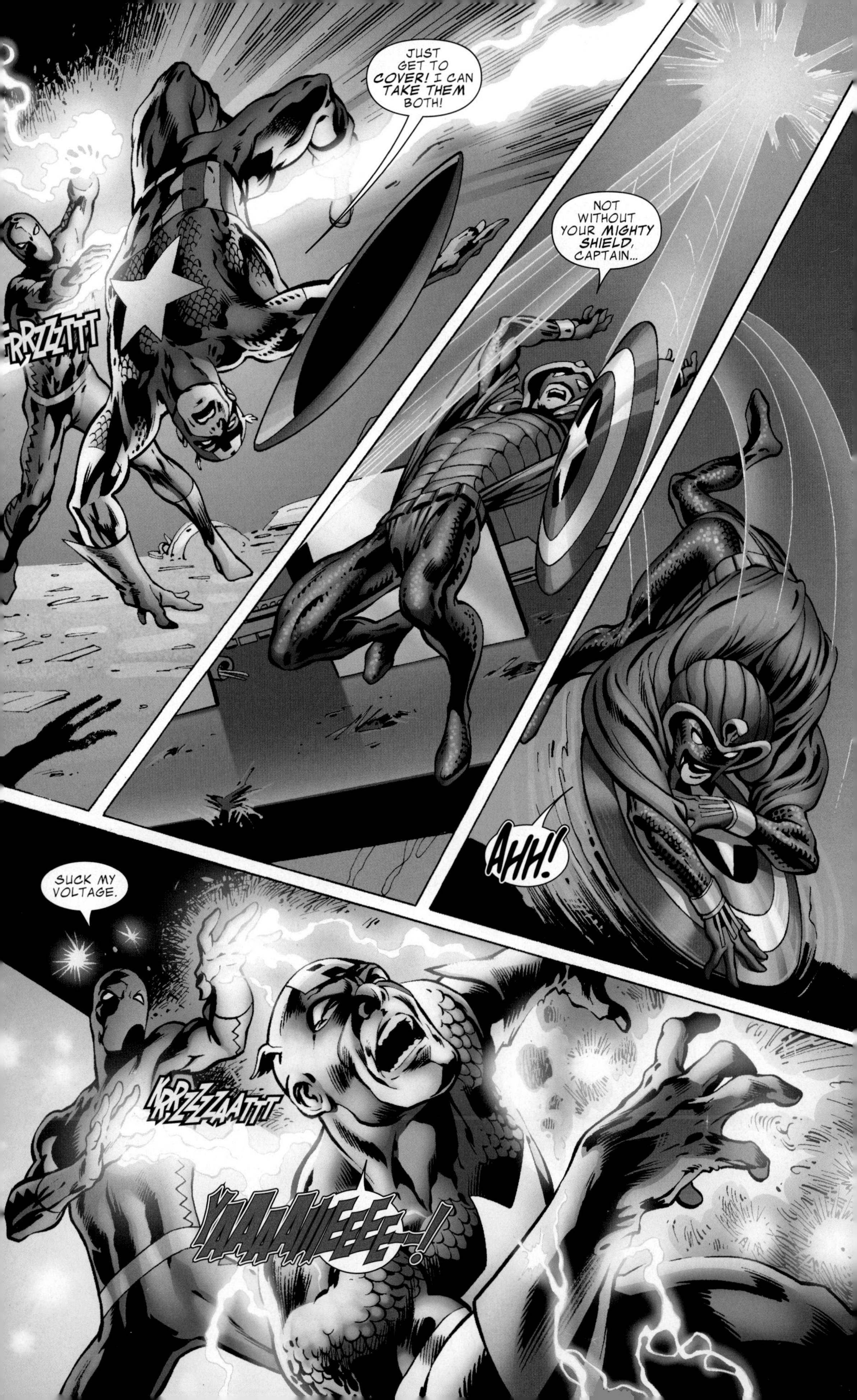
JUST GET TO COVER! I CAN TAKE THEM BOTH!
FRRZZZTTT
NOT WITHOUT YOUR MIGHTY SHIELD, CAPTAIN...
AHH!
SUCK MY VOLTAGE.
KRRZZZZAATTT
YAAAAIIEEEE--!

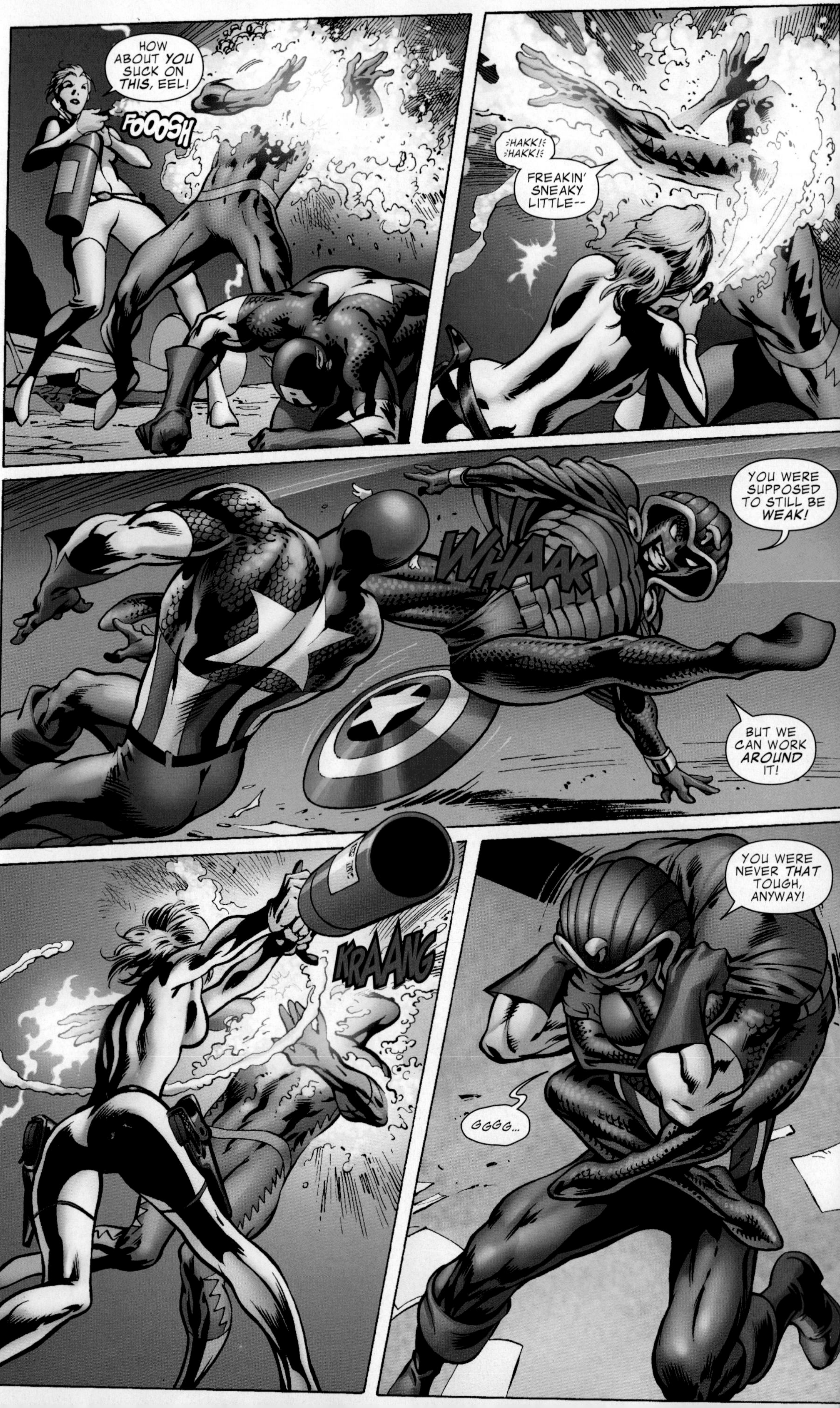
HOW ABOUT YOU SUCK ON THIS, EEL!
FOOOSH
HAKK! HAKK!
FREAKIN' SNEAKY LITTLE--
YOU WERE SUPPOSED TO STILL BE WEAK!
WHAAK
BUT WE CAN WORK AROUND IT!
KRAANG
YOU WERE NEVER THAT TOUGH, ANYWAY!
GGGG...

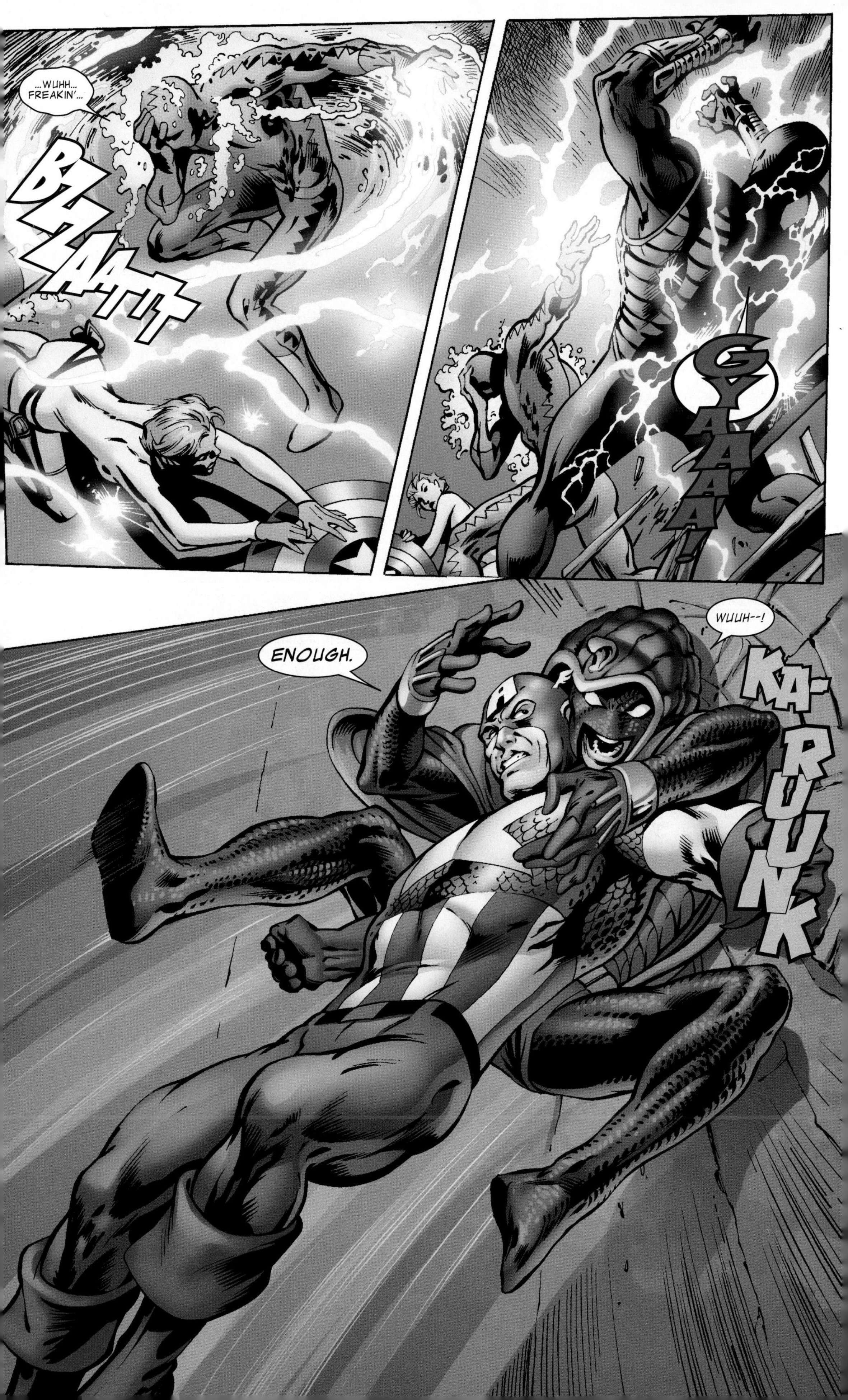
...WUHH... FREAKIN'...
BZZAAATTT
GYAAAA!
ENOUGH.
WUUH--!
KA-RUUNK

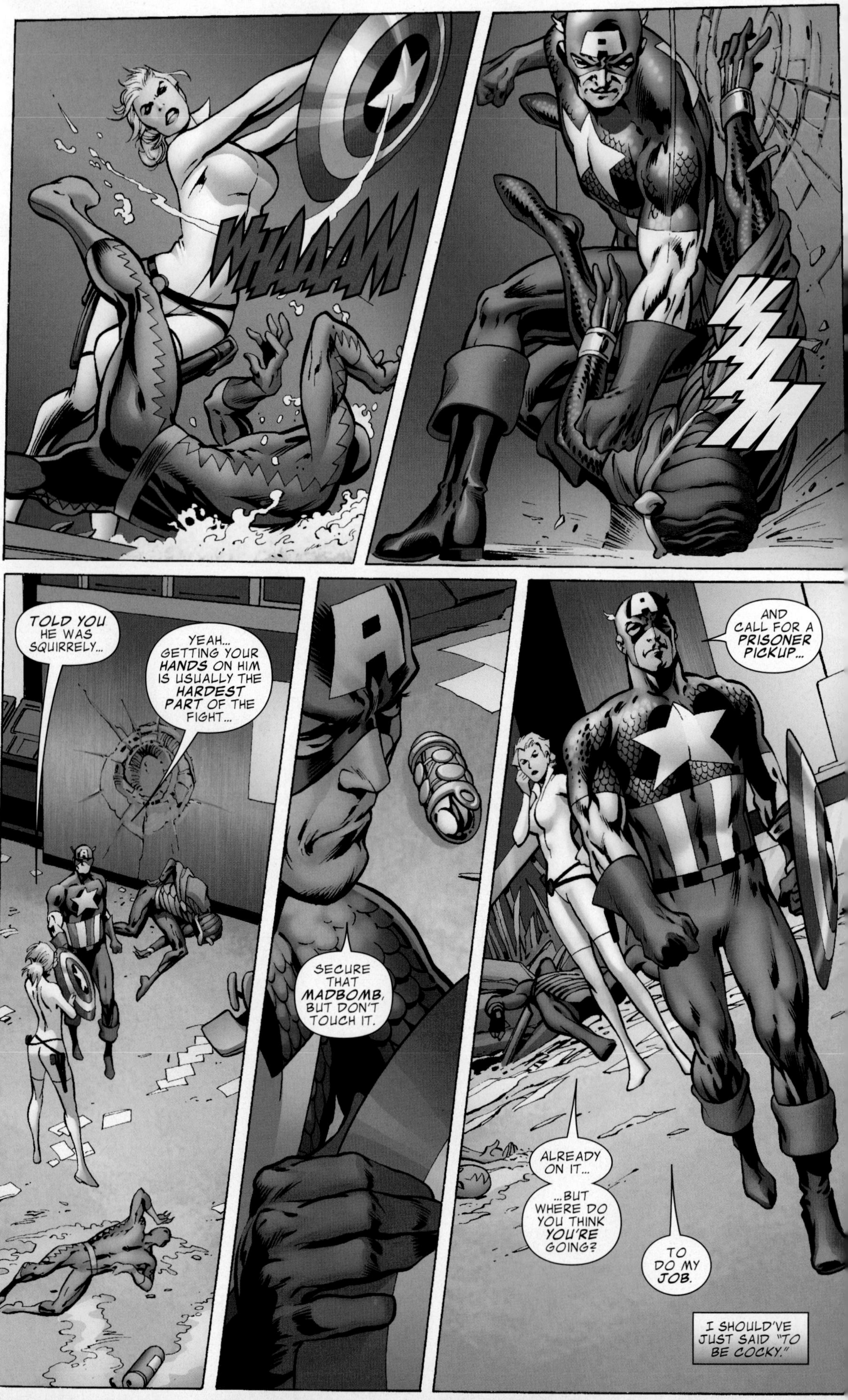
WHAAAM
WHAM
TOLD YOU HE WAS SQUIRRELY...
YEAH... GETTING YOUR HANDS ON HIM IS USUALLY THE HARDEST PART OF THE FIGHT...
SECURE THAT MADBOMB, BUT DON'T TOUCH IT.
AND CALL FOR A PRISONER PICKUP...
ALREADY ON IT...
...BUT WHERE DO YOU THINK YOU'RE GOING?
TO DO MY JOB.
I SHOULD'VE JUST SAID "TO BE COCKY."

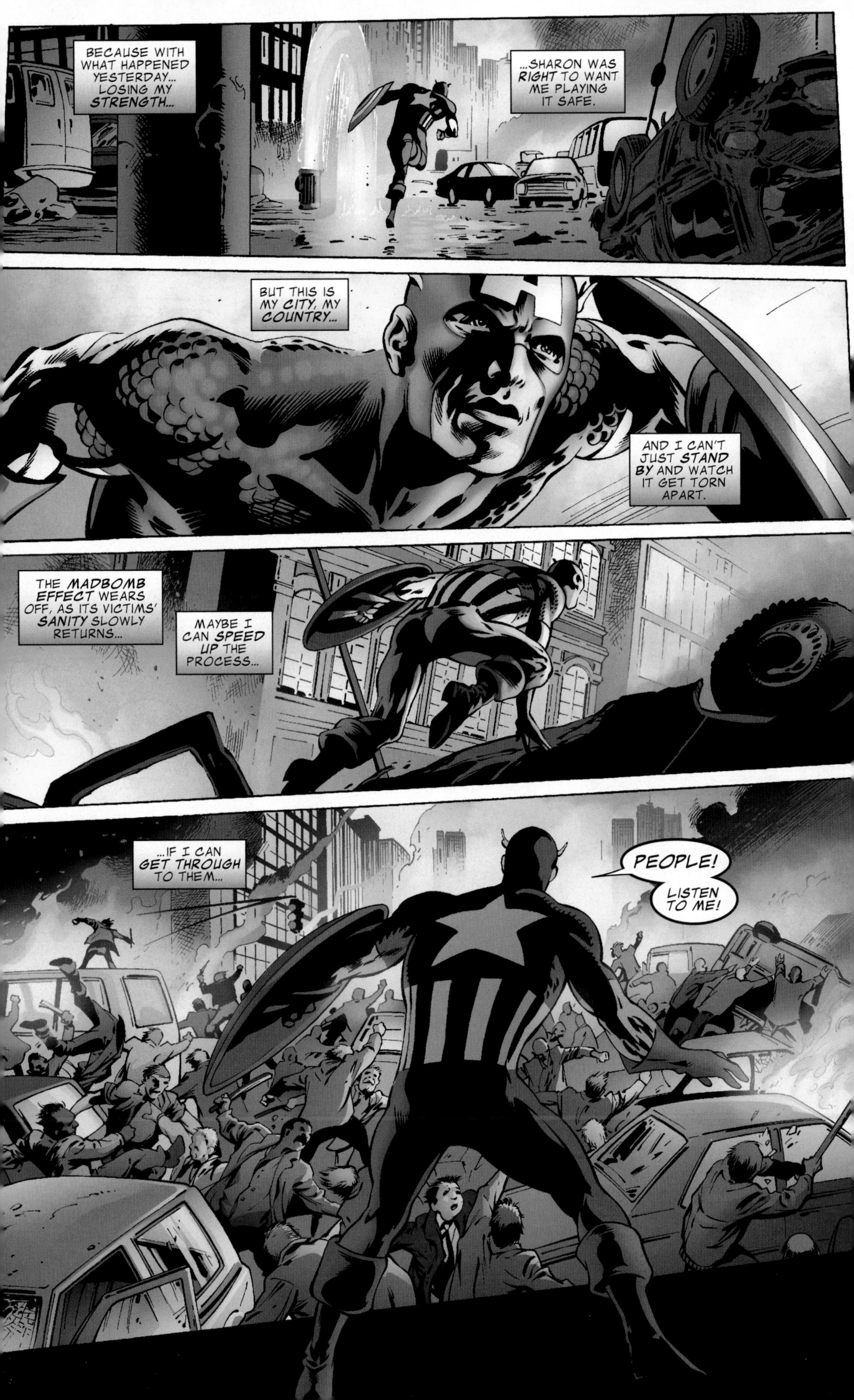
BECAUSE WITH WHAT HAPPENED YESTERDAY... LOSING MY STRENGTH...
...SHARON WAS RIGHT TO WANT ME PLAYING IT SAFE.
BUT THIS IS MY CITY, MY COUNTRY...
AND I CAN'T JUST STAND BY AND WATCH IT GET TORN APART.
THE MADBOMB EFFECT WEARS OFF, AS ITS VICTIMS' SANITY SLOWLY RETURNS...
MAYBE I CAN SPEED UP THE PROCESS...
...IF I CAN GET THROUGH TO THEM...
PEOPLE!
LISTEN TO ME!

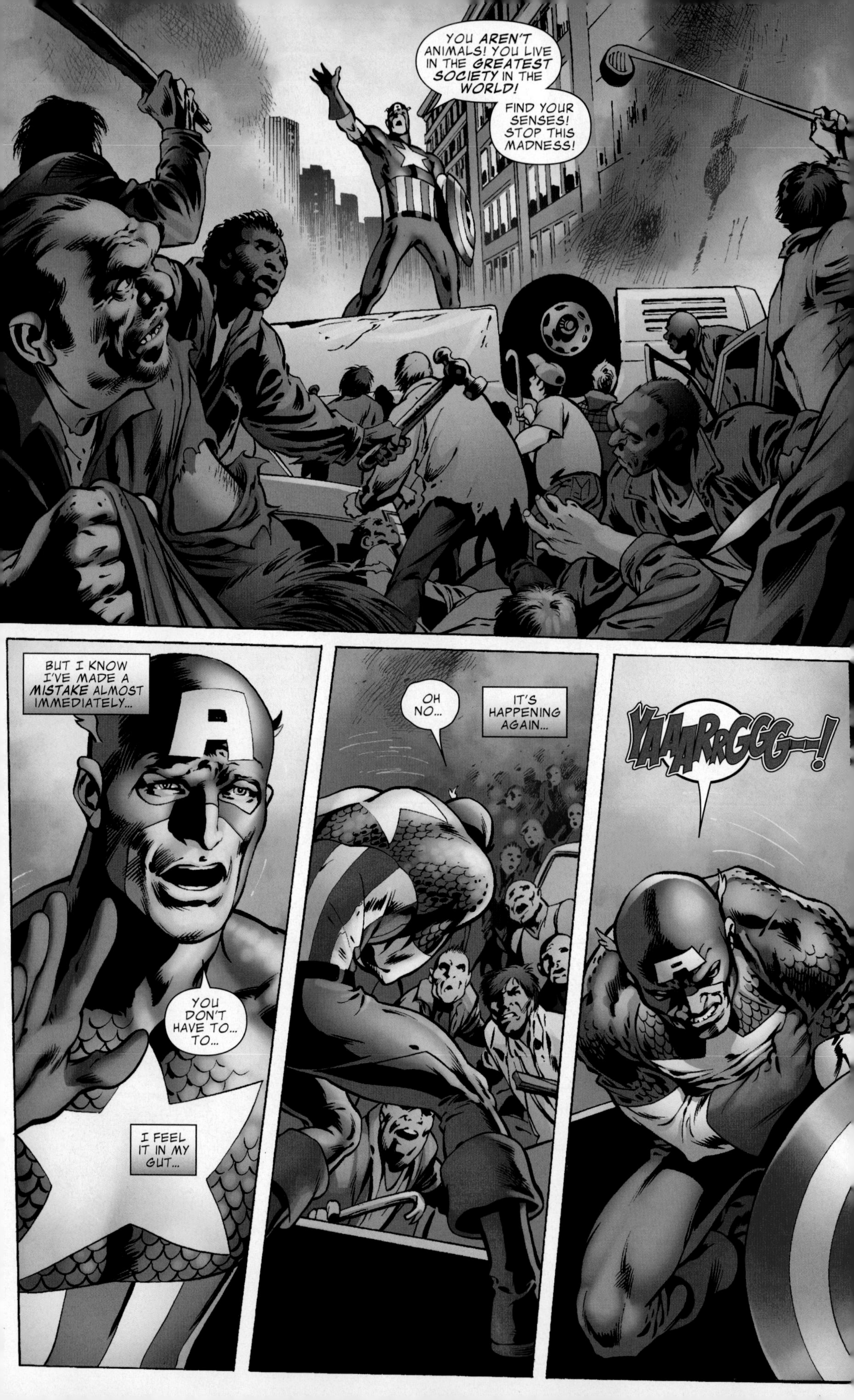
YOU AREN'T ANIMALS! YOU LIVE IN THE GREATEST SOCIETY IN THE WORLD!
FIND YOUR SENSES! STOP THIS MADNESS!
BUT I KNOW I'VE MADE A MISTAKE ALMOST IMMEDIATELY...
YOU DON'T HAVE TO... TO...
I FEEL IT IN MY GUT...
OH NO...
IT'S HAPPENING AGAIN...
YAAARRGGG--!

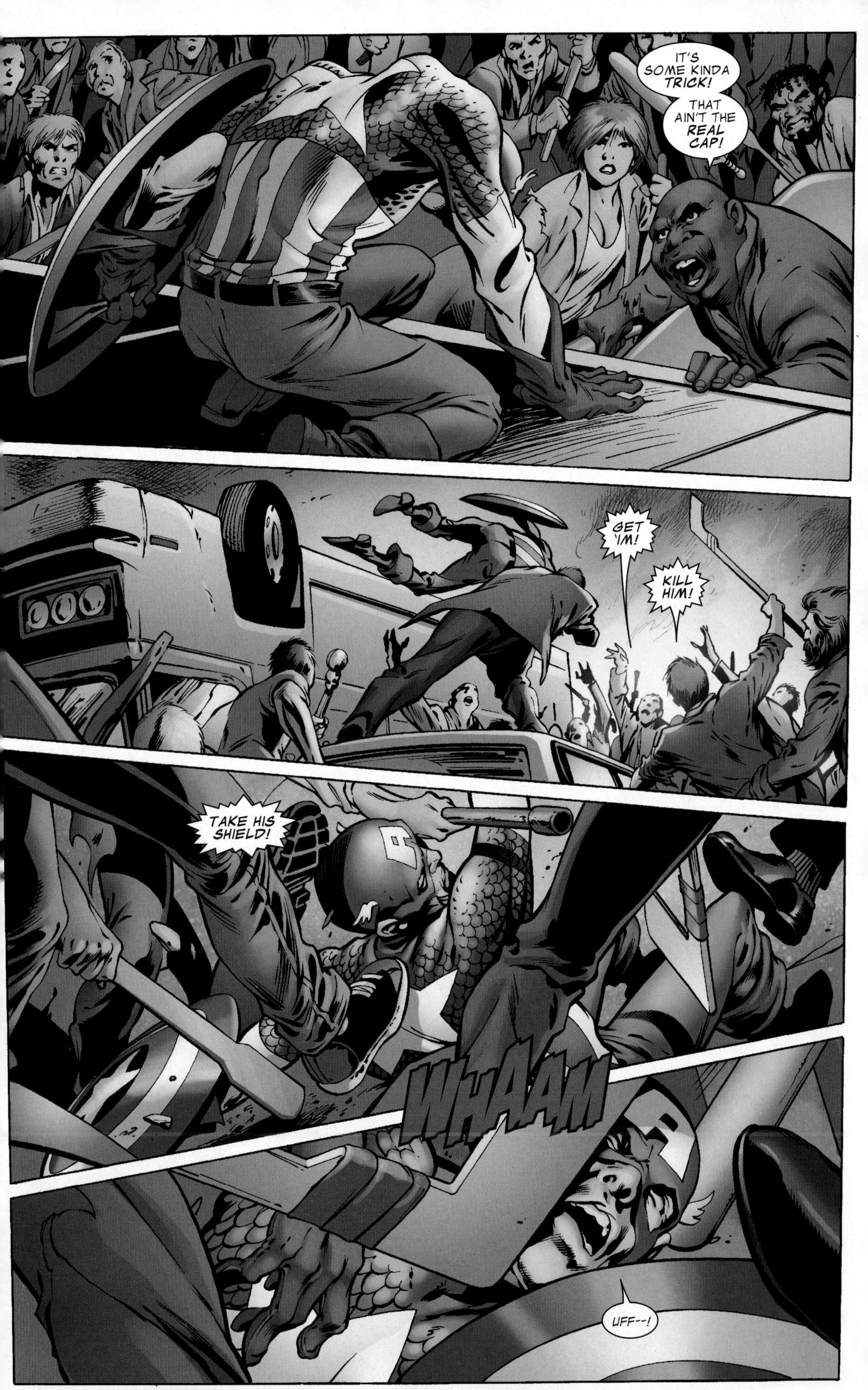
IT'S SOME KINDA TRICK!
THAT AIN'T THE REAL CAP!
GET 'IM!
KILL HIM!
TAKE HIS SHIELD!
WHAAM
UFF--!

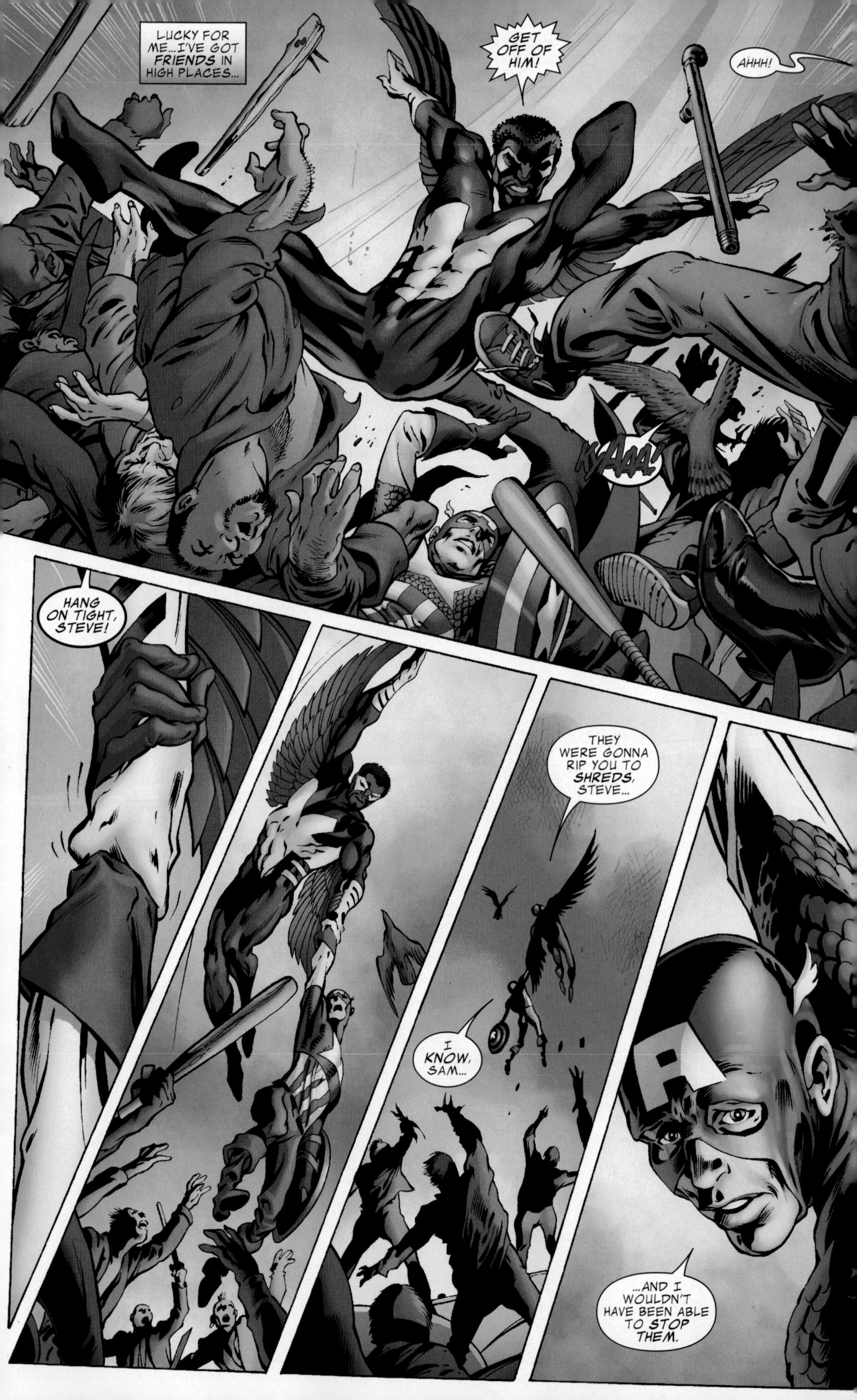
LUCKY FOR ME...I'VE GOT FRIENDS IN HIGH PLACES...
GET OFF OF HIM!
AHHH!
KYAAA!
HANG ON TIGHT, STEVE!
THEY WERE GONNA RIP YOU TO SHREDS, STEVE...
I KNOW, SAM...
...AND I WOULDN'T HAVE BEEN ABLE TO STOP THEM.

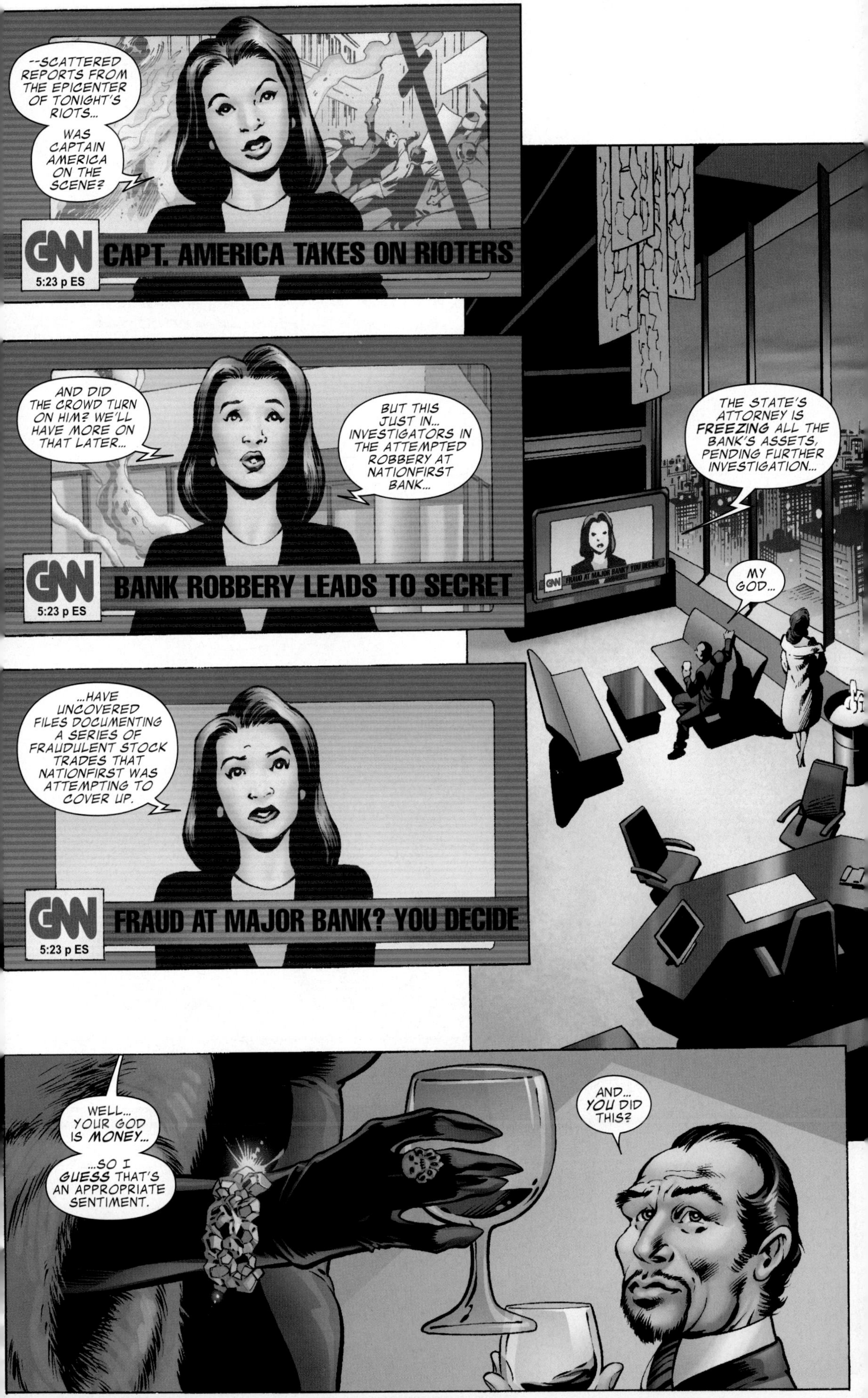
--SCATTERED REPORTS FROM THE EPICENTER OF TONIGHT'S RIOTS...
WAS CAPTAIN AMERICA ON THE SCENE?
GNN 5:23 p ES
CAPT. AMERICA TAKES ON RIOTERS
AND DID THE CROWD TURN ON HIM? WE'LL HAVE MORE ON THAT LATER...
BUT THIS JUST IN... INVESTIGATORS IN THE ATTEMPTED ROBBERY AT NATIONFIRST BANK...
GNN 5:23 p ES
BANK ROBBERY LEADS TO SECRET
...HAVE UNCOVERED FILES DOCUMENTING A SERIES OF FRAUDULENT STOCK TRADES THAT NATIONFIRST WAS ATTEMPTING TO COVER UP.
GNN 5:23 p ES
FRAUD AT MAJOR BANK? YOU DECIDE
THE STATE'S ATTORNEY IS **FREEZING** ALL THE BANK'S ASSETS, PENDING FURTHER INVESTIGATION...
MY GOD...
WELL... YOUR GOD IS ***MONEY***...
...SO I ***GUESS*** THAT'S AN APPROPRIATE SENTIMENT.
AND... ***YOU*** DID THIS?

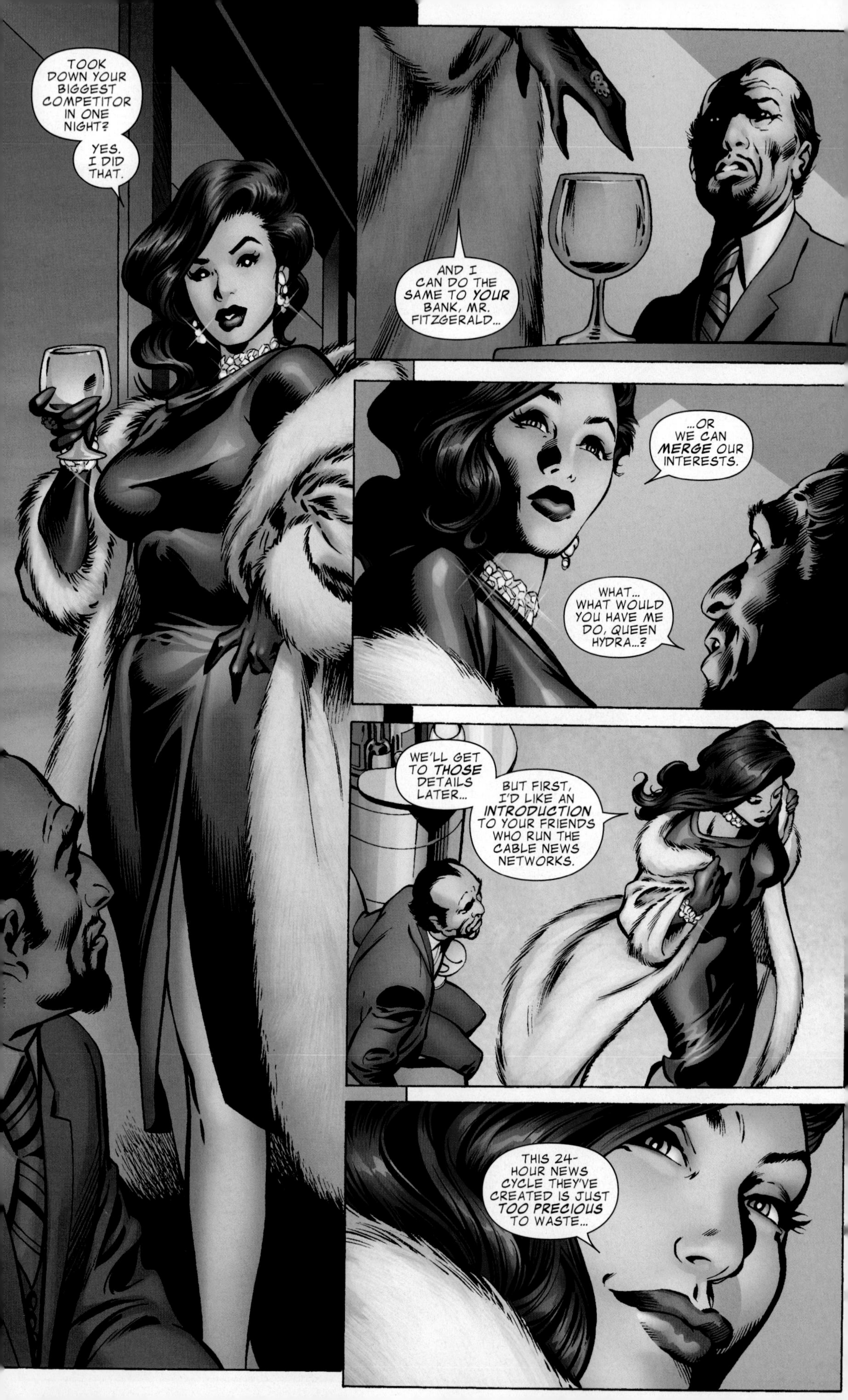
TOOK DOWN YOUR BIGGEST COMPETITOR IN ONE NIGHT?
YES. I DID THAT.
AND I CAN DO THE SAME TO YOUR BANK, MR. FITZGERALD...
...OR WE CAN MERGE OUR INTERESTS.
WHAT... WHAT WOULD YOU HAVE ME DO, QUEEN HYDRA...?
WE'LL GET TO THOSE DETAILS LATER...
BUT FIRST, I'D LIKE AN INTRODUCTION TO YOUR FRIENDS WHO RUN THE CABLE NEWS NETWORKS.
THIS 24-HOUR NEWS CYCLE THEY'VE CREATED IS JUST TOO PRECIOUS TO WASTE...

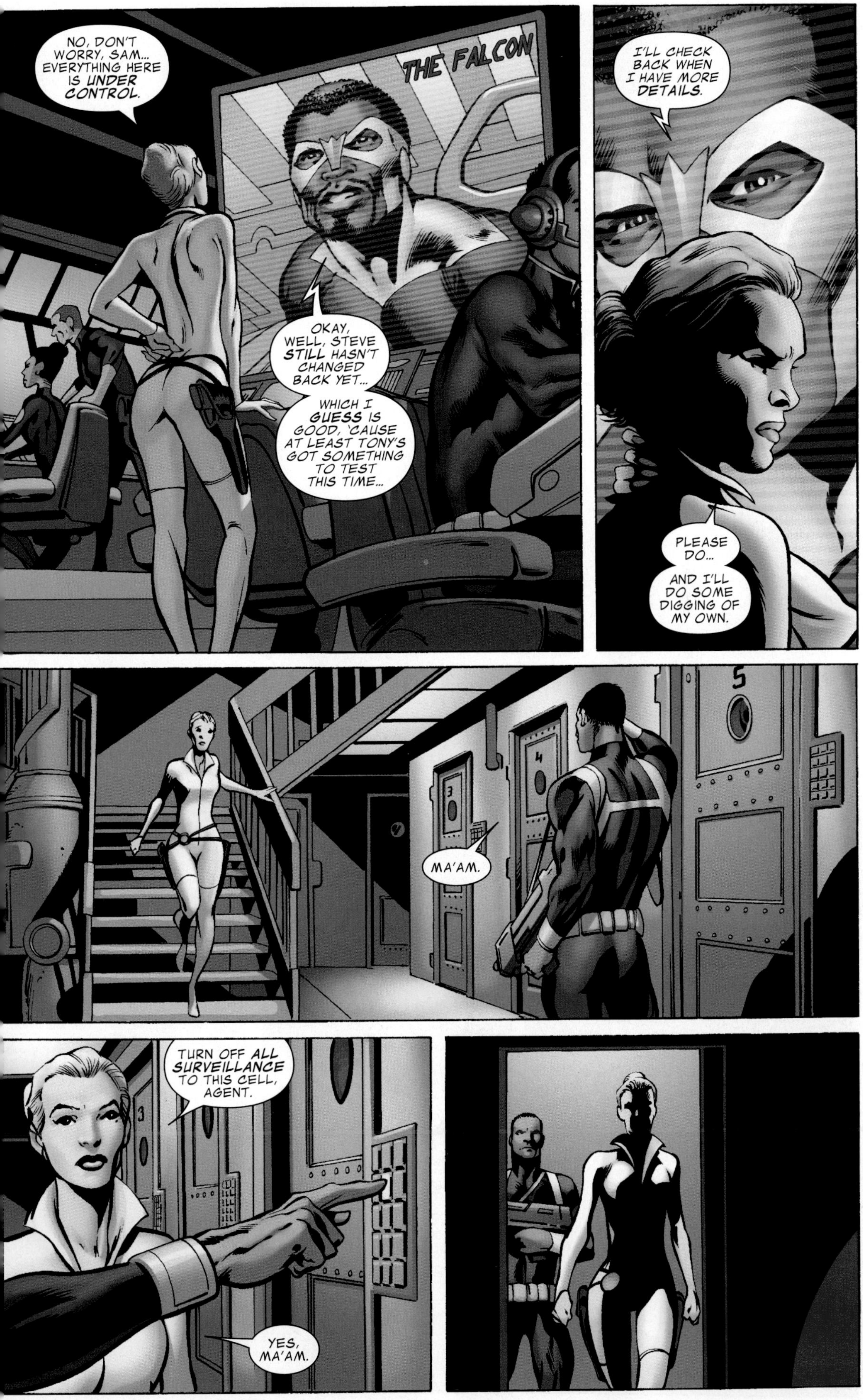
NO, DON'T WORRY, SAM... EVERYTHING HERE IS UNDER CONTROL.
THE FALCON
OKAY, WELL, STEVE STILL HASN'T CHANGED BACK YET...
WHICH I GUESS IS GOOD, 'CAUSE AT LEAST TONY'S GOT SOMETHING TO TEST THIS TIME...
I'LL CHECK BACK WHEN I HAVE MORE DETAILS.
PLEASE DO...
AND I'LL DO SOME DIGGING OF MY OWN.
MA'AM.
TURN OFF ALL SURVEILLANCE TO THIS CELL, AGENT.
YES, MA'AM.

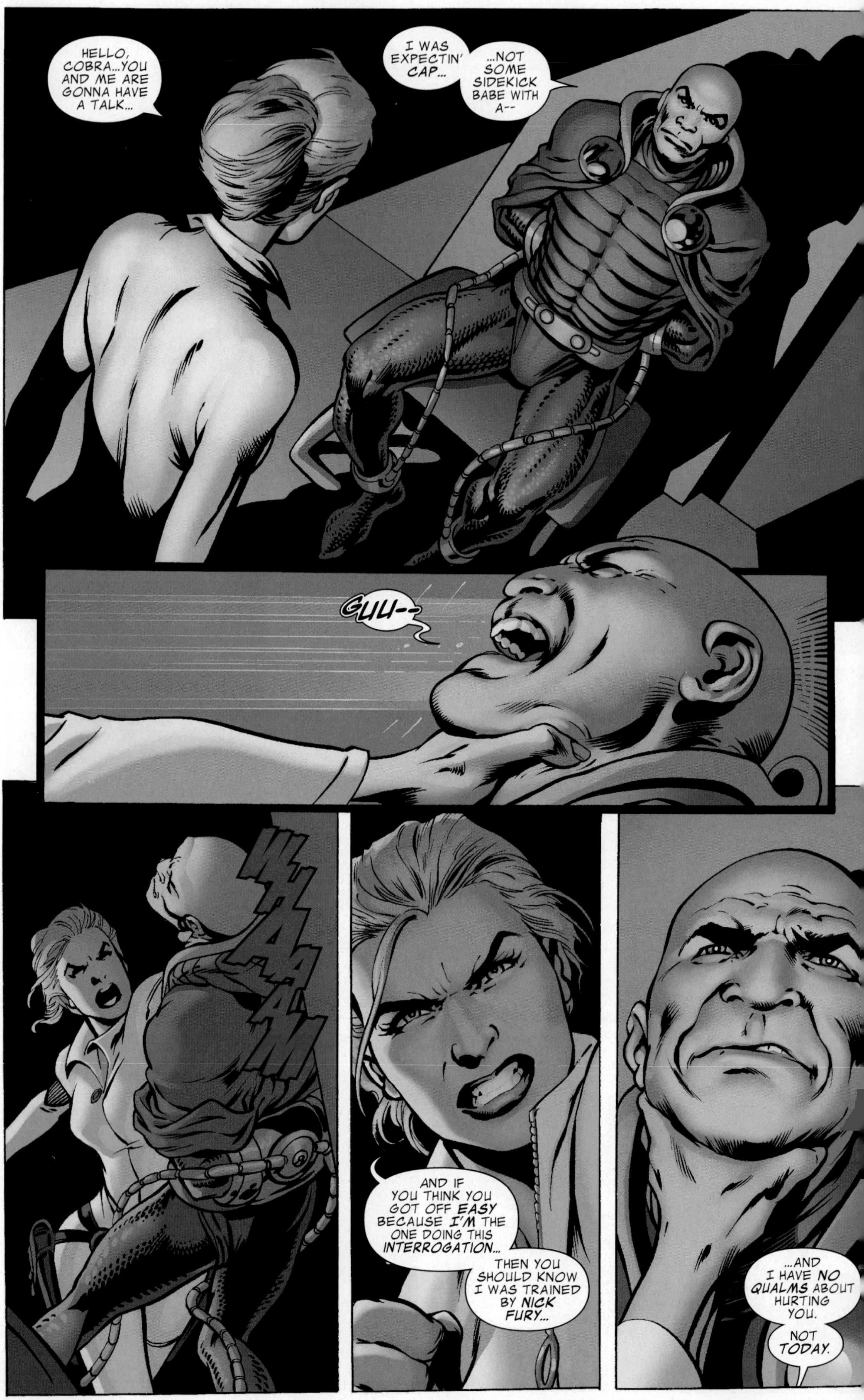
HELLO, COBRA...YOU AND ME ARE GONNA HAVE A TALK...
I WAS EXPECTIN' CAP...
...NOT SOME SIDEKICK BABE WITH A--
GUU--
WHAAAM
AND IF YOU THINK YOU GOT OFF EASY BECAUSE I'M THE ONE DOING THIS INTERROGATION...
THEN YOU SHOULD KNOW I WAS TRAINED BY NICK FURY...
...AND I HAVE NO QUALMS ABOUT HURTING YOU.
NOT TODAY.

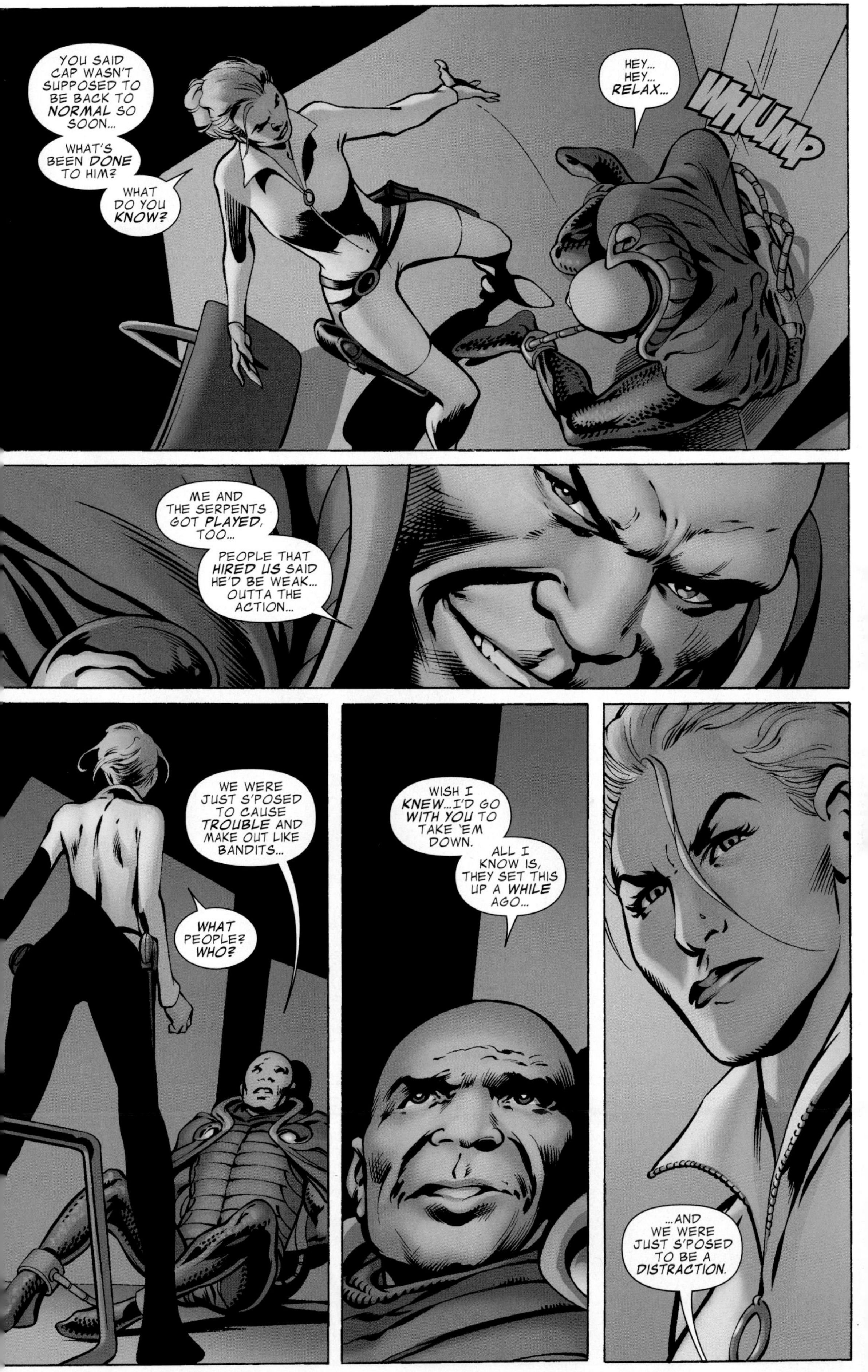
YOU SAID CAP WASN'T SUPPOSED TO BE BACK TO NORMAL SO SOON...
WHAT'S BEEN DONE TO HIM?
WHAT DO YOU KNOW?
HEY... HEY... RELAX...
WHUMP
ME AND THE SERPENTS GOT PLAYED, TOO...
PEOPLE THAT HIRED US SAID HE'D BE WEAK... OUTTA THE ACTION...
WE WERE JUST S'POSED TO CAUSE TROUBLE AND MAKE OUT LIKE BANDITS...
WHAT PEOPLE? WHO?
WISH I KNEW...I'D GO WITH YOU TO TAKE 'EM DOWN.
ALL I KNOW IS, THEY SET THIS UP A WHILE AGO...
...AND WE WERE JUST S'POSED TO BE A DISTRACTION.

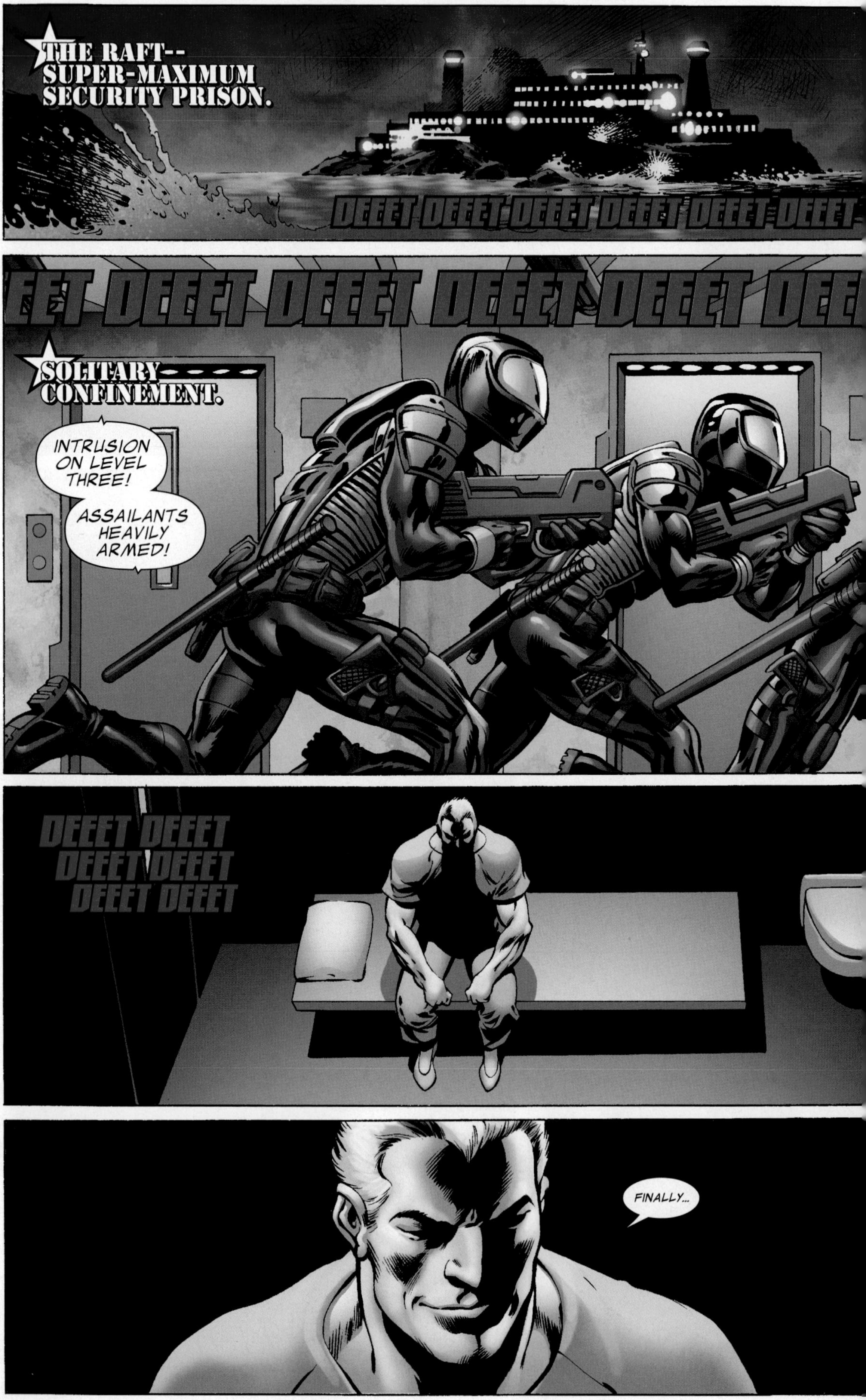
THE RAFT-- SUPER-MAXIMUM SECURITY PRISON.
DEEET DEEET DEEET DEEET DEEET DEEET
DEEET DEEET DEEET DEEET DEEET
SOLITARY CONFINEMENT.
INTRUSION ON LEVEL THREE!
ASSAILANTS HEAVILY ARMED!
DEEET DEEET DEEET DEEET DEEET DEEET
FINALLY...

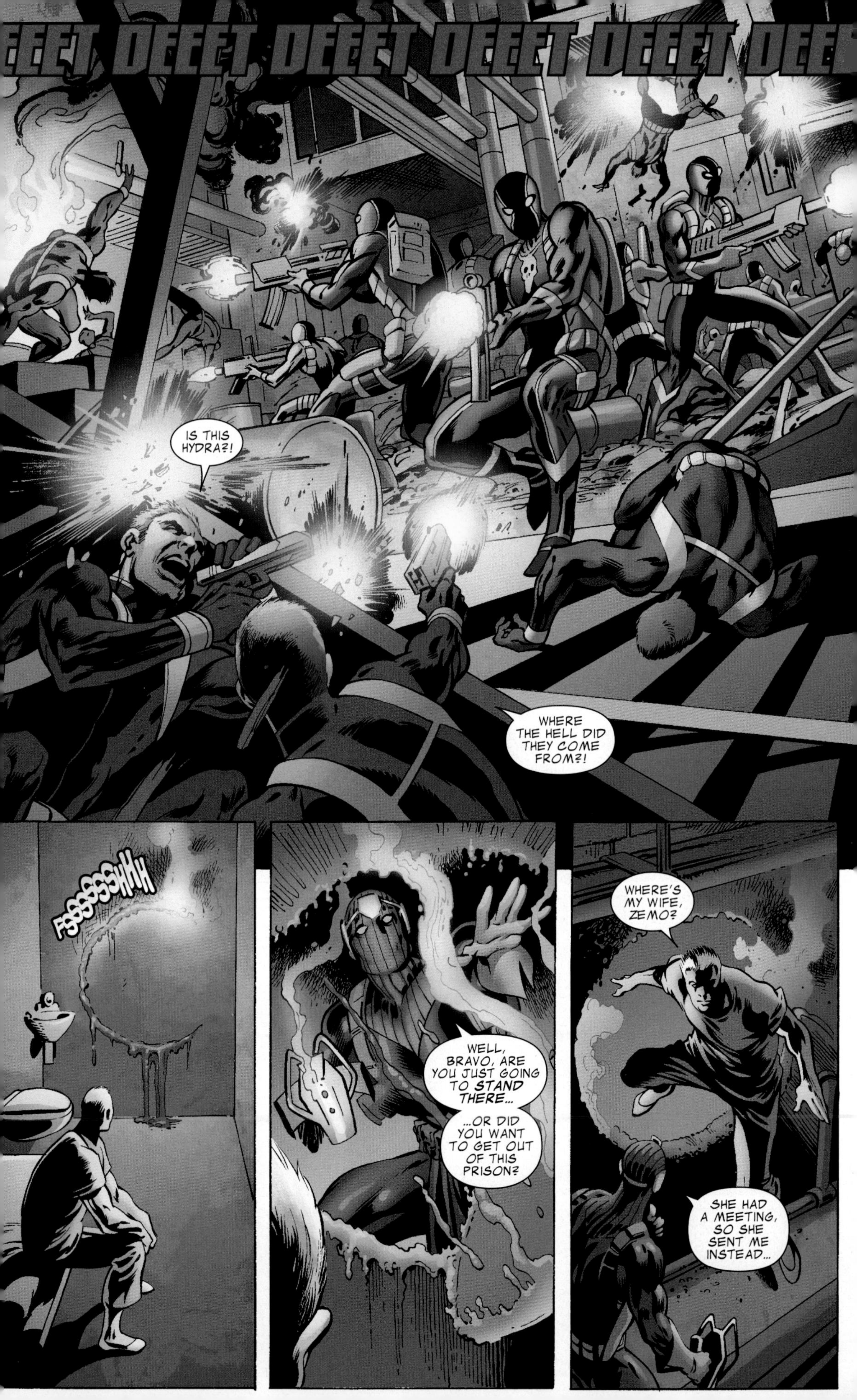
DEEET DEEET DEEET DEEET DEEET DEEET
IS THIS HYDRA?!
WHERE THE HELL DID THEY COME FROM?!
FSSSSSHHH
WELL, BRAVO, ARE YOU JUST GOING TO STAND THERE...
...OR DID YOU WANT TO GET OUT OF THIS PRISON?
WHERE'S MY WIFE, ZEMO?
SHE HAD A MEETING, SO SHE SENT ME INSTEAD...

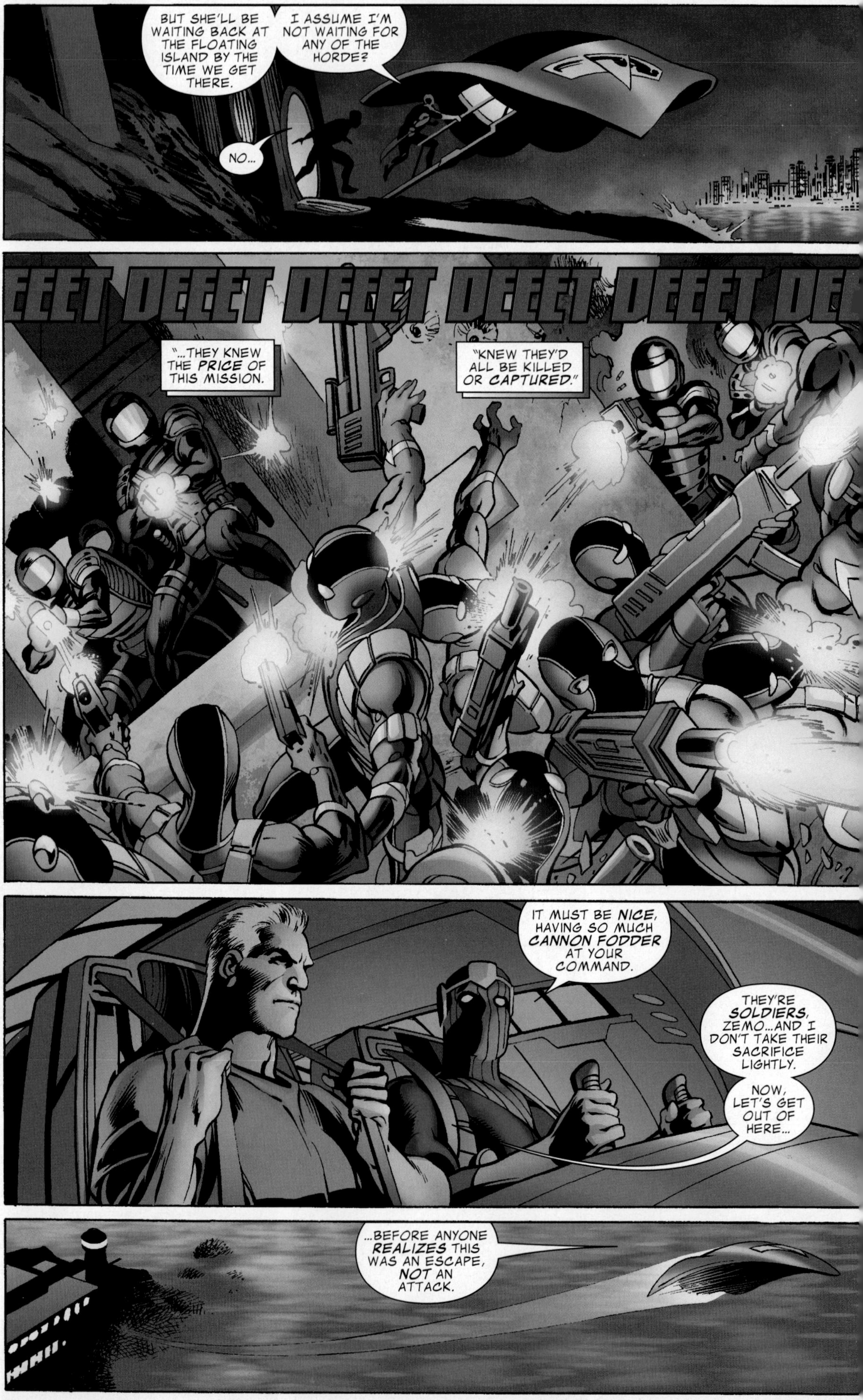
BUT SHE'LL BE WAITING BACK AT THE FLOATING ISLAND BY THE TIME WE GET THERE.
I ASSUME I'M NOT WAITING FOR ANY OF THE HORDE?
NO...
DEEET DEEET DEEET DEEET DEEET
"...THEY KNEW THE PRICE OF THIS MISSION.
"KNEW THEY'D ALL BE KILLED OR CAPTURED."
IT MUST BE NICE, HAVING SO MUCH CANNON FODDER AT YOUR COMMAND.
THEY'RE SOLDIERS, ZEMO...AND I DON'T TAKE THEIR SACRIFICE LIGHTLY.
NOW, LET'S GET OUT OF HERE...
...BEFORE ANYONE REALIZES THIS WAS AN ESCAPE, NOT AN ATTACK.

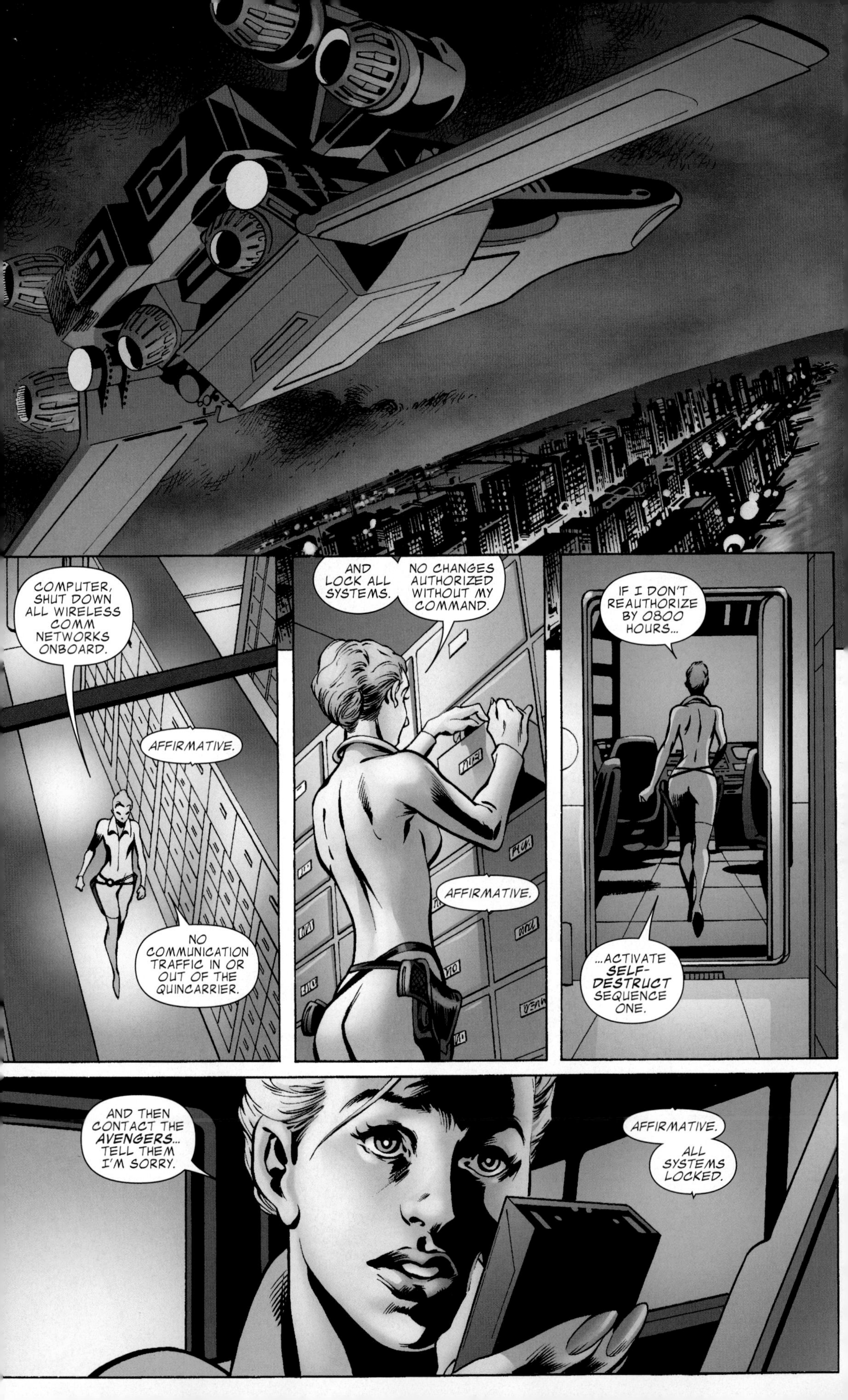
COMPUTER, SHUT DOWN ALL WIRELESS COMM NETWORKS ONBOARD.
AFFIRMATIVE.
NO COMMUNICATION TRAFFIC IN OR OUT OF THE QUINCARRIER.
AND LOCK ALL SYSTEMS.
NO CHANGES AUTHORIZED WITHOUT MY COMMAND.
AFFIRMATIVE.
IF I DON'T REAUTHORIZE BY 0800 HOURS...
...ACTIVATE SELF-DESTRUCT SEQUENCE ONE.
AND THEN CONTACT THE AVENGERS... TELL THEM I'M SORRY.
AFFIRMATIVE.
ALL SYSTEMS LOCKED.

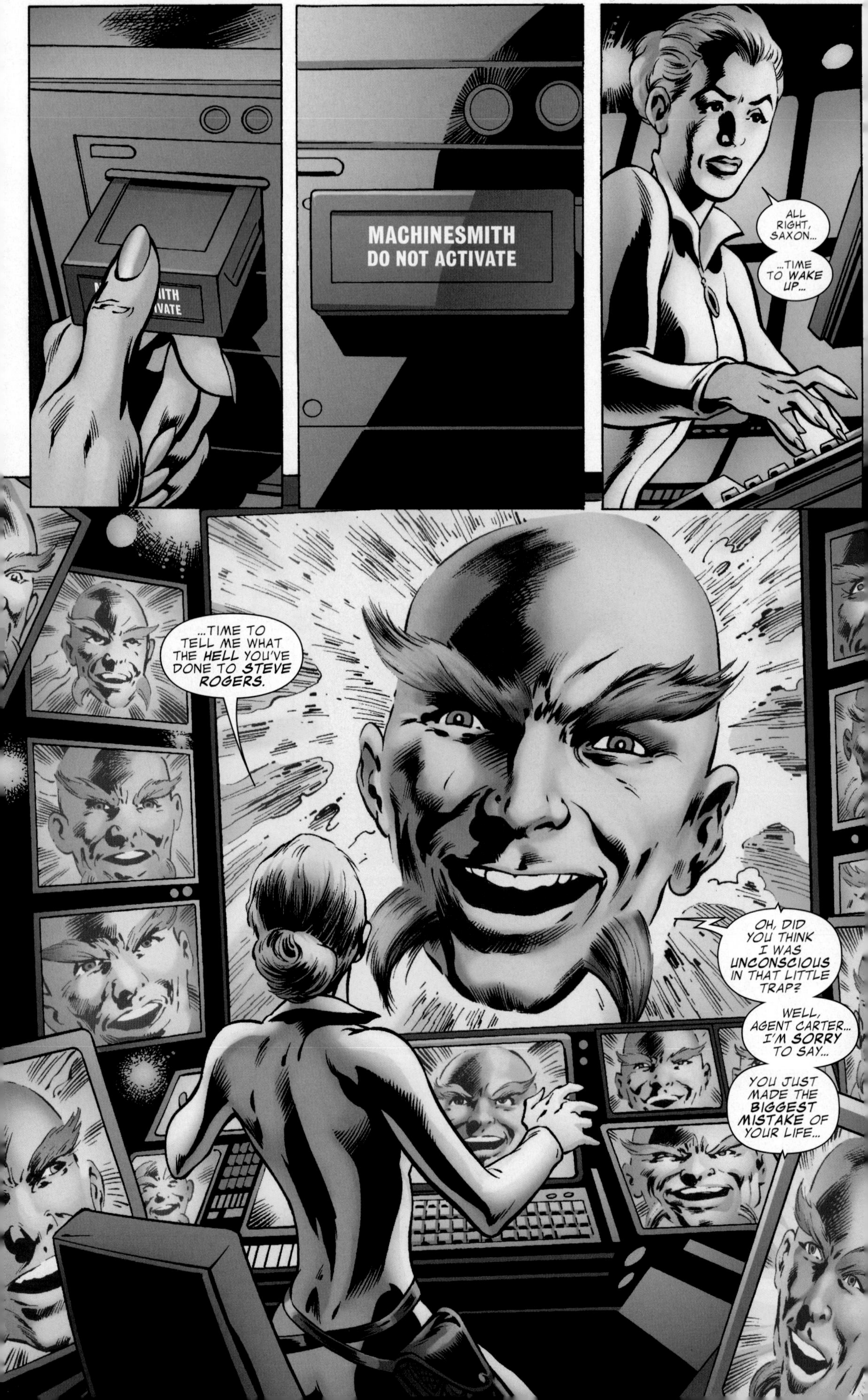
MACHINESMITH
DO NOT ACTIVATE
ALL RIGHT, SAXON...
...TIME TO WAKE UP...
...TIME TO TELL ME WHAT THE HELL YOU'VE DONE TO STEVE ROGERS.
OH, DID YOU THINK I WAS UNCONSCIOUS IN THAT LITTLE TRAP?
WELL, AGENT CARTER... I'M SORRY TO SAY...
YOU JUST MADE THE BIGGEST MISTAKE OF YOUR LIFE...

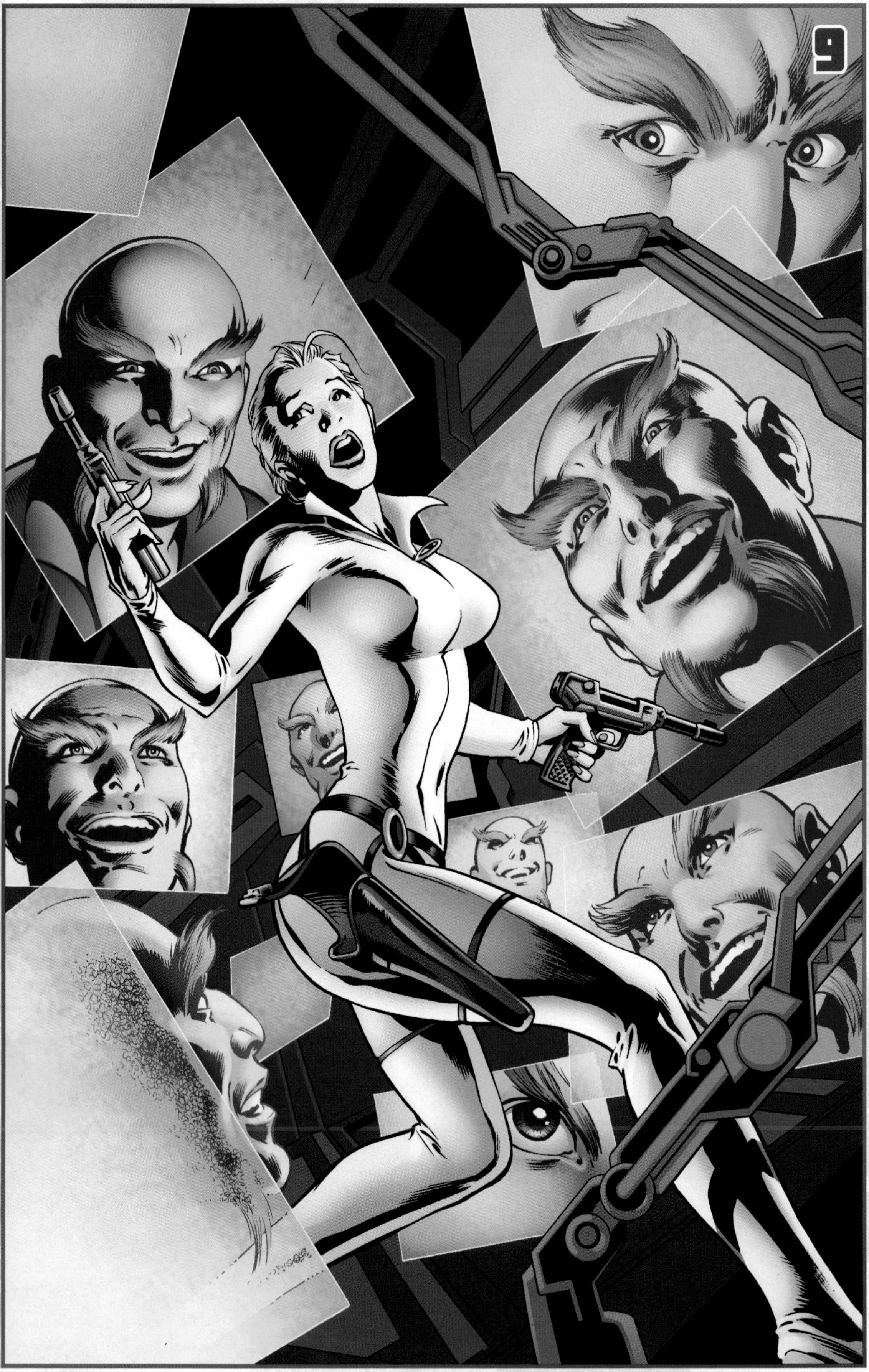
9

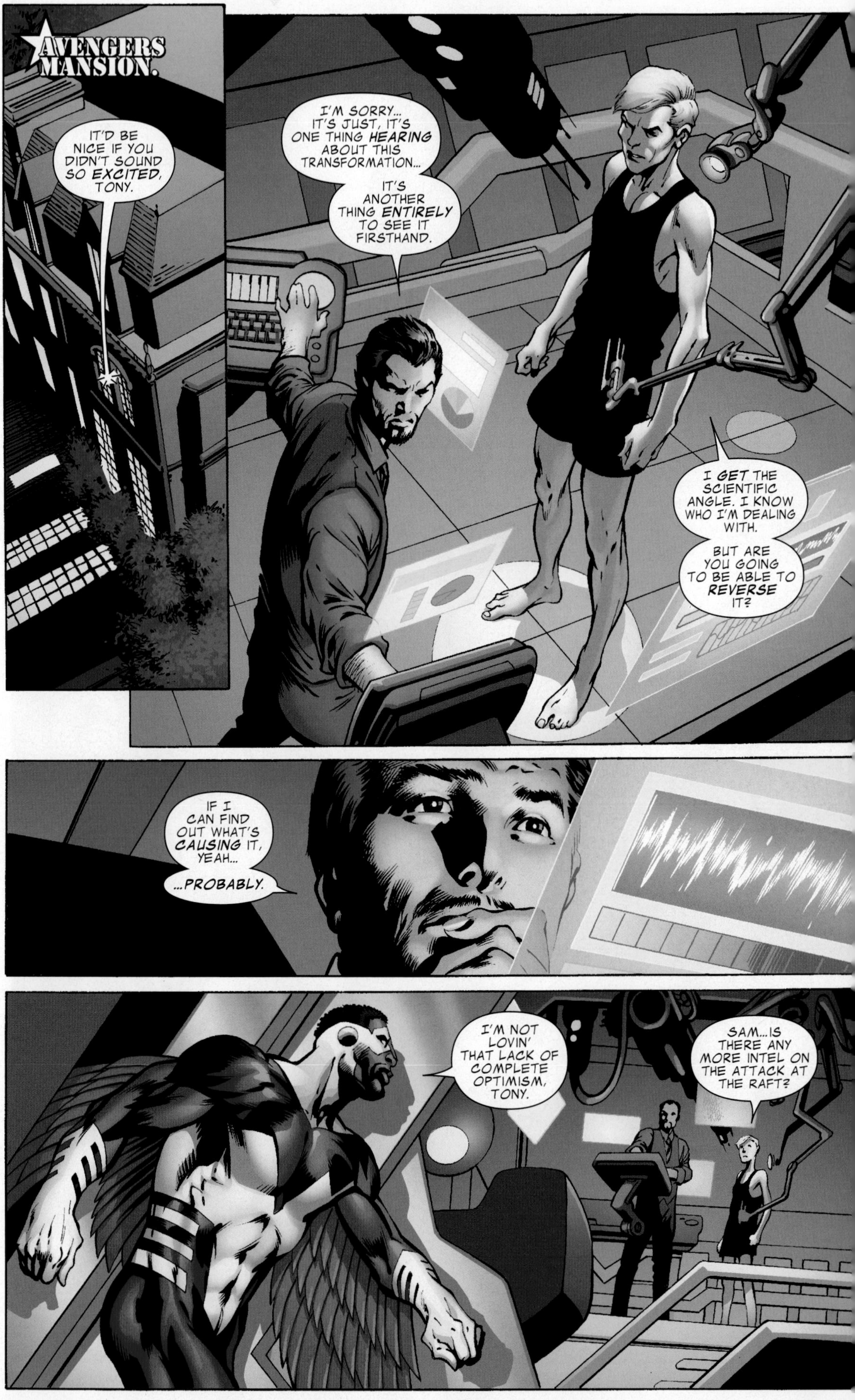
AVENGERS MANSION.
IT'D BE NICE IF YOU DIDN'T SOUND SO EXCITED, TONY.
I'M SORRY... IT'S JUST, IT'S ONE THING HEARING ABOUT THIS TRANSFORMATION...
IT'S ANOTHER THING ENTIRELY TO SEE IT FIRSTHAND.
I GET THE SCIENTIFIC ANGLE. I KNOW WHO I'M DEALING WITH.
BUT ARE YOU GOING TO BE ABLE TO REVERSE IT?
IF I CAN FIND OUT WHAT'S CAUSING IT, YEAH...
...PROBABLY.
I'M NOT LOVIN' THAT LACK OF COMPLETE OPTIMISM, TONY.
SAM...IS THERE ANY MORE INTEL ON THE ATTACK AT THE RAFT?

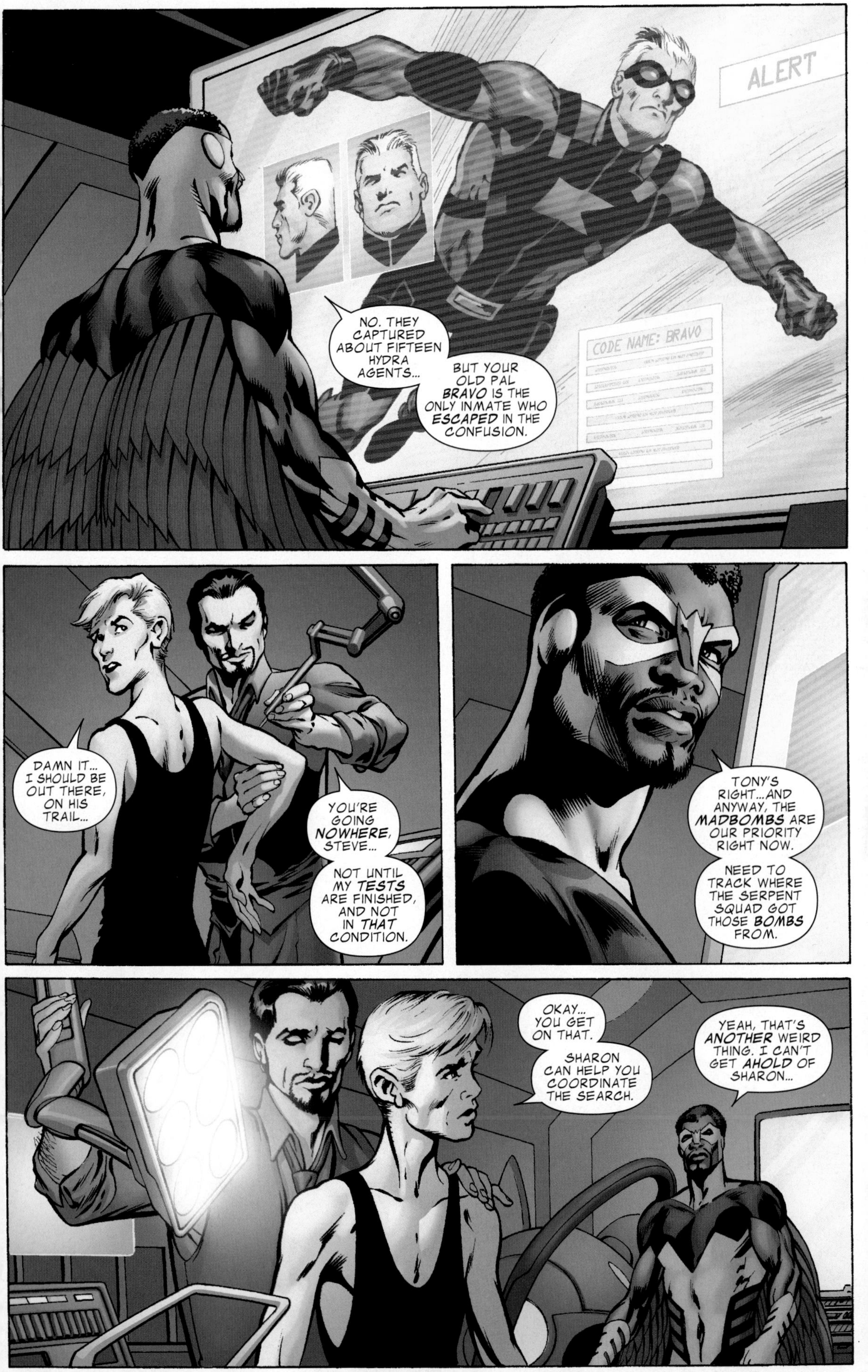
ALERT
CODE NAME: BRAVO
NO. THEY CAPTURED ABOUT FIFTEEN HYDRA AGENTS...
BUT YOUR OLD PAL BRAVO IS THE ONLY INMATE WHO ESCAPED IN THE CONFUSION.
DAMN IT... I SHOULD BE OUT THERE, ON HIS TRAIL...
YOU'RE GOING NOWHERE, STEVE...
NOT UNTIL MY TESTS ARE FINISHED, AND NOT IN THAT CONDITION.
TONY'S RIGHT...AND ANYWAY, THE MADBOMBS ARE OUR PRIORITY RIGHT NOW.
NEED TO TRACK WHERE THE SERPENT SQUAD GOT THOSE BOMBS FROM.
OKAY... YOU GET ON THAT.
SHARON CAN HELP YOU COORDINATE THE SEARCH.
YEAH, THAT'S ANOTHER WEIRD THING. I CAN'T GET AHOLD OF SHARON...

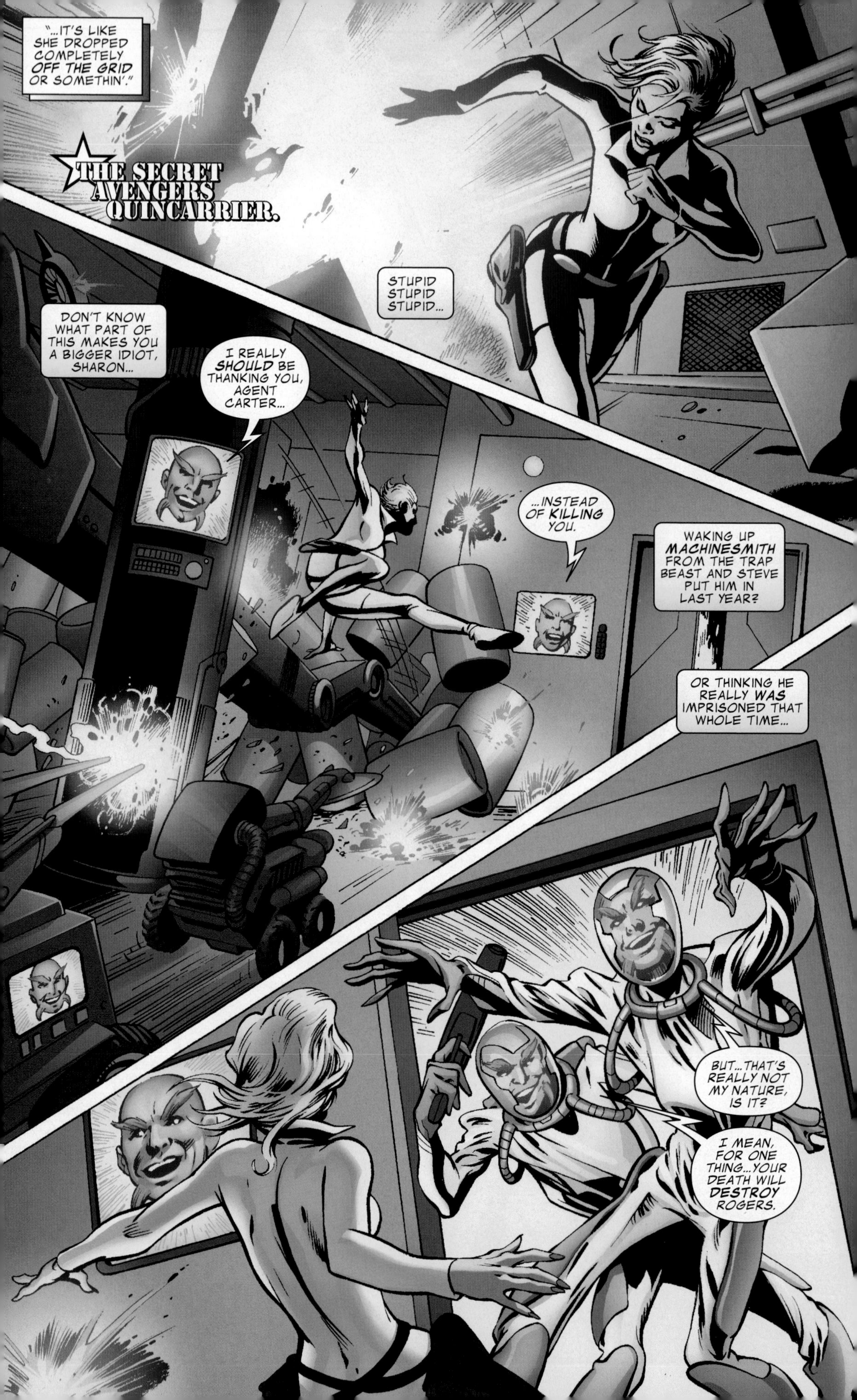
"...IT'S LIKE SHE DROPPED COMPLETELY OFF THE GRID OR SOMETHIN'."
THE SECRET AVENGERS QUINCARRIER.
STUPID STUPID STUPID...
DON'T KNOW WHAT PART OF THIS MAKES YOU A BIGGER IDIOT, SHARON...
I REALLY SHOULD BE THANKING YOU, AGENT CARTER...
...INSTEAD OF KILLING YOU.
WAKING UP MACHINESMITH FROM THE TRAP BEAST AND STEVE PUT HIM IN LAST YEAR?
OR THINKING HE REALLY WAS IMPRISONED THAT WHOLE TIME...
BUT...THAT'S REALLY NOT MY NATURE, IS IT?
I MEAN, FOR ONE THING...YOUR DEATH WILL DESTROY ROGERS.

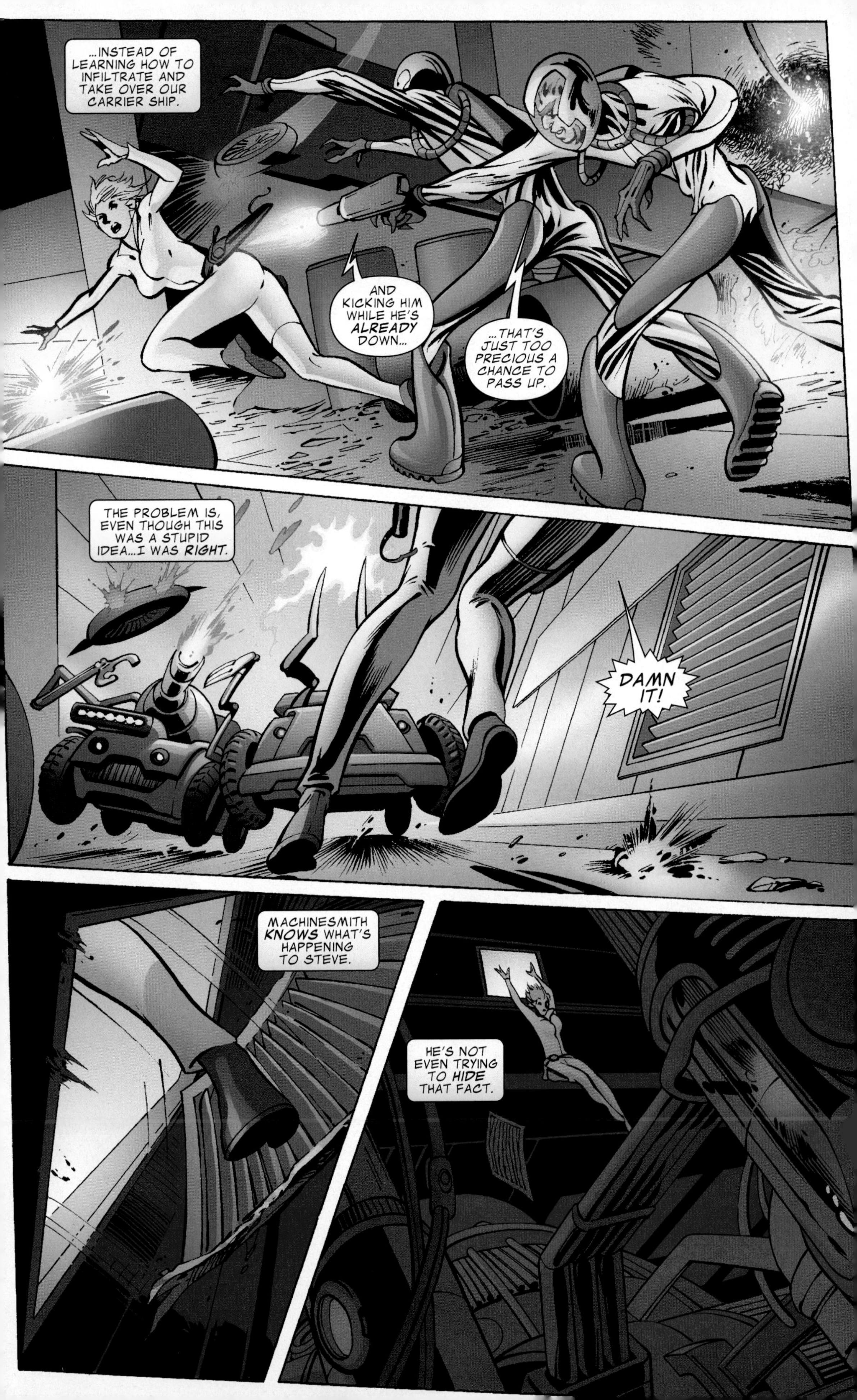
...INSTEAD OF LEARNING HOW TO INFILTRATE AND TAKE OVER OUR CARRIER SHIP.
AND KICKING HIM WHILE HE'S ALREADY DOWN...
...THAT'S JUST TOO PRECIOUS A CHANCE TO PASS UP.
THE PROBLEM IS, EVEN THOUGH THIS WAS A STUPID IDEA...I WAS RIGHT.
DAMN IT!
MACHINESMITH KNOWS WHAT'S HAPPENING TO STEVE.
HE'S NOT EVEN TRYING TO HIDE THAT FACT.

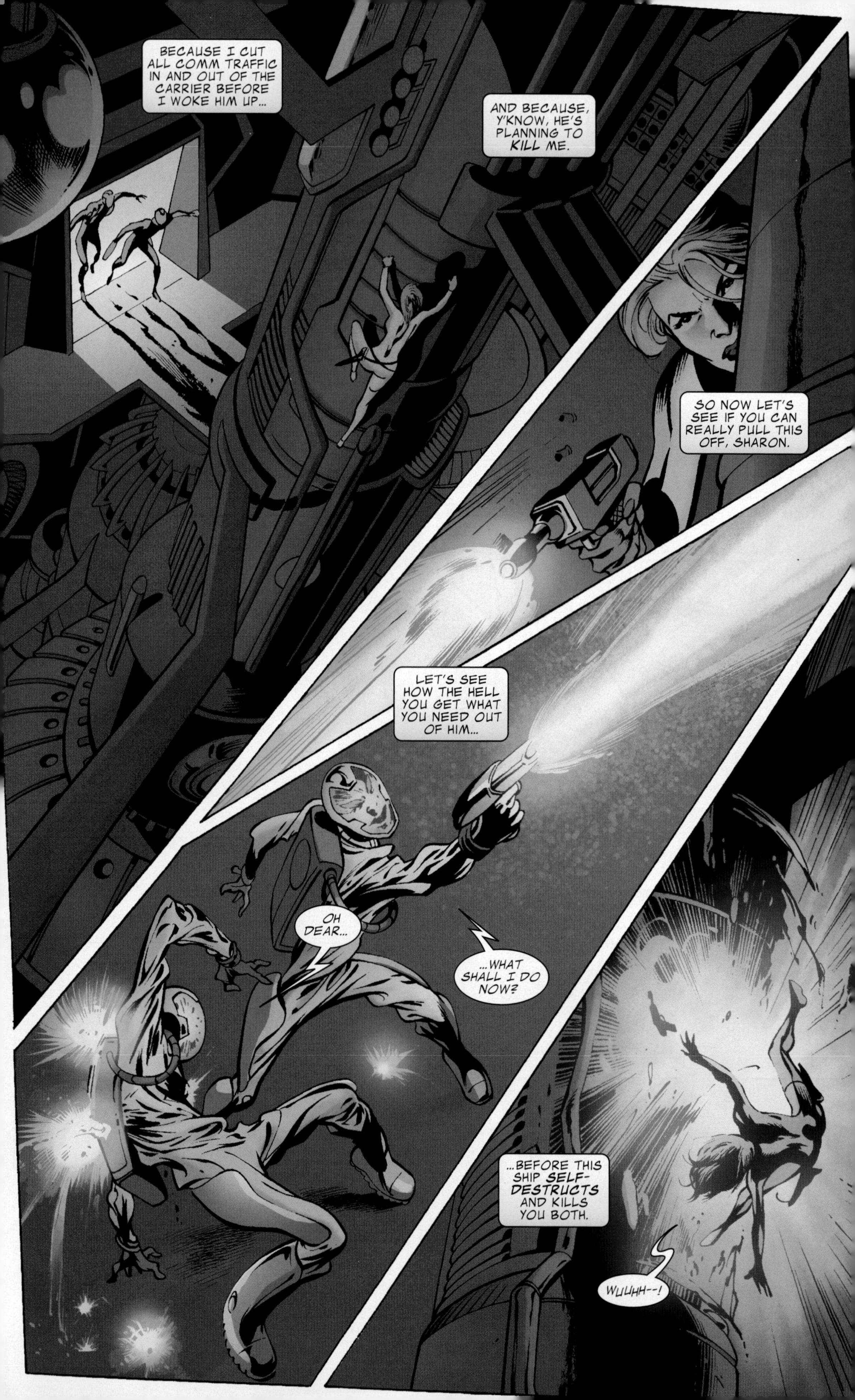
BECAUSE I CUT ALL COMM TRAFFIC IN AND OUT OF THE CARRIER BEFORE I WOKE HIM UP...
AND BECAUSE, Y'KNOW, HE'S PLANNING TO KILL ME.
SO NOW LET'S SEE IF YOU CAN REALLY PULL THIS OFF, SHARON.
LET'S SEE HOW THE HELL YOU GET WHAT YOU NEED OUT OF HIM...
OH DEAR...
...WHAT SHALL I DO NOW?
...BEFORE THIS SHIP SELF-DESTRUCTS AND KILLS YOU BOTH.
WUUHH--!

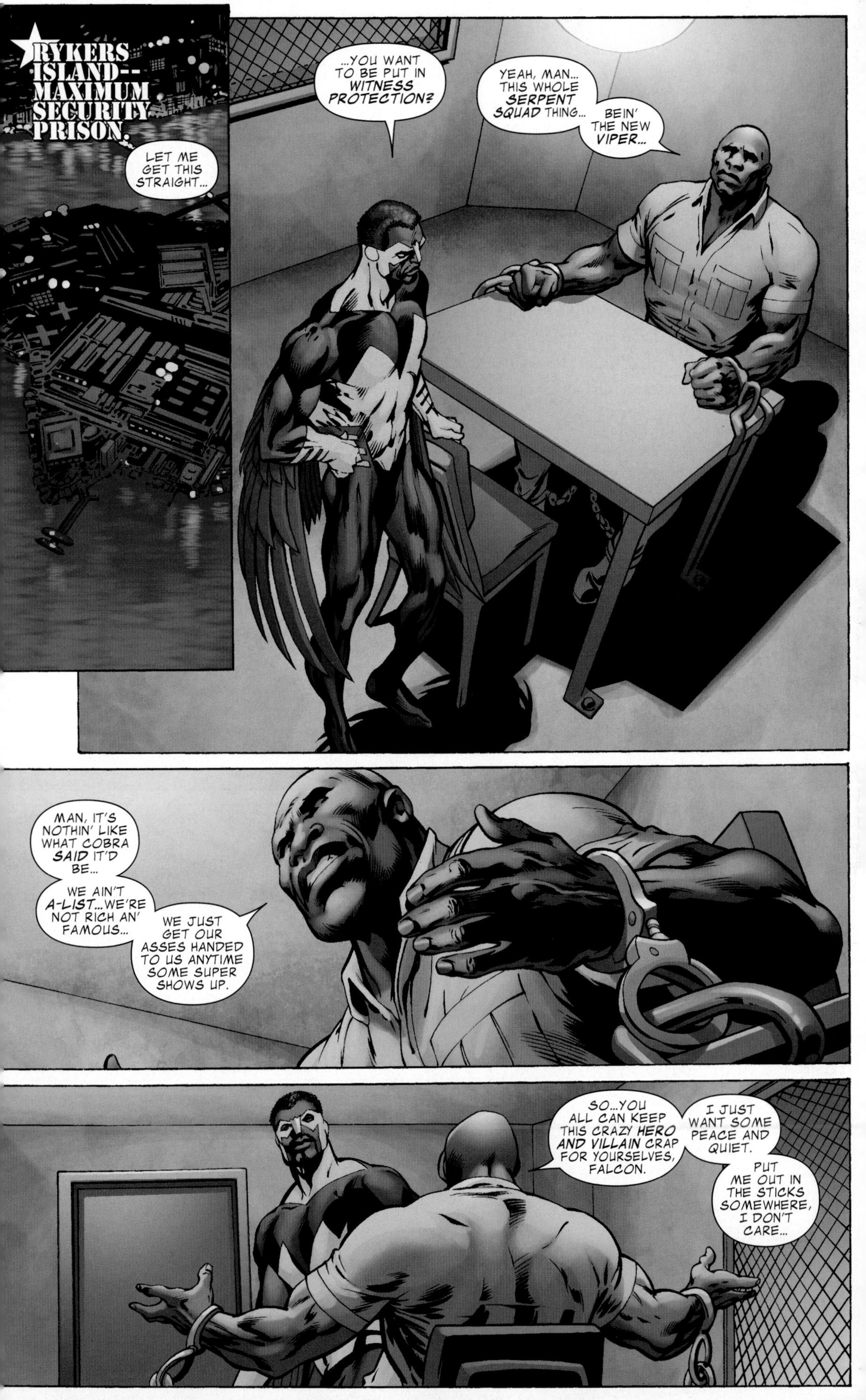
RYKERS ISLAND-- MAXIMUM SECURITY PRISON.
LET ME GET THIS STRAIGHT...
...YOU WANT TO BE PUT IN WITNESS PROTECTION?
YEAH, MAN... THIS WHOLE SERPENT SQUAD THING...
BEIN' THE NEW VIPER...
MAN, IT'S NOTHIN' LIKE WHAT COBRA SAID IT'D BE...
WE AIN'T A-LIST...WE'RE NOT RICH AN' FAMOUS...
WE JUST GET OUR ASSES HANDED TO US ANYTIME SOME SUPER SHOWS UP.
SO...YOU ALL CAN KEEP THIS CRAZY HERO AND VILLAIN CRAP FOR YOURSELVES, FALCON.
I JUST WANT SOME PEACE AND QUIET.
PUT ME OUT IN THE STICKS SOMEWHERE, I DON'T CARE...

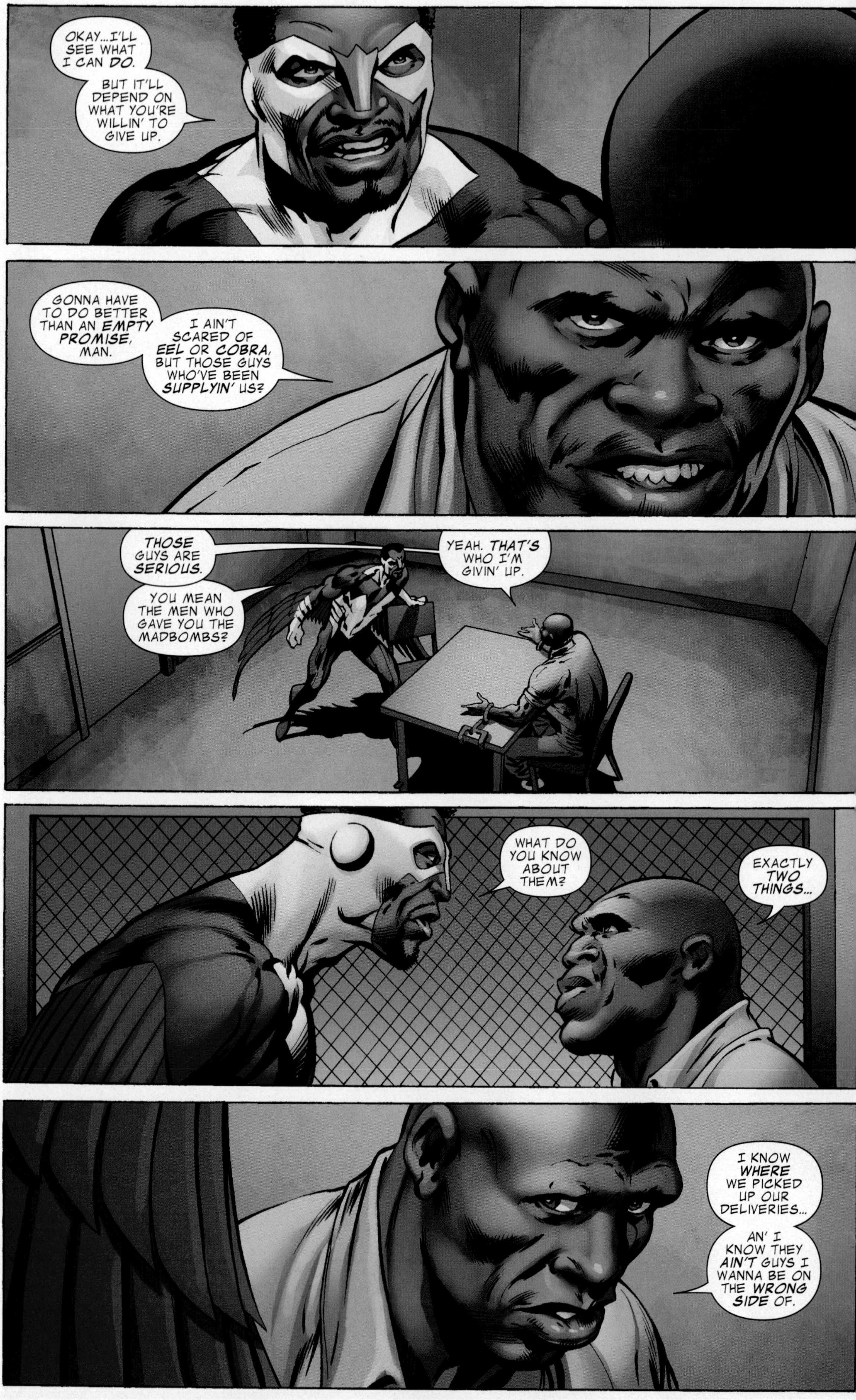
OKAY...I'LL SEE WHAT I CAN DO.
BUT IT'LL DEPEND ON WHAT YOU'RE WILLIN' TO GIVE UP.
GONNA HAVE TO DO BETTER THAN AN EMPTY PROMISE, MAN.
I AIN'T SCARED OF EEL OR COBRA, BUT THOSE GUYS WHO'VE BEEN SUPPLYIN' US?
THOSE GUYS ARE SERIOUS.
YOU MEAN THE MEN WHO GAVE YOU THE MADBOMBS?
YEAH. THAT'S WHO I'M GIVIN' UP.
WHAT DO YOU KNOW ABOUT THEM?
EXACTLY TWO THINGS...
I KNOW WHERE WE PICKED UP OUR DELIVERIES...
AN' I KNOW THEY AIN'T GUYS I WANNA BE ON THE WRONG SIDE OF.

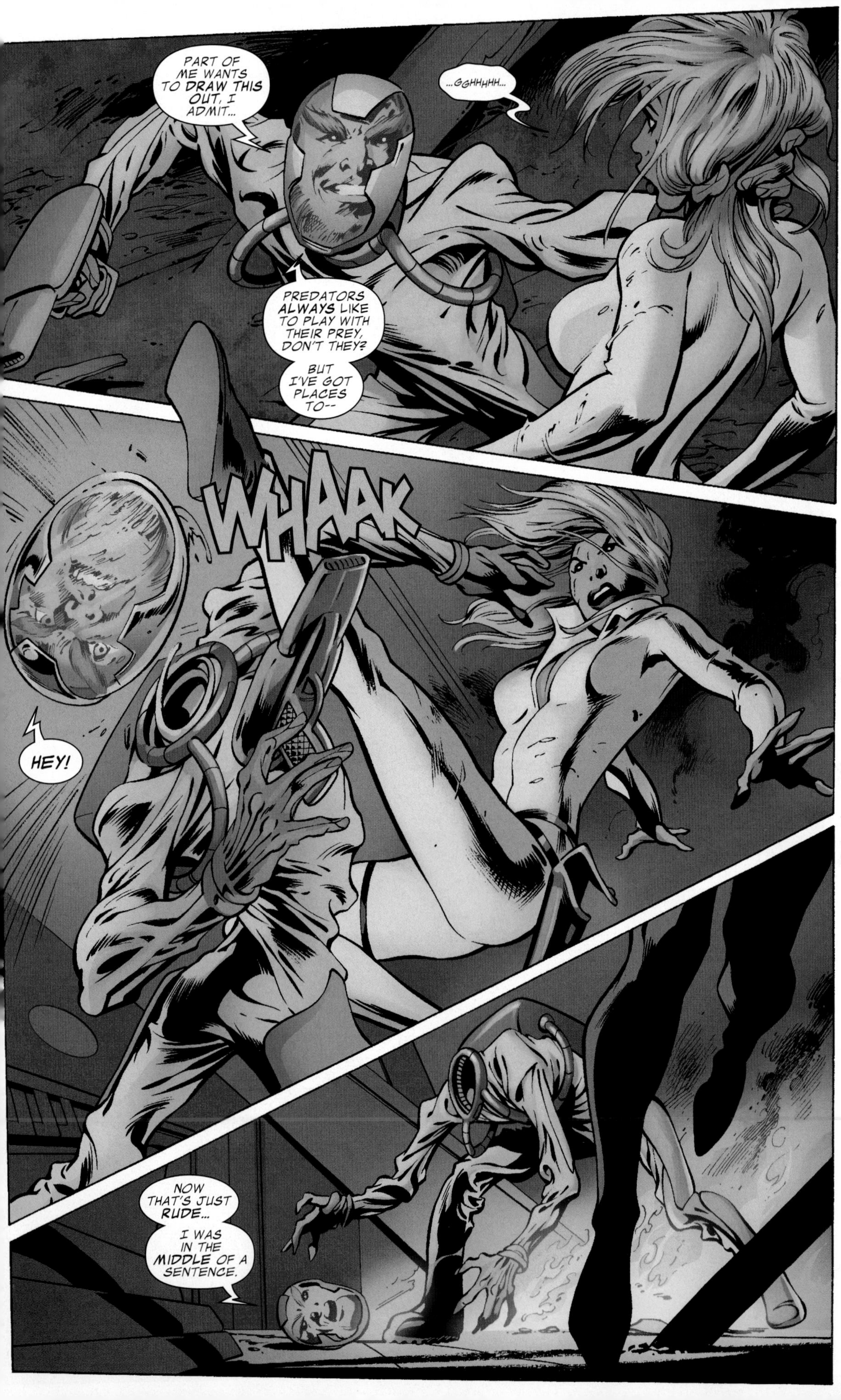
PART OF ME WANTS TO DRAW THIS OUT, I ADMIT...
...GGHHHHH...
PREDATORS ALWAYS LIKE TO PLAY WITH THEIR PREY, DON'T THEY?
BUT I'VE GOT PLACES TO--
WHAAK
HEY!
NOW THAT'S JUST RUDE...
I WAS IN THE MIDDLE OF A SENTENCE.

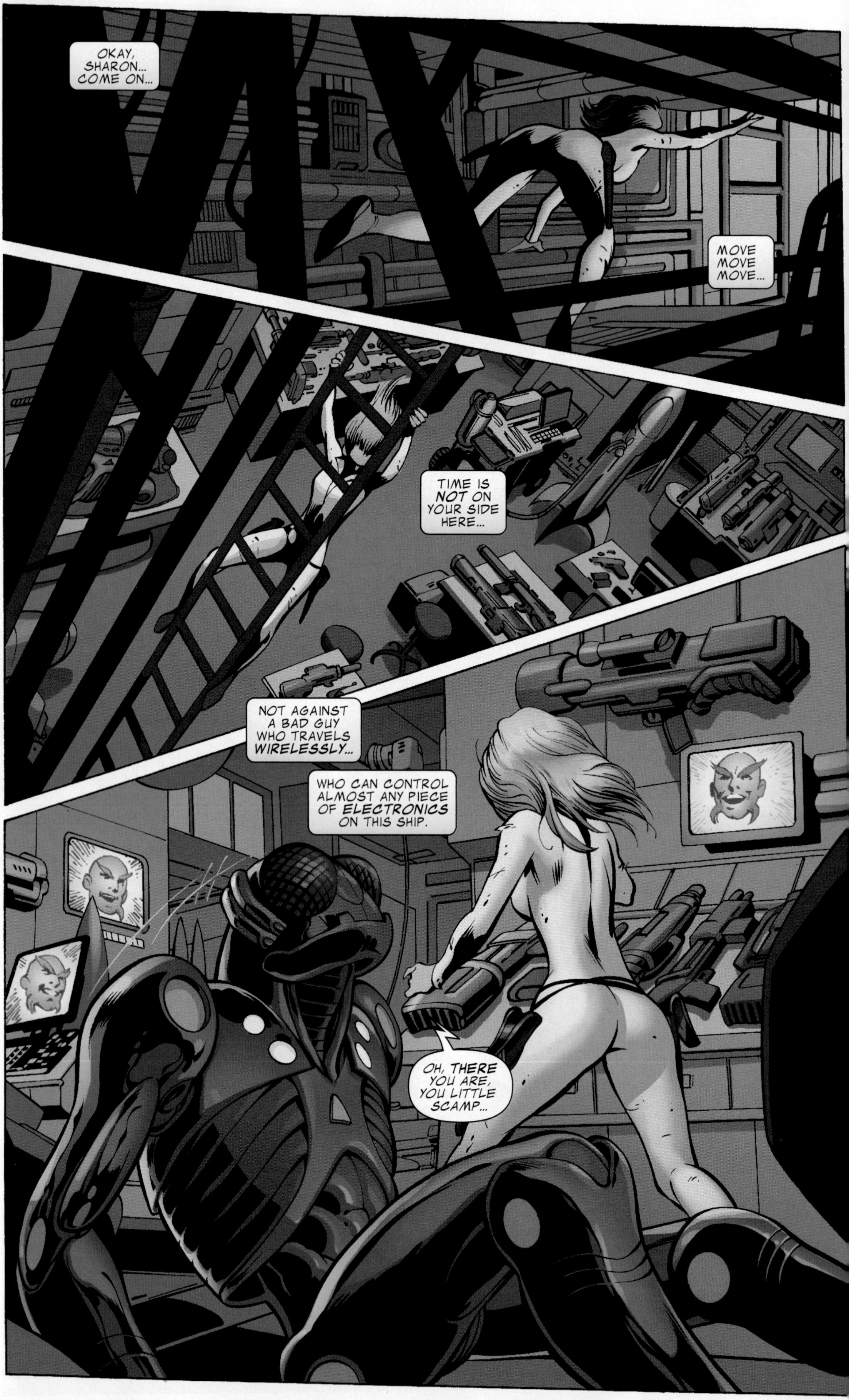
OKAY, SHARON... COME ON...
MOVE MOVE MOVE...
TIME IS NOT ON YOUR SIDE HERE...
NOT AGAINST A BAD GUY WHO TRAVELS WIRELESSLY...
WHO CAN CONTROL ALMOST ANY PIECE OF ELECTRONICS ON THIS SHIP.
OH, THERE YOU ARE, YOU LITTLE SCAMP...

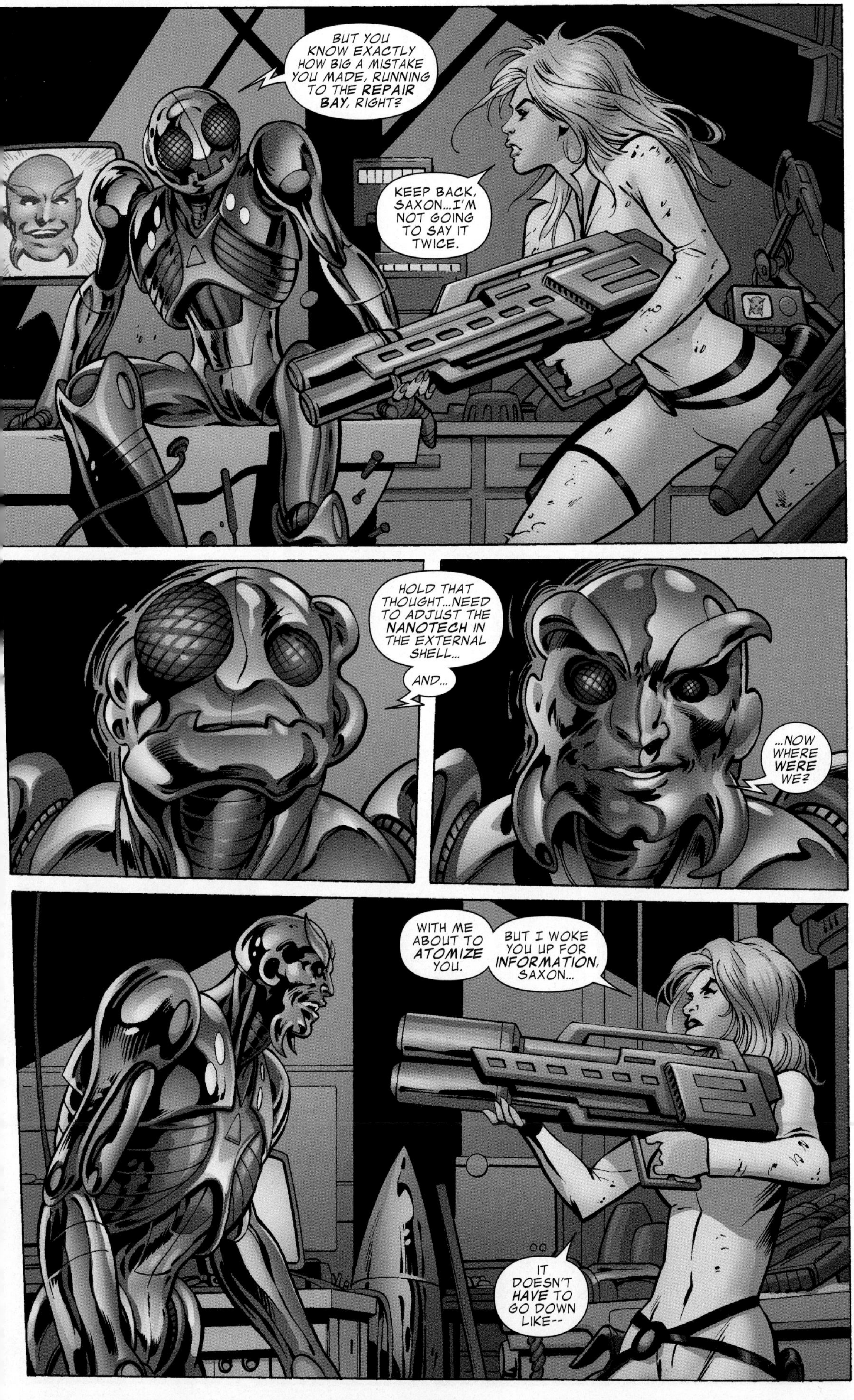
BUT YOU KNOW EXACTLY HOW BIG A MISTAKE YOU MADE, RUNNING TO THE REPAIR BAY, RIGHT?
KEEP BACK, SAXON...I'M NOT GOING TO SAY IT TWICE.
HOLD THAT THOUGHT...NEED TO ADJUST THE NANOTECH IN THE EXTERNAL SHELL...
AND...
...NOW WHERE WERE WE?
WITH ME ABOUT TO ATOMIZE YOU.
BUT I WOKE YOU UP FOR INFORMATION, SAXON...
IT DOESN'T HAVE TO GO DOWN LIKE--

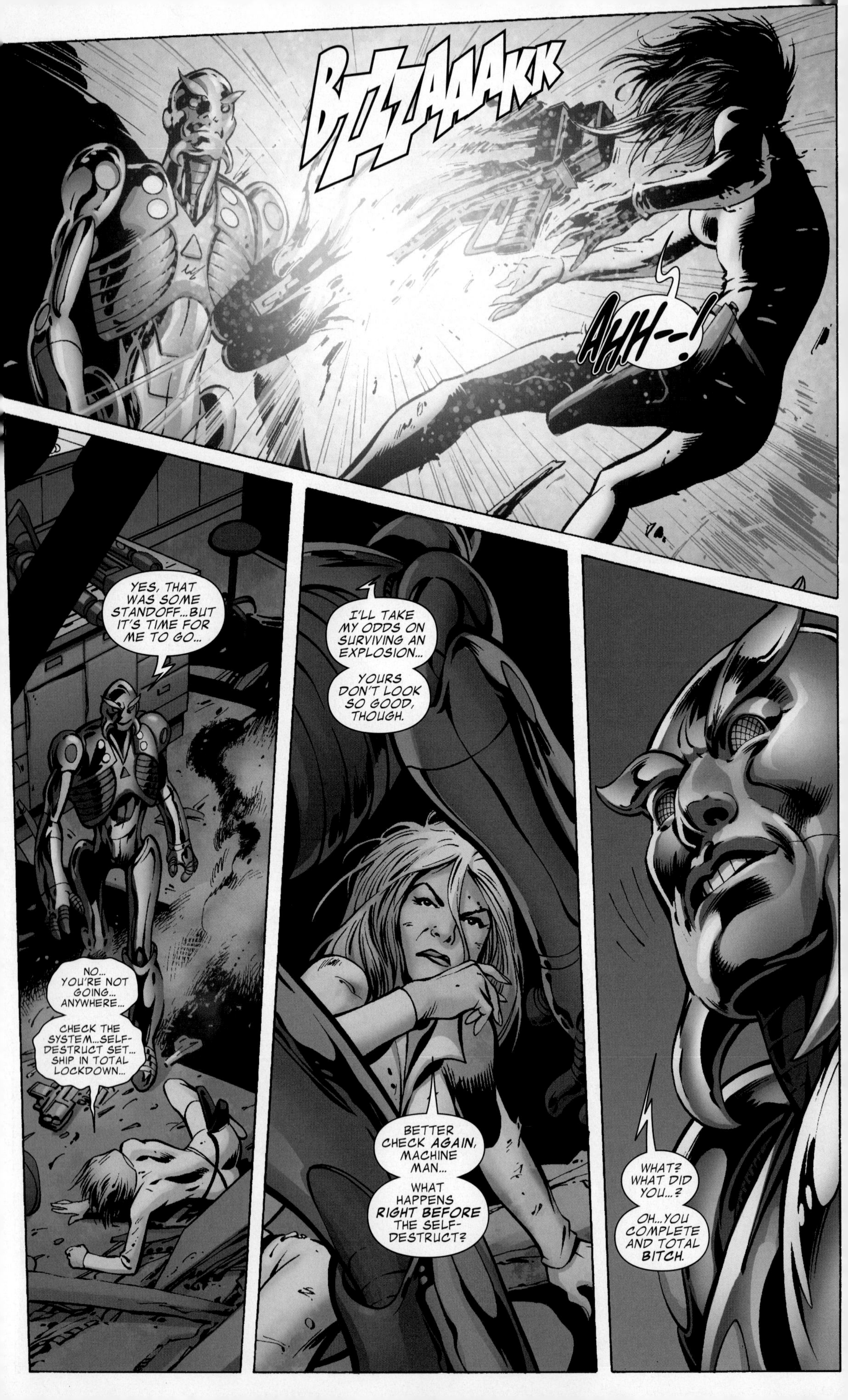
BZZZAAAKK
AHH--!
YES, THAT WAS SOME STANDOFF...BUT IT'S TIME FOR ME TO GO...
NO... YOU'RE NOT GOING... ANYWHERE...
CHECK THE SYSTEM...SELF-DESTRUCT SET... SHIP IN TOTAL LOCKDOWN...
I'LL TAKE MY ODDS ON SURVIVING AN EXPLOSION...
YOURS DON'T LOOK SO GOOD, THOUGH.
BETTER CHECK AGAIN, MACHINE MAN...
WHAT HAPPENS RIGHT BEFORE THE SELF-DESTRUCT?
WHAT? WHAT DID YOU...?
OH...YOU COMPLETE AND TOTAL BITCH.

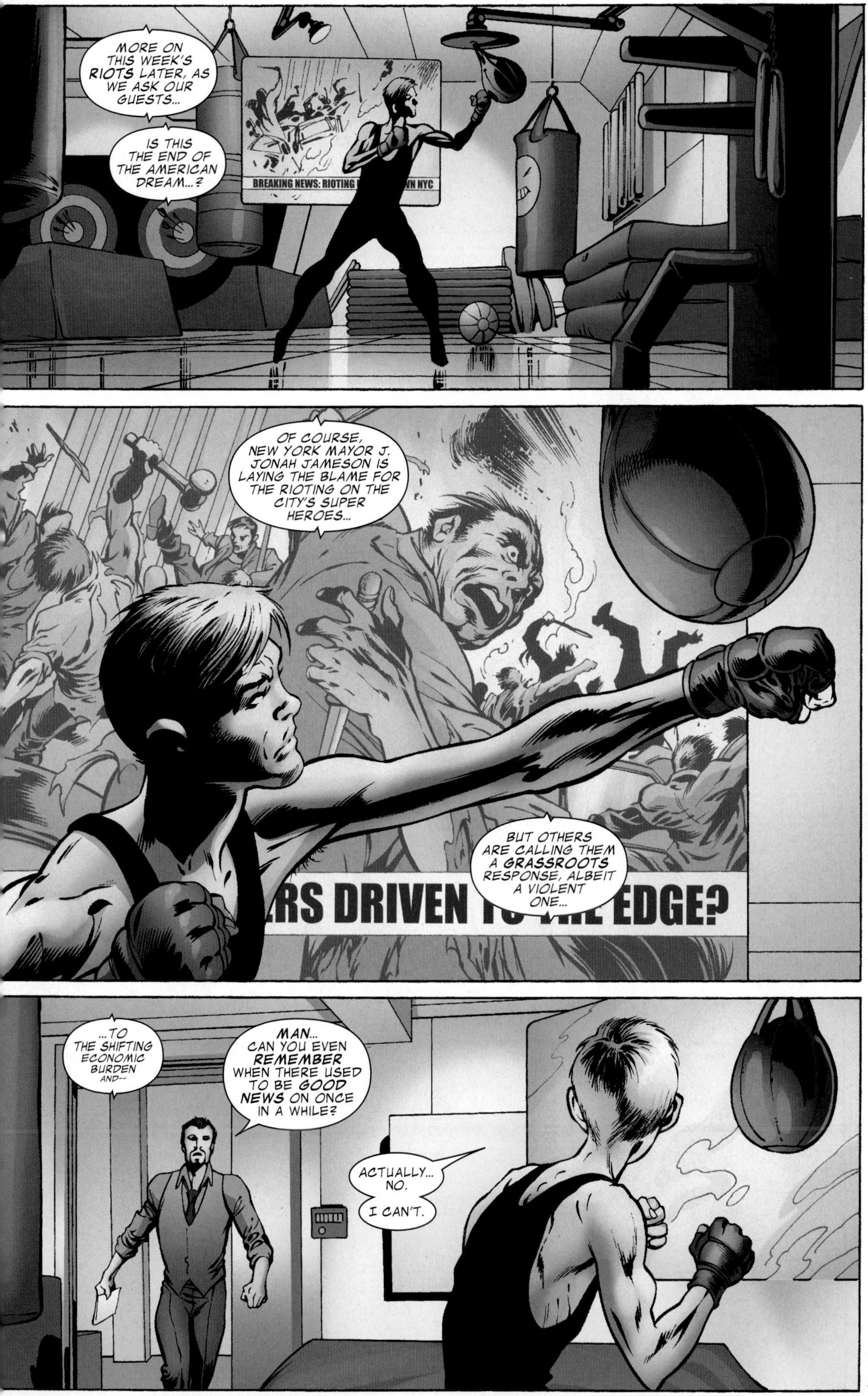

MORE ON THIS WEEK'S **RIOTS** LATER, AS WE ASK OUR GUESTS...
IS THIS THE END OF THE AMERICAN DREAM...?
BREAKING NEWS: RIOTING
WN NYC
OF COURSE, NEW YORK MAYOR J. JONAH JAMESON IS LAYING THE BLAME FOR THE RIOTING ON THE CITY'S SUPER HEROES...
BUT OTHERS ARE CALLING THEM A **GRASSROOTS** RESPONSE, ALBEIT A VIOLENT ONE...
ERS DRIVEN
EDGE?
...TO THE SHIFTING ECONOMIC BURDEN AND--
MAN... CAN YOU EVEN ***REMEMBER*** WHEN THERE USED TO BE ***GOOD NEWS*** ON ONCE IN A WHILE?
ACTUALLY... NO.
I CAN'T.

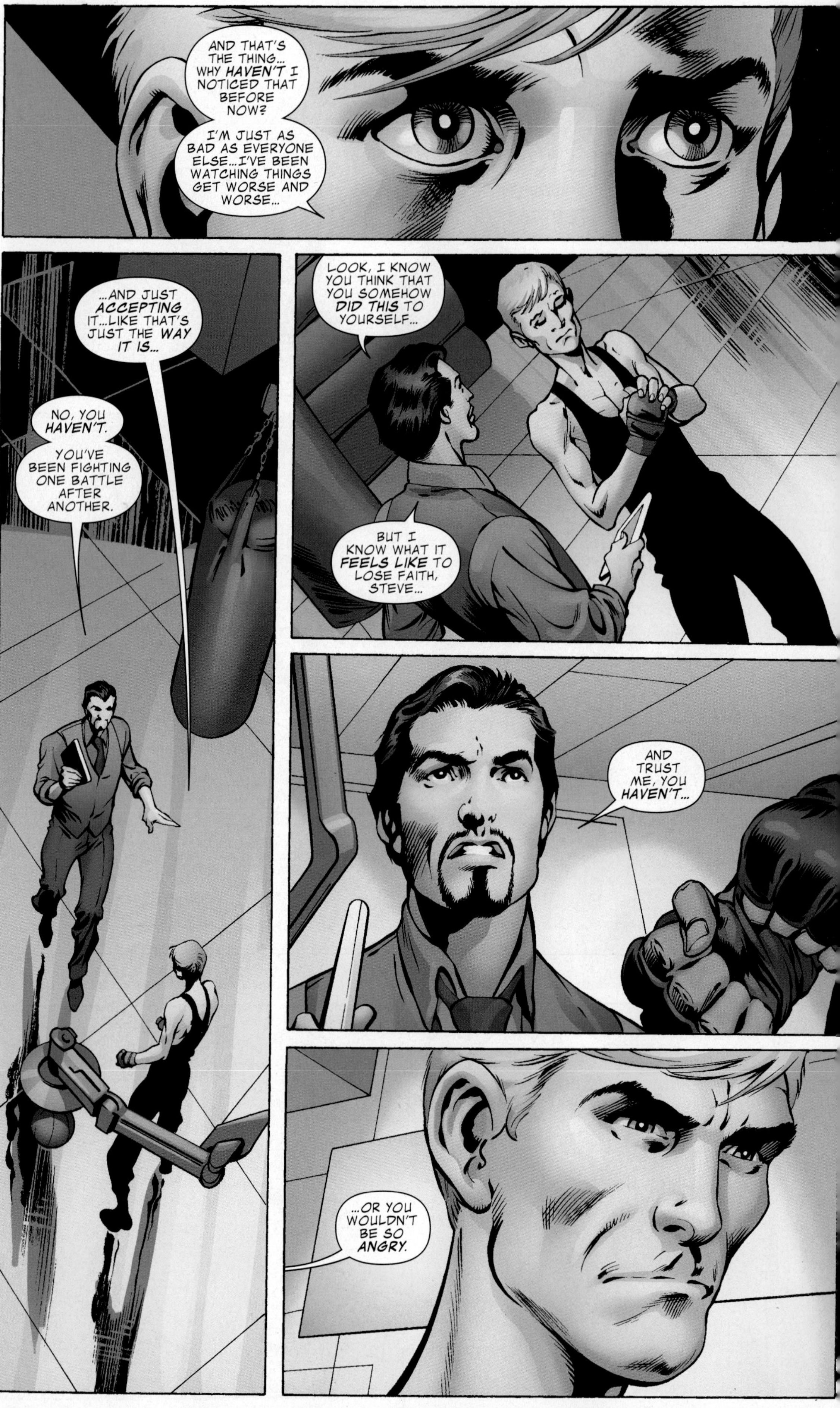
AND THAT'S THE THING... WHY HAVEN'T I NOTICED THAT BEFORE NOW?
I'M JUST AS BAD AS EVERYONE ELSE...I'VE BEEN WATCHING THINGS GET WORSE AND WORSE...
...AND JUST ACCEPTING IT...LIKE THAT'S JUST THE WAY IT IS...
NO, YOU HAVEN'T.
YOU'VE BEEN FIGHTING ONE BATTLE AFTER ANOTHER.
LOOK, I KNOW YOU THINK THAT YOU SOMEHOW DID THIS TO YOURSELF...
BUT I KNOW WHAT IT FEELS LIKE TO LOSE FAITH, STEVE...
AND TRUST ME, YOU HAVEN'T...
...OR YOU WOULDN'T BE SO ANGRY.

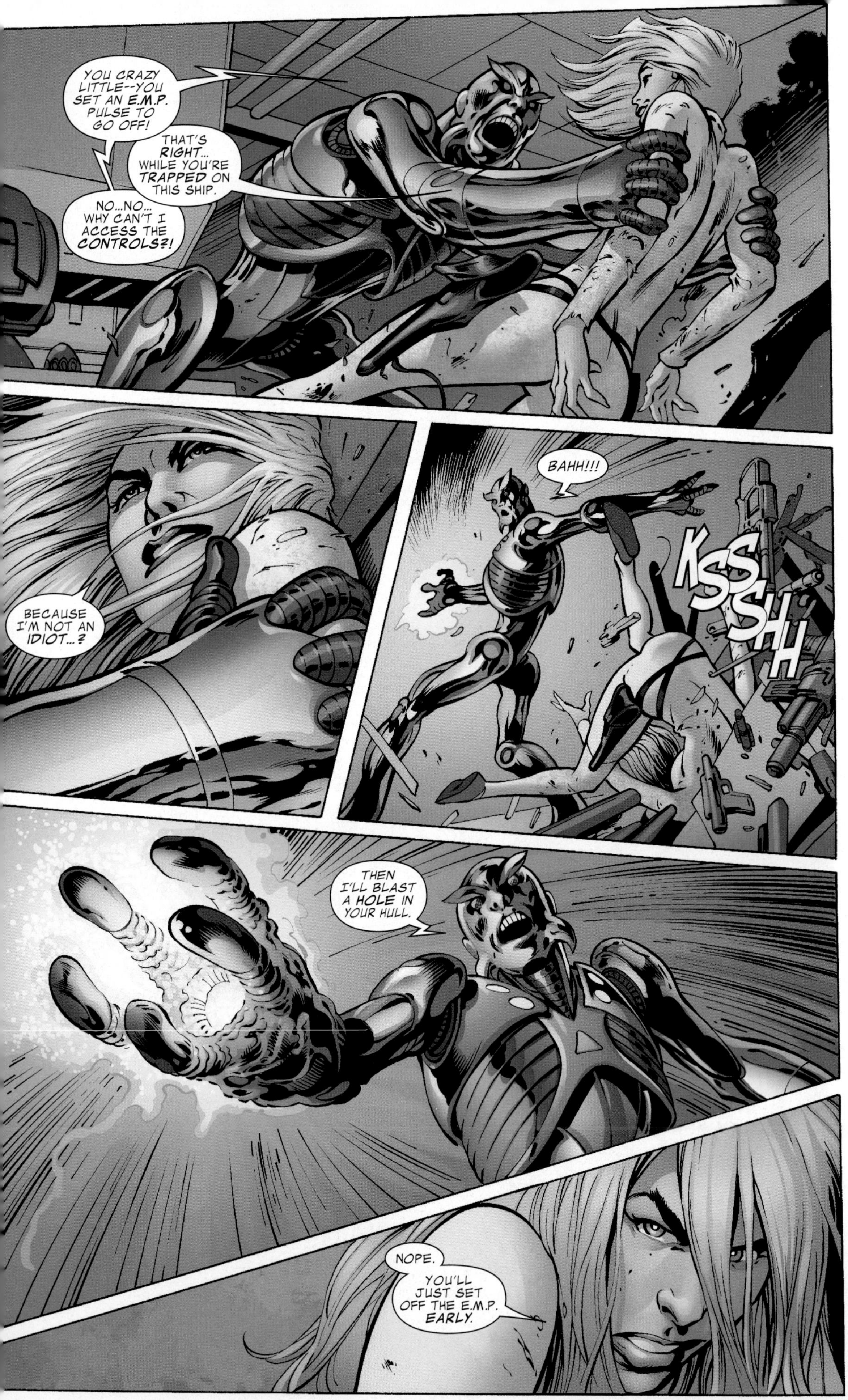
YOU CRAZY LITTLE--YOU SET AN E.M.P. PULSE TO GO OFF!
THAT'S RIGHT... WHILE YOU'RE TRAPPED ON THIS SHIP.
NO...NO... WHY CAN'T I ACCESS THE CONTROLS?!
BECAUSE I'M NOT AN IDIOT...?
BAHH!!!
KSSSHH
THEN I'LL BLAST A HOLE IN YOUR HULL.
NOPE.
YOU'LL JUST SET OFF THE E.M.P. EARLY.

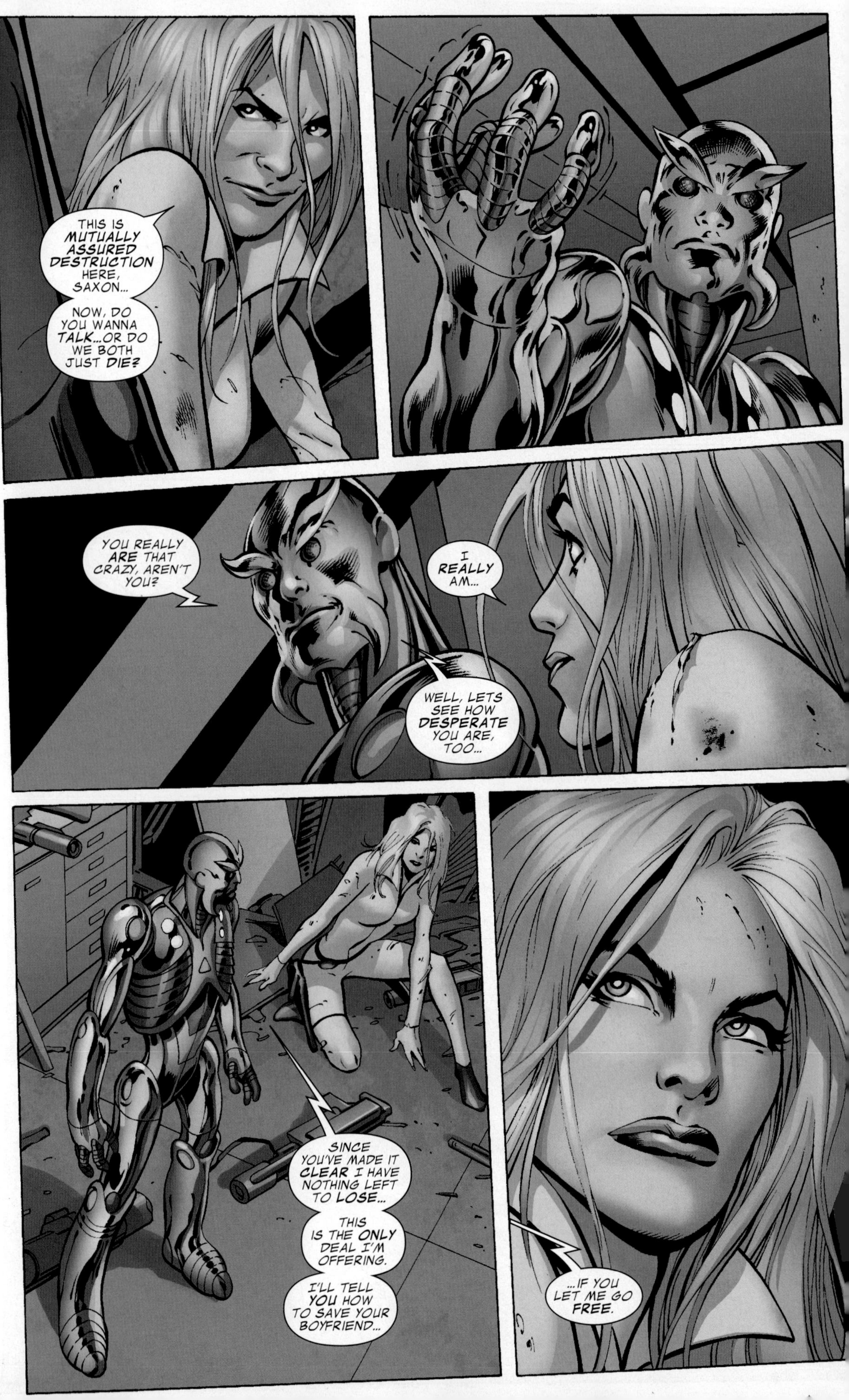
THIS IS MUTUALLY ASSURED DESTRUCTION HERE, SAXON...
NOW, DO YOU WANNA TALK...OR DO WE BOTH JUST DIE?
YOU REALLY ARE THAT CRAZY, AREN'T YOU?
I REALLY AM...
WELL, LETS SEE HOW DESPERATE YOU ARE, TOO...
SINCE YOU'VE MADE IT CLEAR I HAVE NOTHING LEFT TO LOSE...
THIS IS THE ONLY DEAL I'M OFFERING.
I'LL TELL YOU HOW TO SAVE YOUR BOYFRIEND...
...IF YOU LET ME GO FREE.

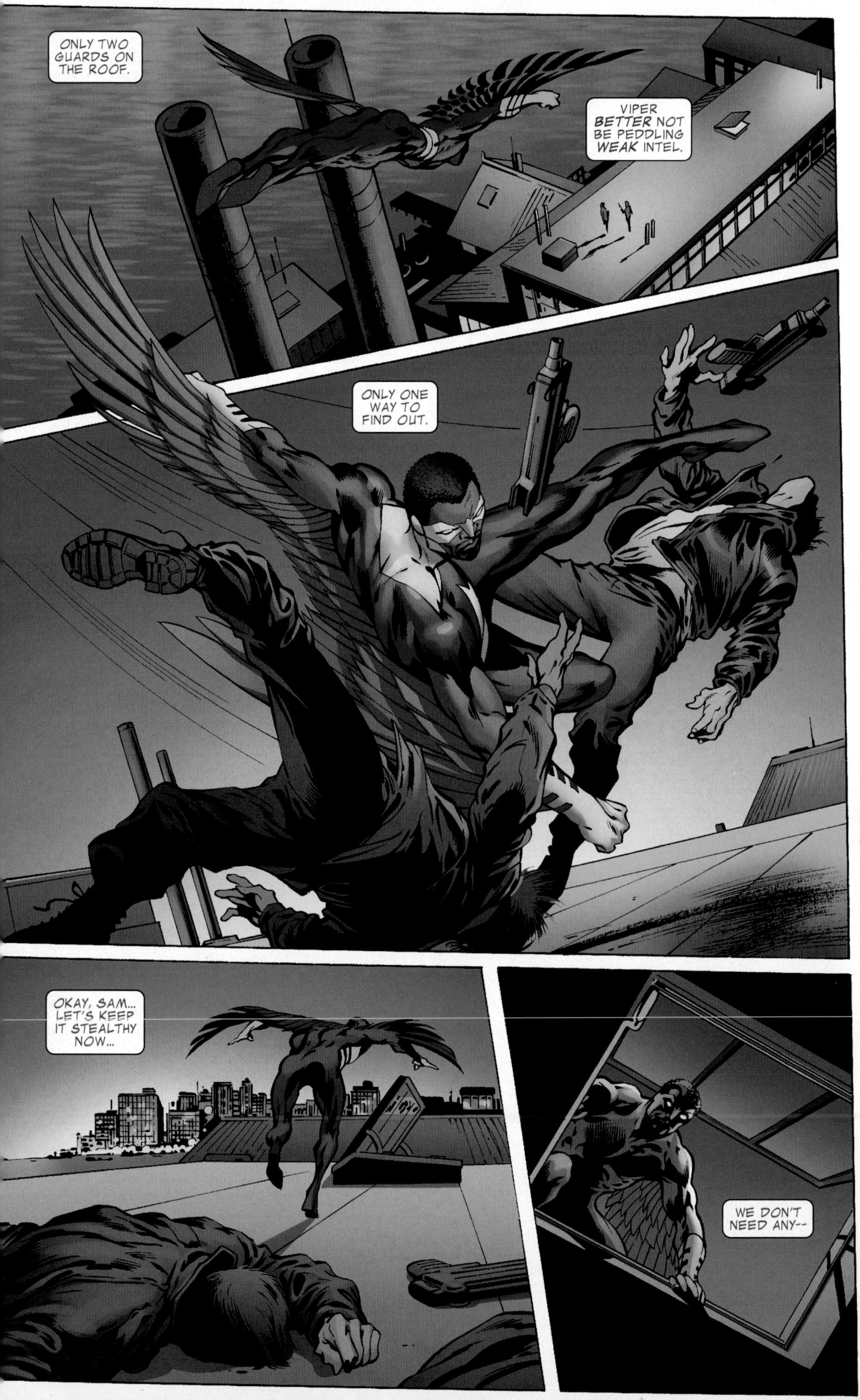
ONLY TWO GUARDS ON THE ROOF.
VIPER BETTER NOT BE PEDDLING WEAK INTEL.
ONLY ONE WAY TO FIND OUT.
OKAY, SAM... LET'S KEEP IT STEALTHY NOW...
WE DON'T NEED ANY--

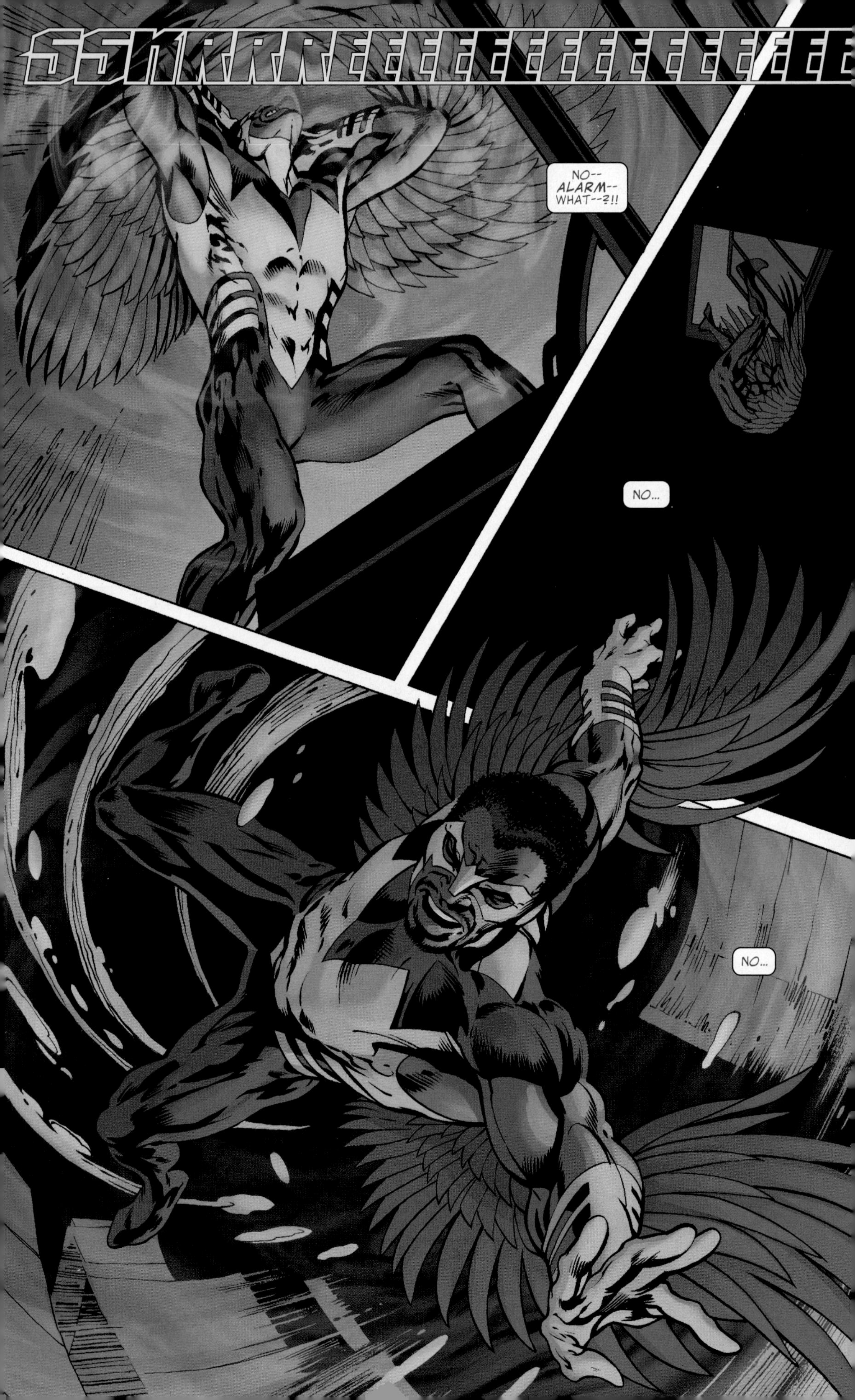
SSKRRREEEEEEEEEEEEE
NO--
ALARM--
WHAT--?!!
NO...
NO...

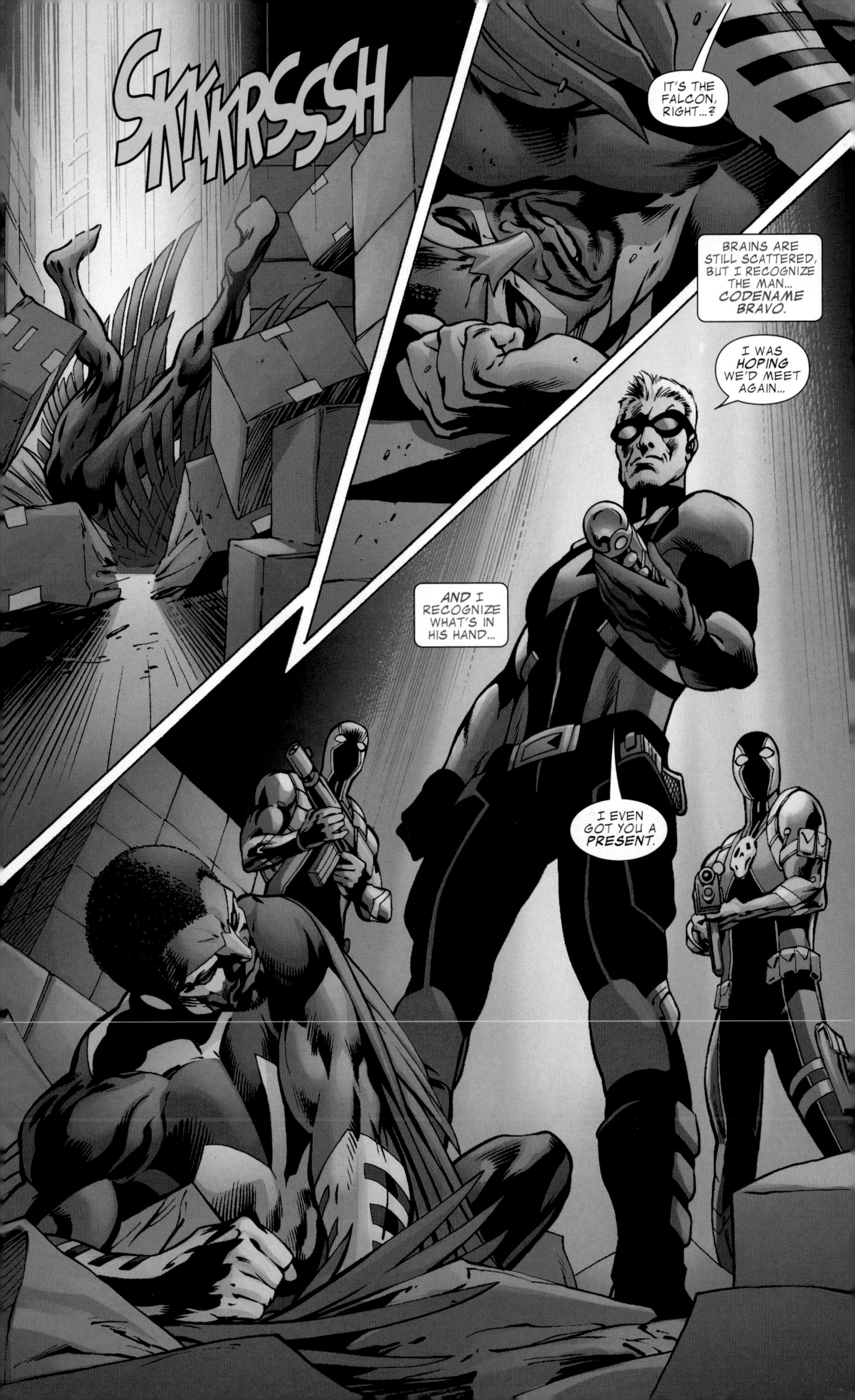
SKKKRSSSH
IT'S THE FALCON, RIGHT...?
BRAINS ARE STILL SCATTERED, BUT I RECOGNIZE THE MAN... CODENAME BRAVO.
I WAS HOPING WE'D MEET AGAIN...
AND I RECOGNIZE WHAT'S IN HIS HAND...
I EVEN GOT YOU A PRESENT.

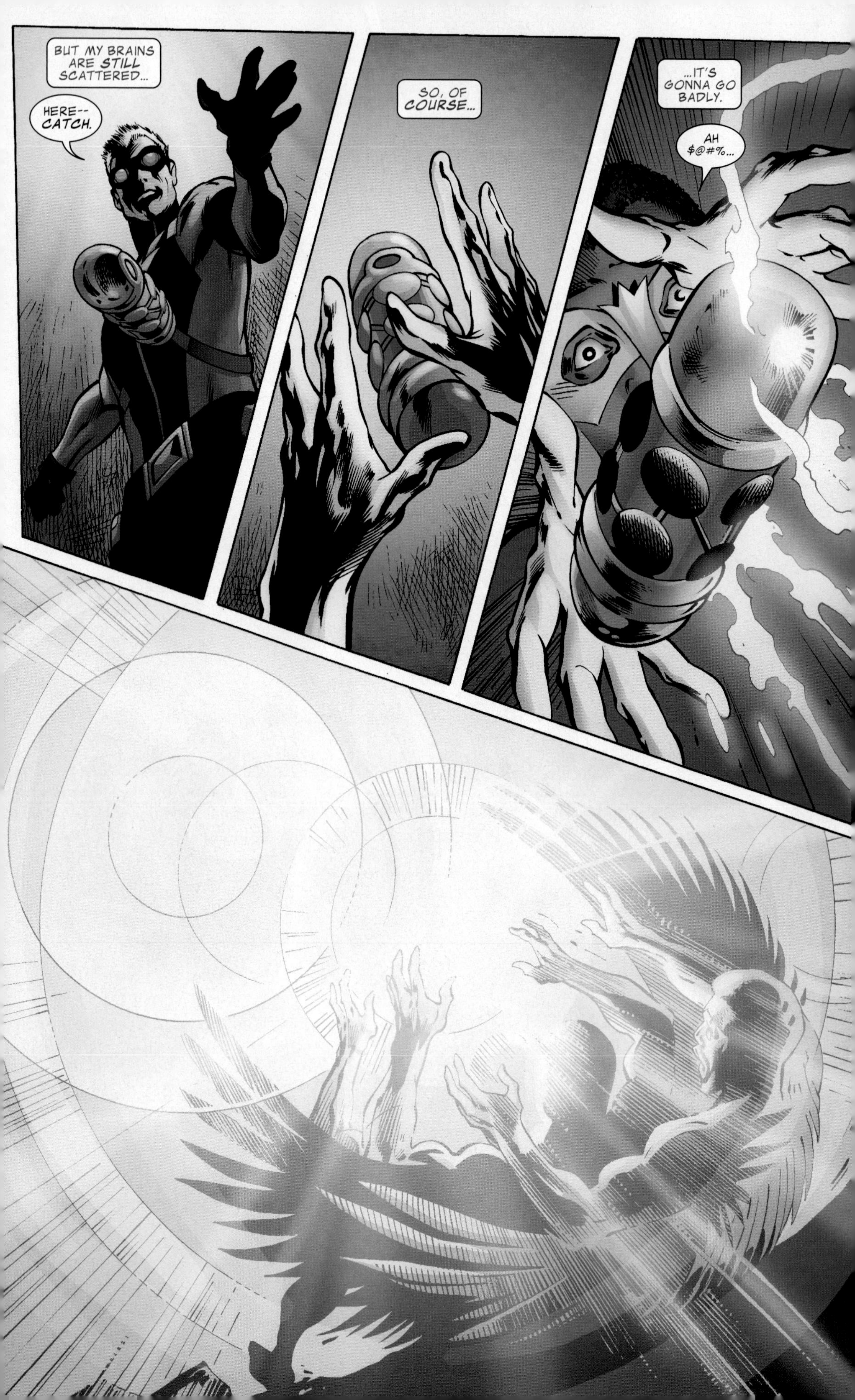
BUT MY BRAINS ARE STILL SCATTERED...
HERE-- CATCH.
SO, OF COURSE...
...IT'S GONNA GO BADLY.
AH $@#%...

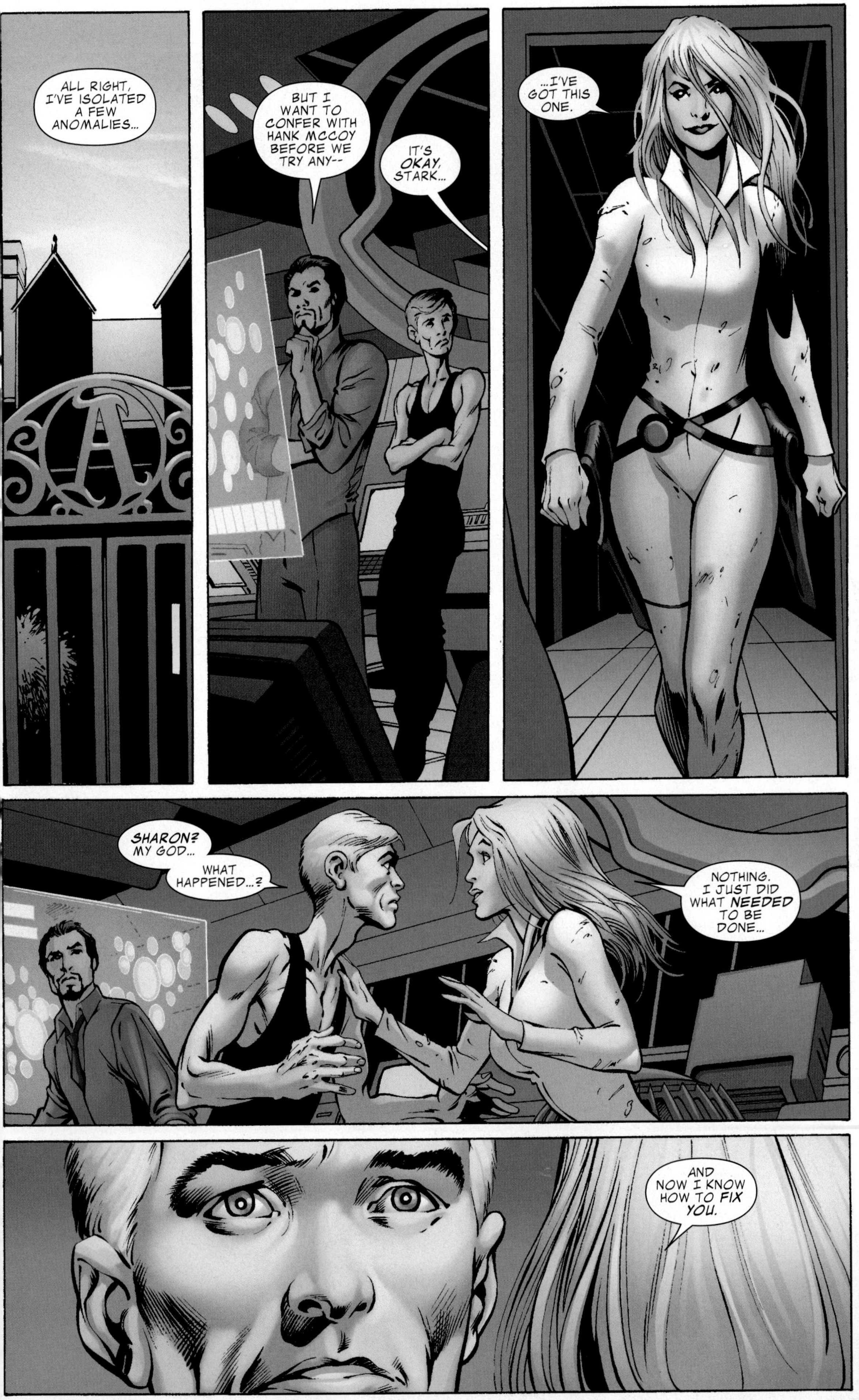
ALL RIGHT, I'VE ISOLATED A FEW ANOMALIES...
BUT I WANT TO CONFER WITH HANK MCCOY BEFORE WE TRY ANY--
IT'S OKAY, STARK...
...I'VE GOT THIS ONE.
SHARON? MY GOD...
WHAT HAPPENED...?
NOTHING. I JUST DID WHAT NEEDED TO BE DONE...
AND NOW I KNOW HOW TO FIX YOU.

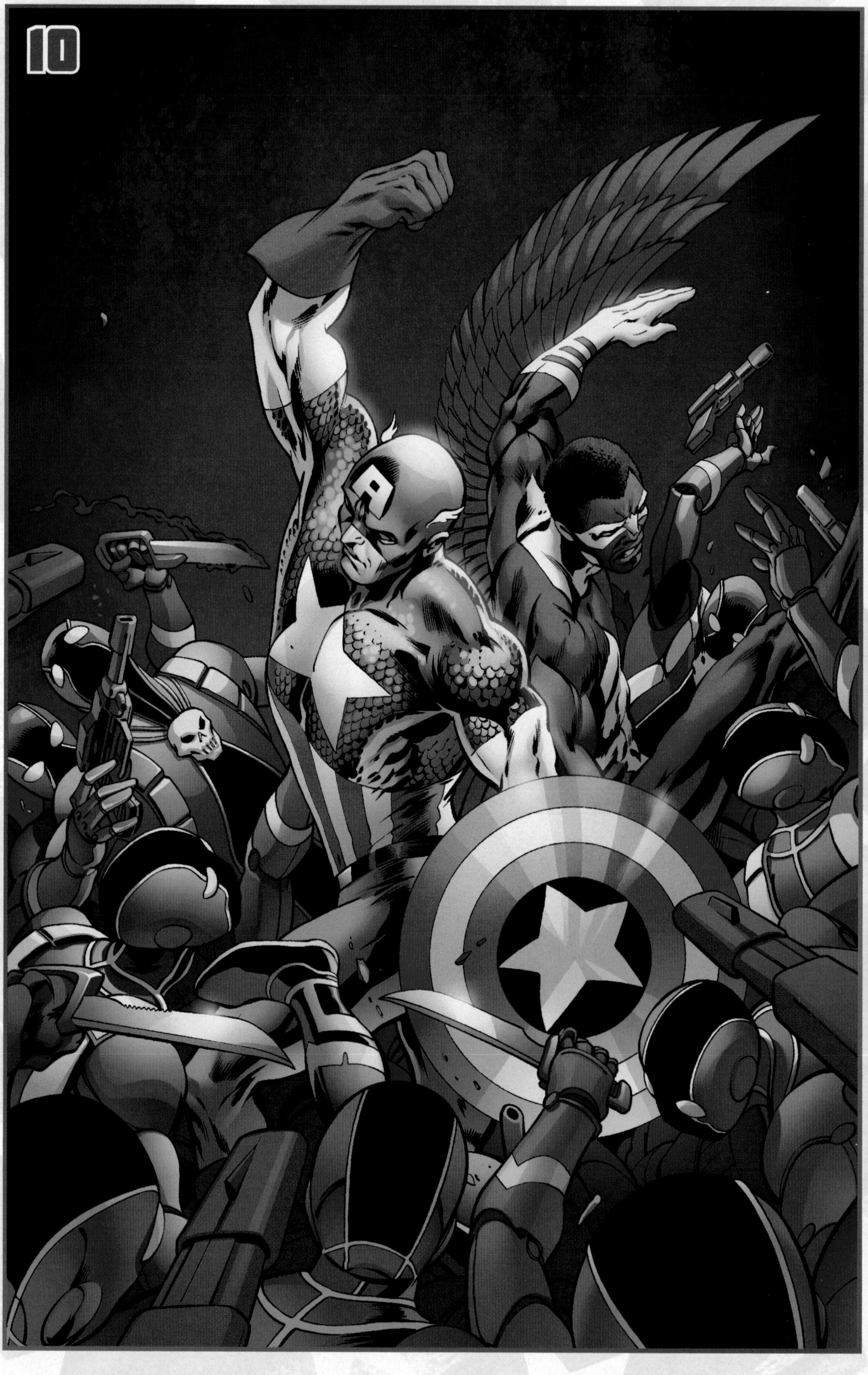
10

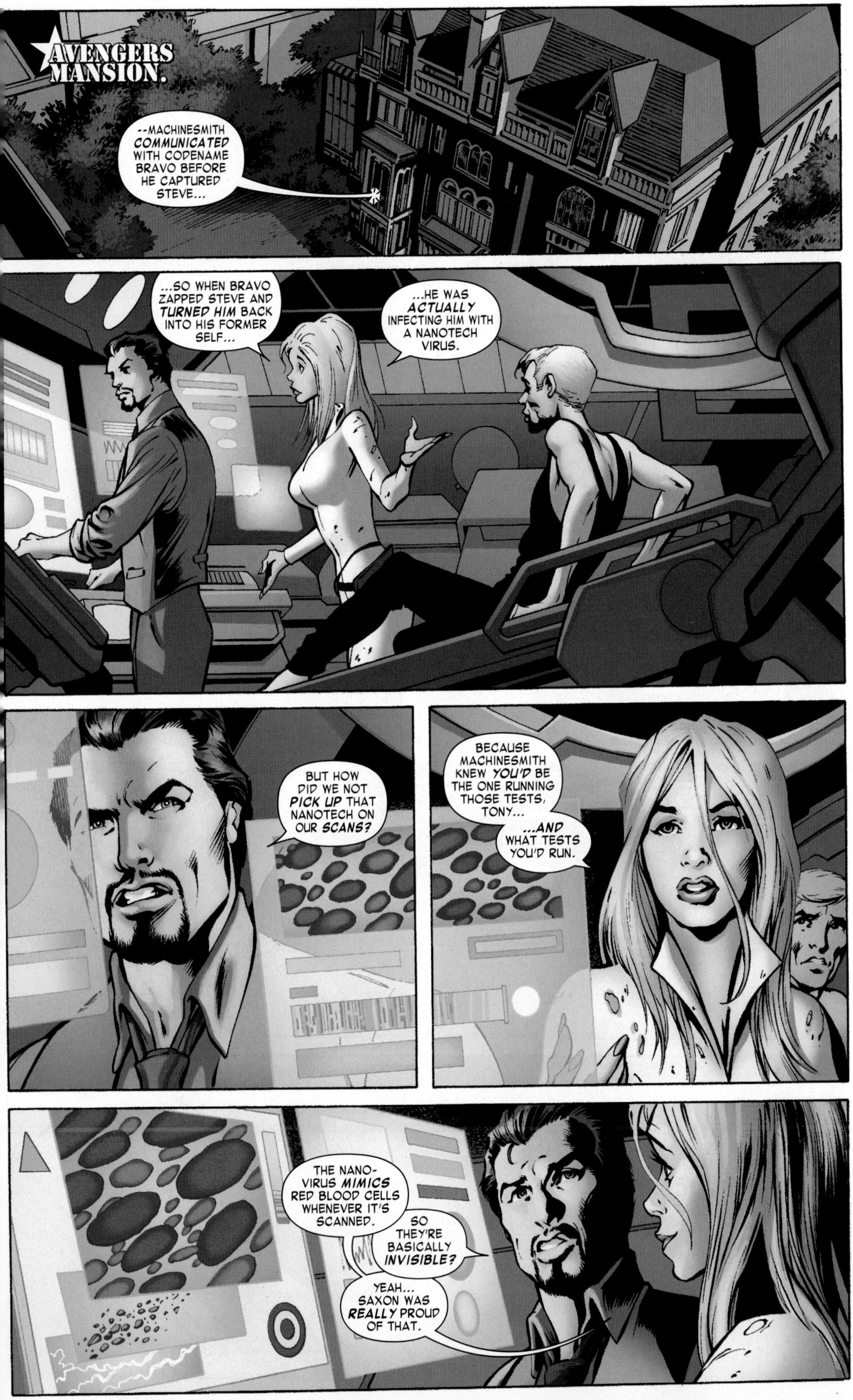
AVENGERS MANSION.
--MACHINESMITH COMMUNICATED WITH CODENAME BRAVO BEFORE HE CAPTURED STEVE...
...SO WHEN BRAVO ZAPPED STEVE AND TURNED HIM BACK INTO HIS FORMER SELF...
...HE WAS ACTUALLY INFECTING HIM WITH A NANOTECH VIRUS.
BUT HOW DID WE NOT PICK UP THAT NANOTECH ON OUR SCANS?
BECAUSE MACHINESMITH KNEW YOU'D BE THE ONE RUNNING THOSE TESTS, TONY...
...AND WHAT TESTS YOU'D RUN.
THE NANO-VIRUS MIMICS RED BLOOD CELLS WHENEVER IT'S SCANNED.
SO THEY'RE BASICALLY INVISIBLE?
YEAH... SAXON WAS REALLY PROUD OF THAT.

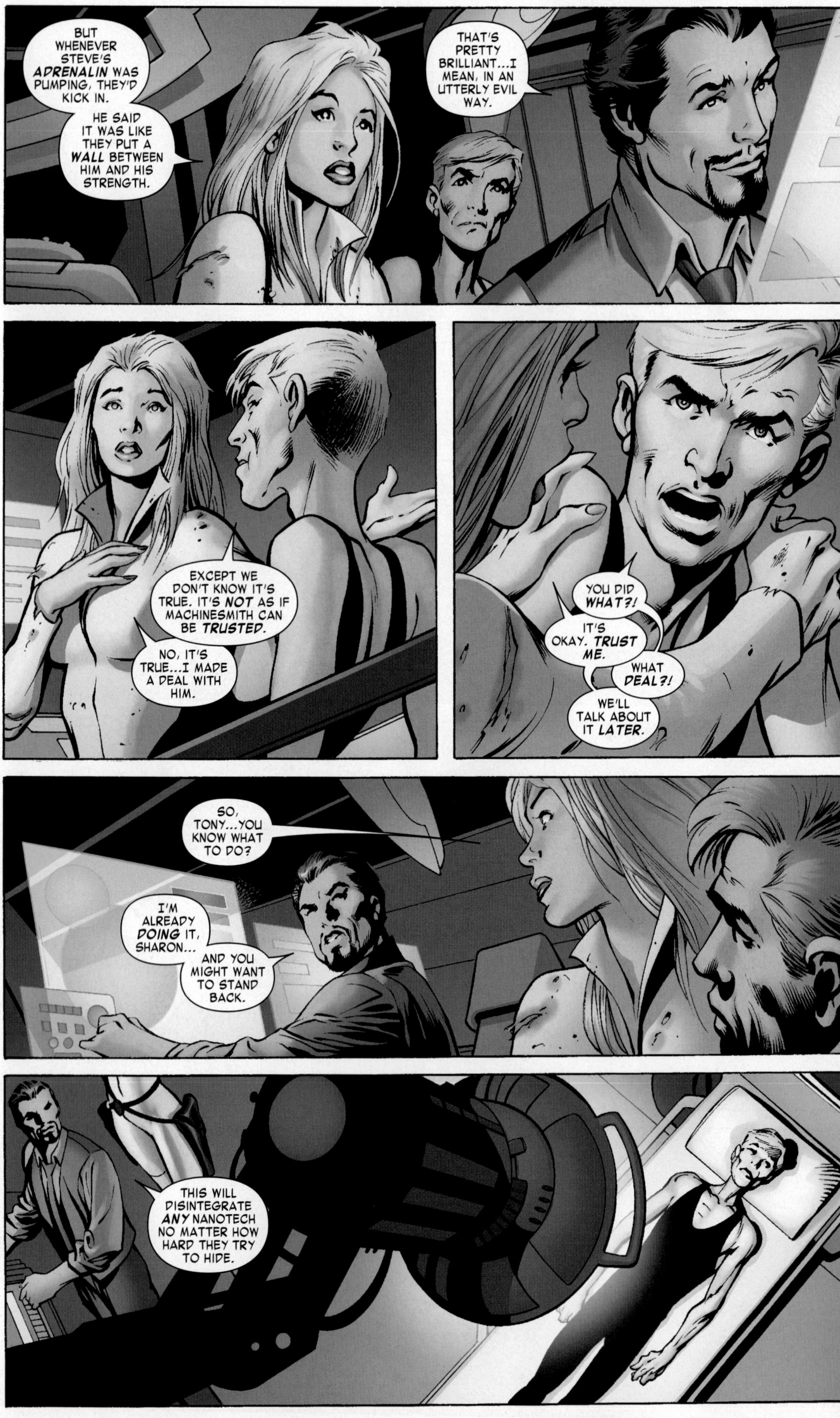

BUT WHENEVER STEVE'S ADRENALIN WAS PUMPING, THEY'D KICK IN.
HE SAID IT WAS LIKE THEY PUT A WALL BETWEEN HIM AND HIS STRENGTH.
THAT'S PRETTY BRILLIANT...I MEAN, IN AN UTTERLY EVIL WAY.
EXCEPT WE DON'T KNOW IT'S TRUE. IT'S NOT AS IF MACHINESMITH CAN BE TRUSTED.
NO, IT'S TRUE...I MADE A DEAL WITH HIM.
YOU DID WHAT?!
IT'S OKAY. TRUST ME.
WHAT DEAL?!
WE'LL TALK ABOUT IT LATER.
SO, TONY...YOU KNOW WHAT TO DO?
I'M ALREADY DOING IT, SHARON...
AND YOU MIGHT WANT TO STAND BACK.
THIS WILL DISINTEGRATE ANY NANOTECH NO MATTER HOW HARD THEY TRY TO HIDE.

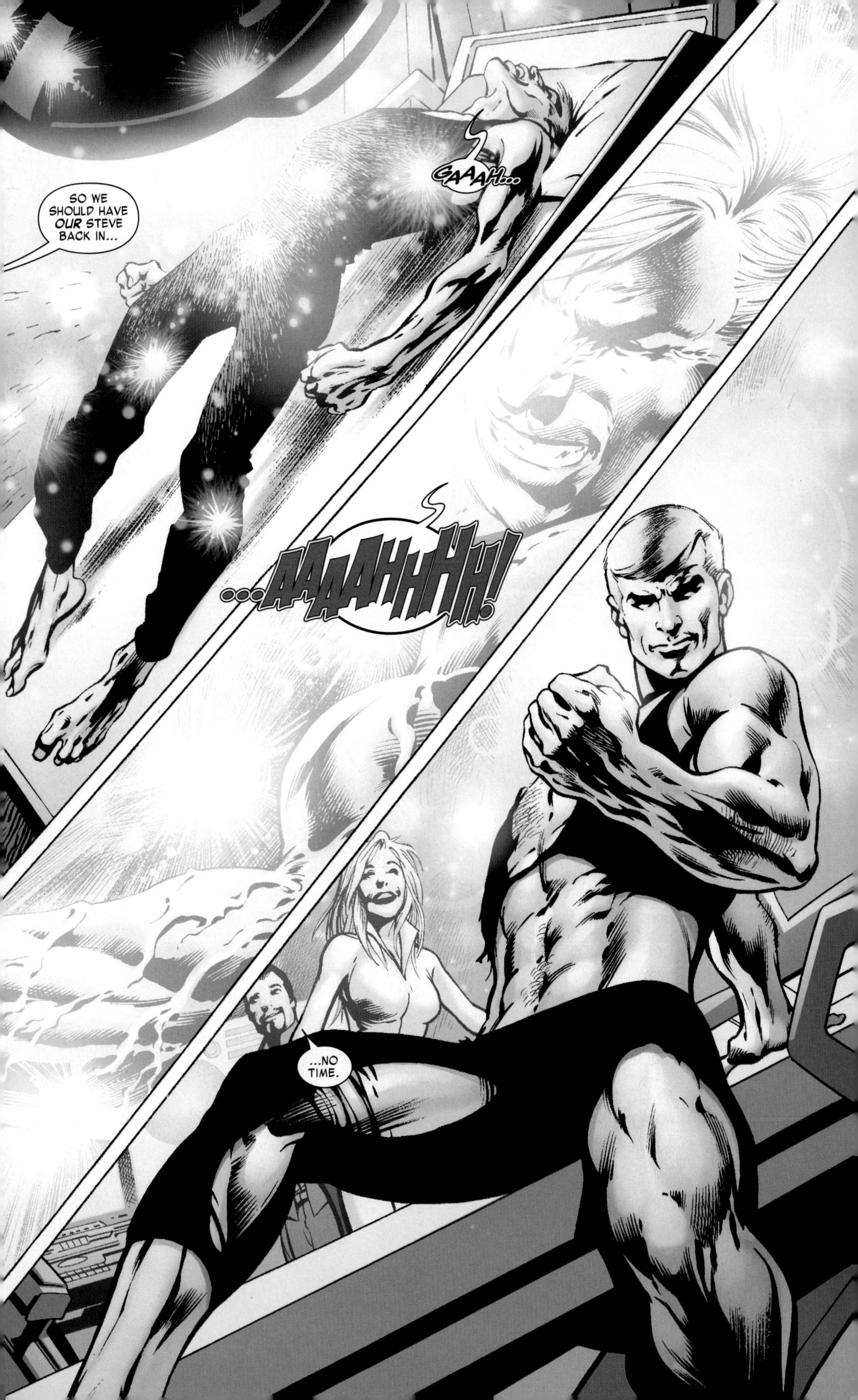
SO WE SHOULD HAVE OUR STEVE BACK IN...
GAAAH...
...AAAAHHHH!
...NO TIME.

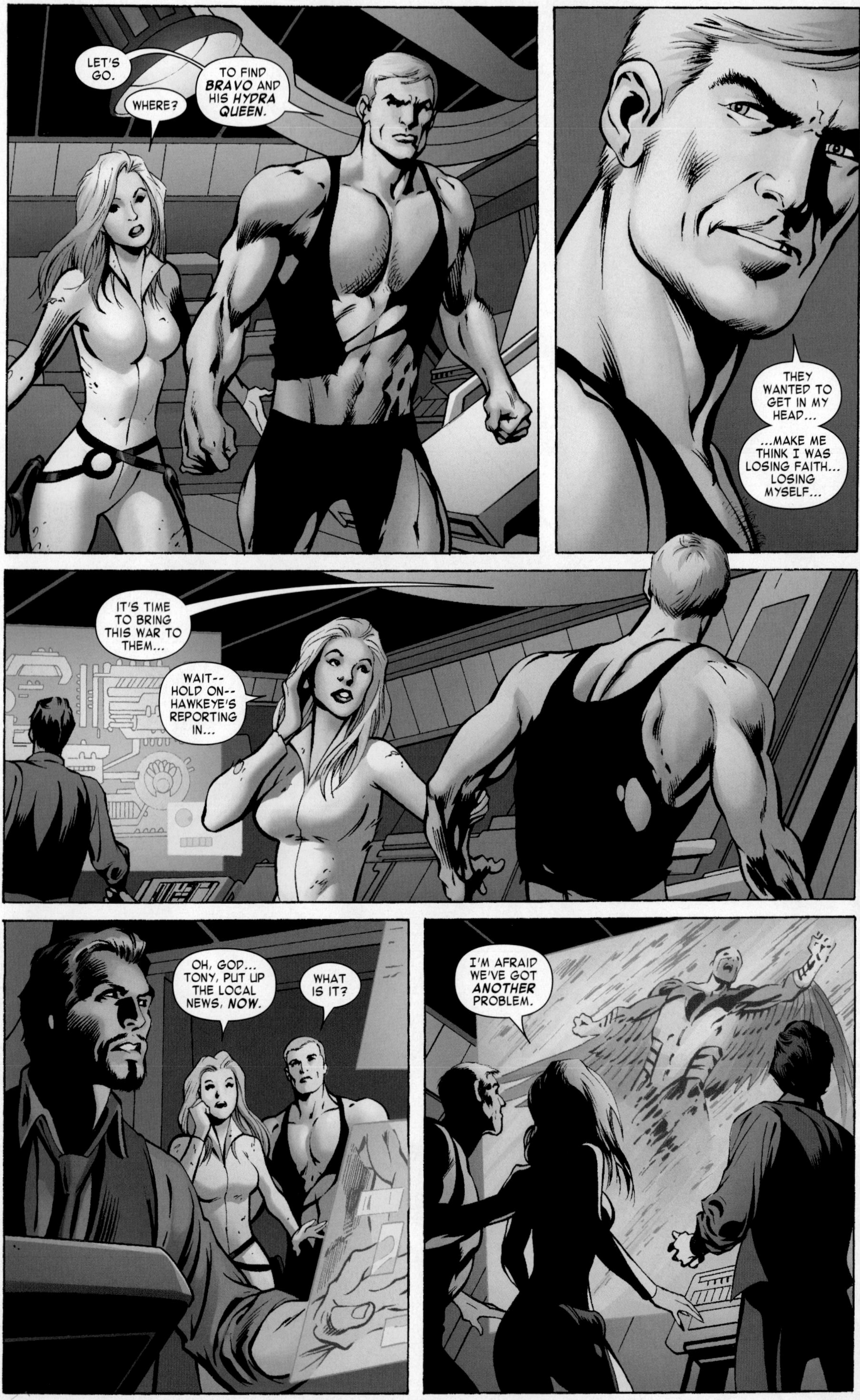
LET'S GO.
WHERE?
TO FIND BRAVO AND HIS HYDRA QUEEN.
THEY WANTED TO GET IN MY HEAD...
...MAKE ME THINK I WAS LOSING FAITH... LOSING MYSELF...
IT'S TIME TO BRING THIS WAR TO THEM...
WAIT-- HOLD ON-- HAWKEYE'S REPORTING IN...
OH, GOD... TONY, PUT UP THE LOCAL NEWS, NOW.
WHAT IS IT?
I'M AFRAID WE'VE GOT ANOTHER PROBLEM.

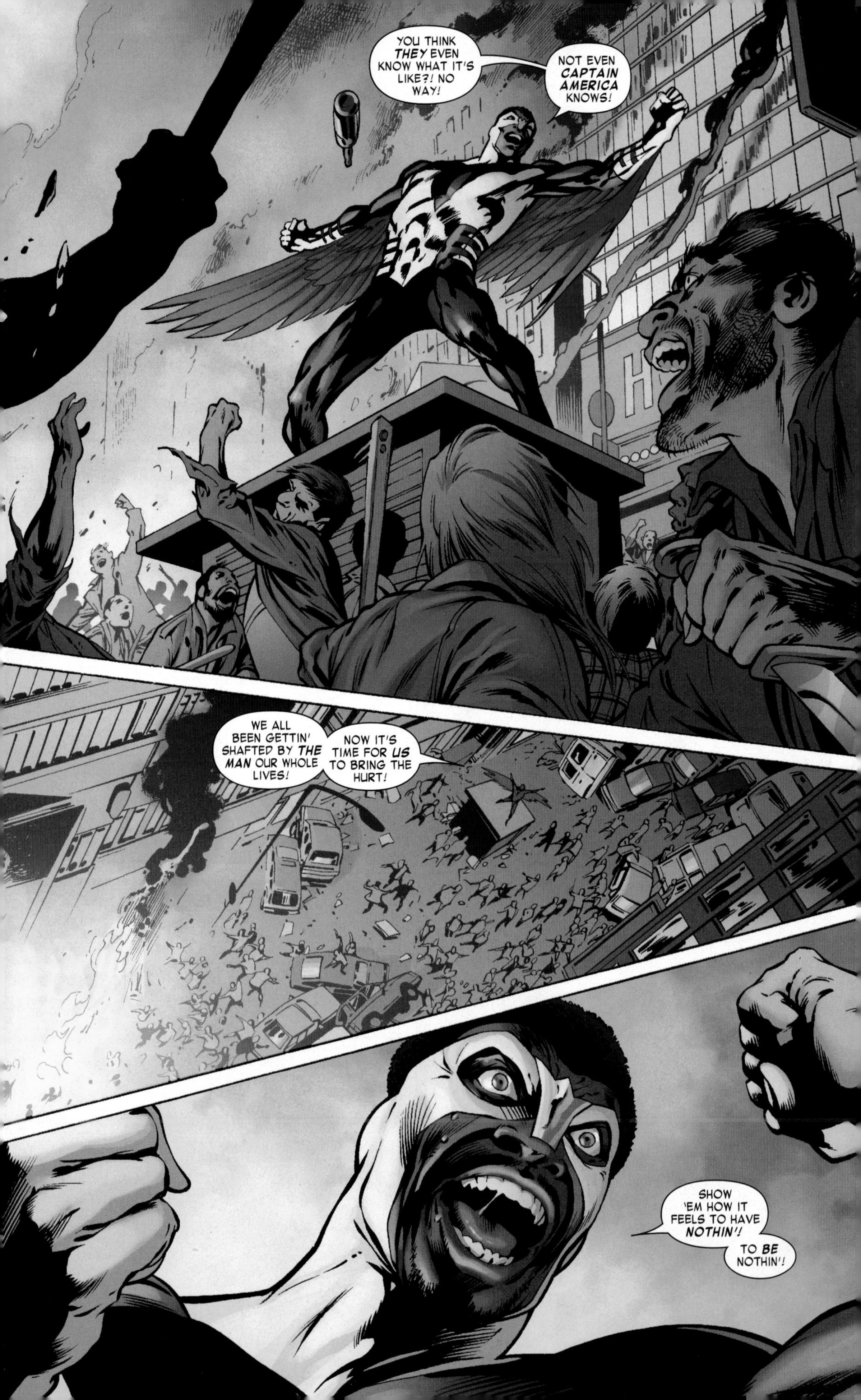
YOU THINK THEY EVEN KNOW WHAT IT'S LIKE?! NO WAY!
NOT EVEN CAPTAIN AMERICA KNOWS!
WE ALL BEEN GETTIN' SHAFTED BY THE MAN OUR WHOLE LIVES!
NOW IT'S TIME FOR US TO BRING THE HURT!
SHOW 'EM HOW IT FEELS TO HAVE NOTHIN'!
TO BE NOTHIN'!

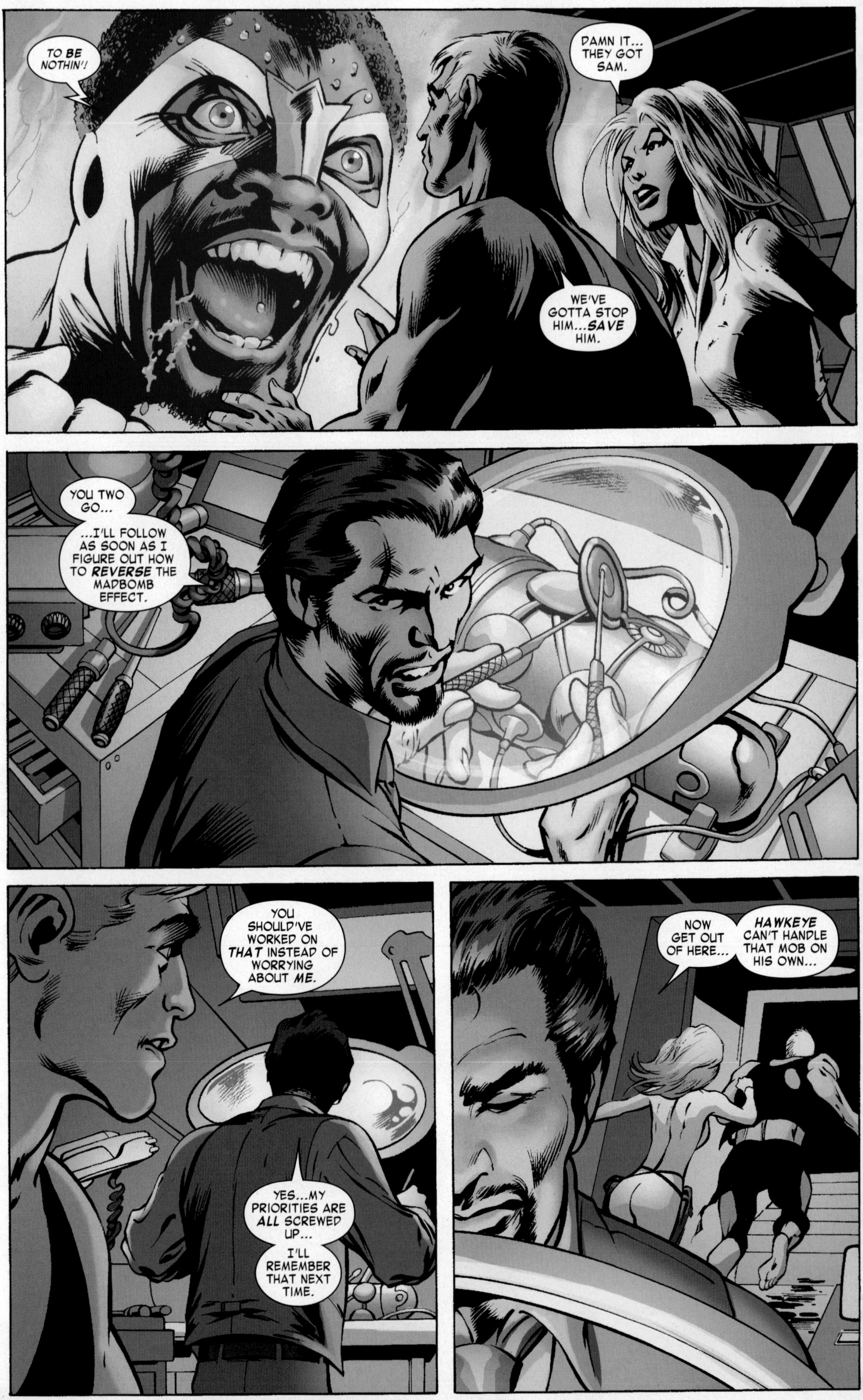
TO BE NOTHIN'!
DAMN IT... THEY GOT SAM.
WE'VE GOTTA STOP HIM...SAVE HIM.
YOU TWO GO...
...I'LL FOLLOW AS SOON AS I FIGURE OUT HOW TO REVERSE THE MADBOMB EFFECT.
YOU SHOULD'VE WORKED ON THAT INSTEAD OF WORRYING ABOUT ME.
YES...MY PRIORITIES ARE ALL SCREWED UP...
I'LL REMEMBER THAT NEXT TIME.
NOW GET OUT OF HERE...
HAWKEYE CAN'T HANDLE THAT MOB ON HIS OWN...

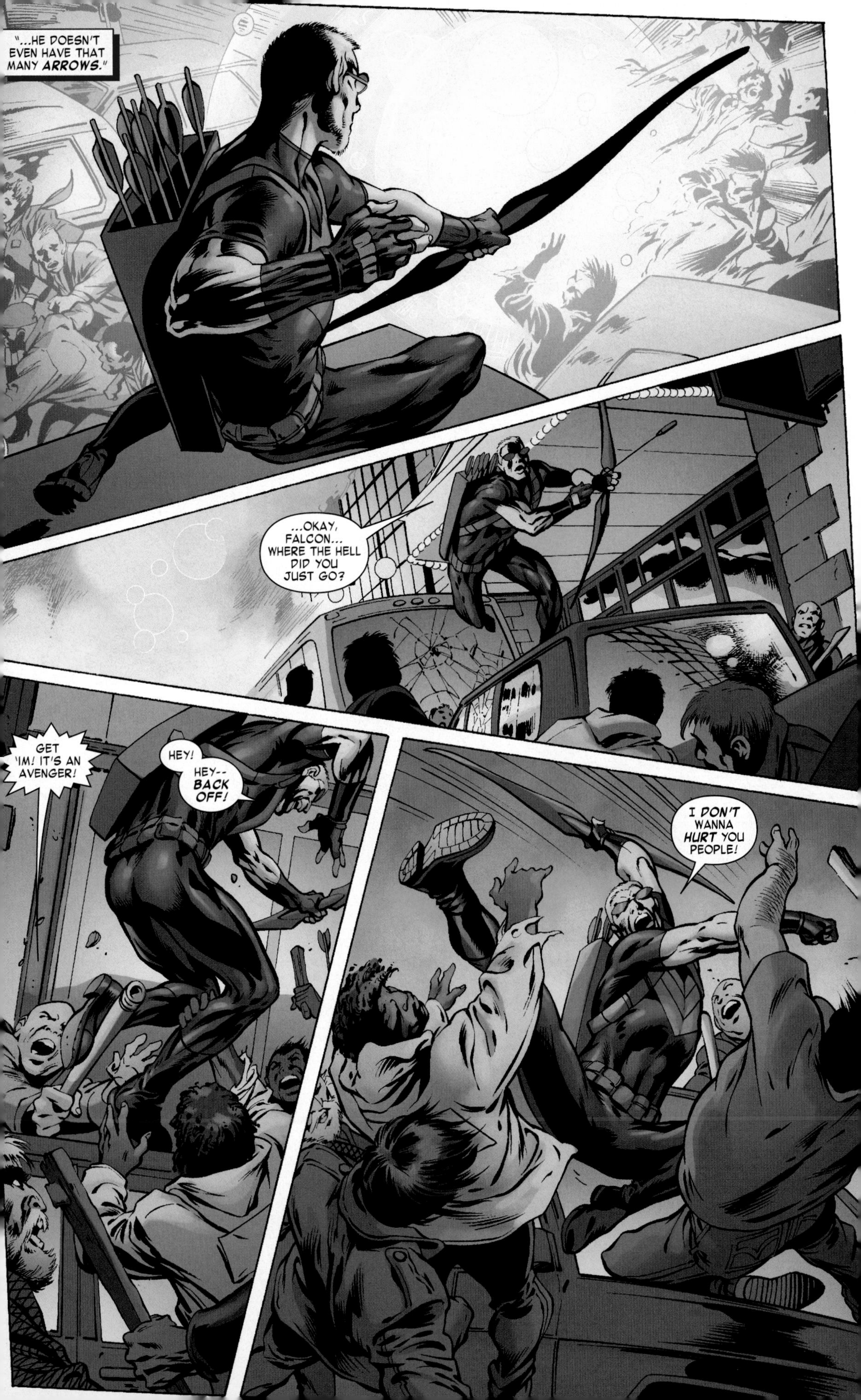
"...HE DOESN'T EVEN HAVE THAT MANY ARROWS."
...OKAY, FALCON... WHERE THE HELL DID YOU JUST GO?
GET 'IM! IT'S AN AVENGER!
HEY!
HEY-- BACK OFF!
I DON'T WANNA HURT YOU PEOPLE!

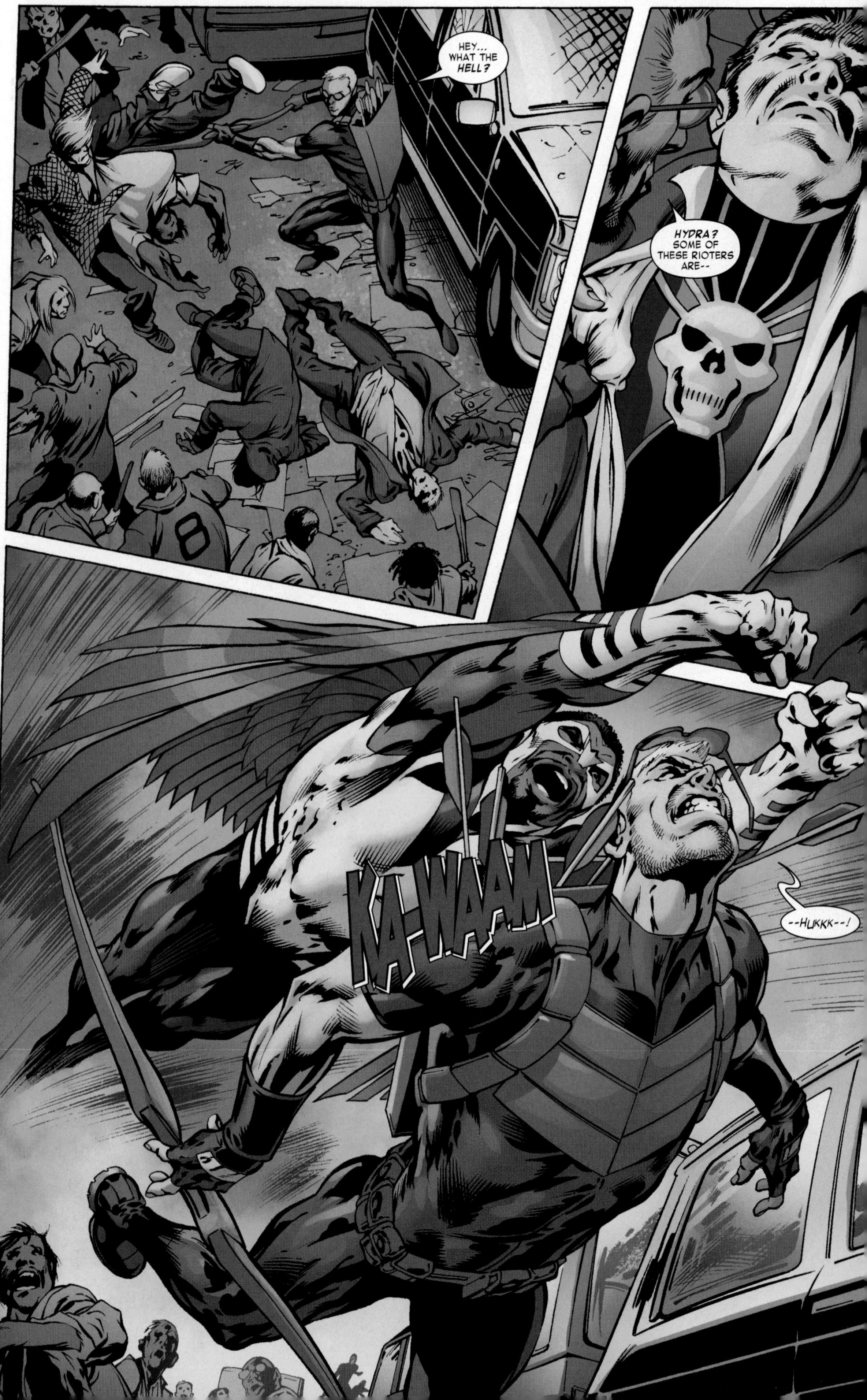
HEY... WHAT THE HELL?
HYDRA? SOME OF THESE RIOTERS ARE--
KA-WAAM
--HUKKK--!

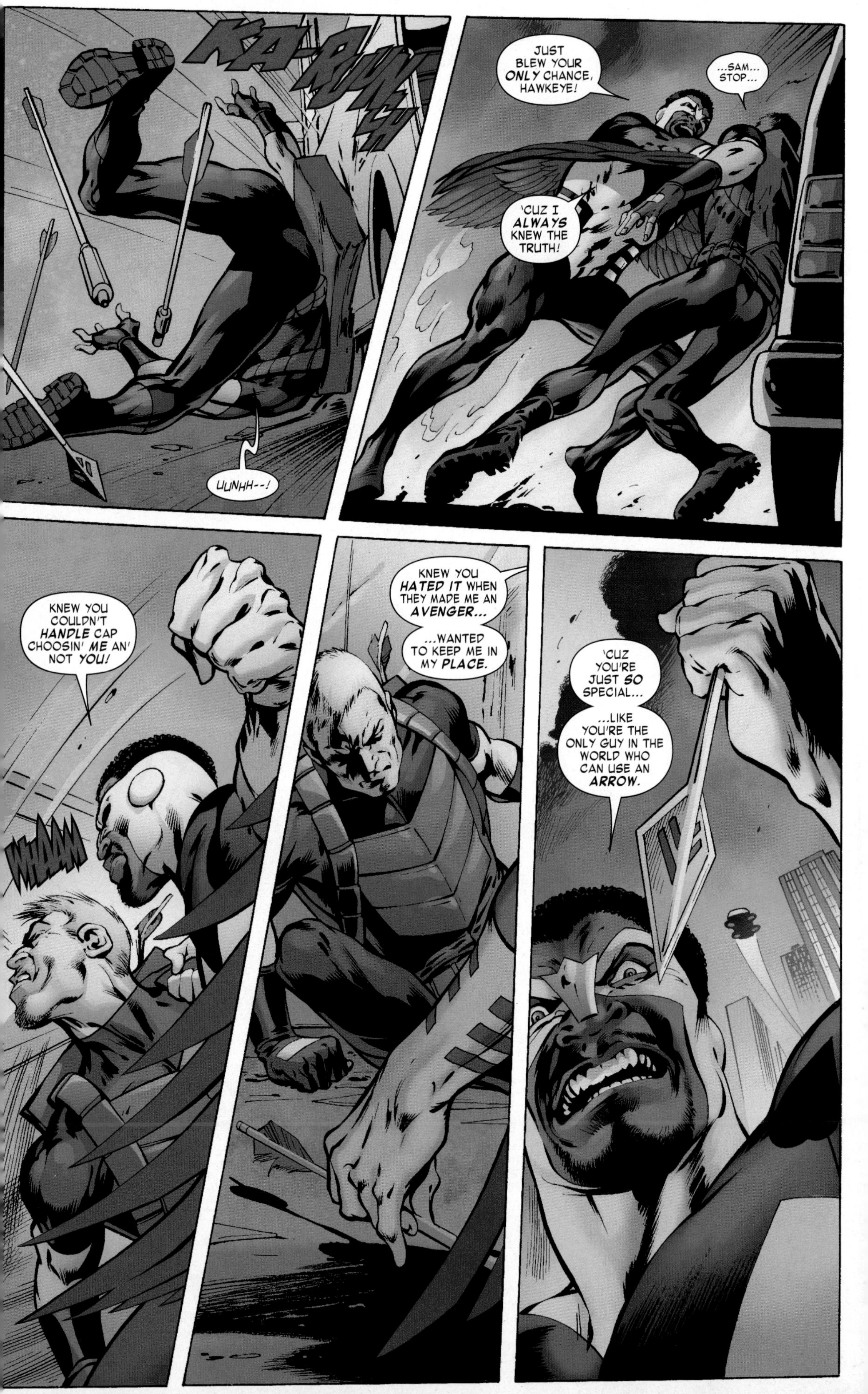
KA-BUM
UUNHH--!
JUST BLEW YOUR ONLY CHANCE, HAWKEYE!
...SAM... STOP...
'CUZ I ALWAYS KNEW THE TRUTH!
KNEW YOU COULDN'T HANDLE CAP CHOOSIN' ME AN' NOT YOU!
WHAAM
KNEW YOU HATED IT WHEN THEY MADE ME AN AVENGER...
...WANTED TO KEEP ME IN MY PLACE.
'CUZ YOU'RE JUST SO SPECIAL...
...LIKE YOU'RE THE ONLY GUY IN THE WORLD WHO CAN USE AN ARROW.

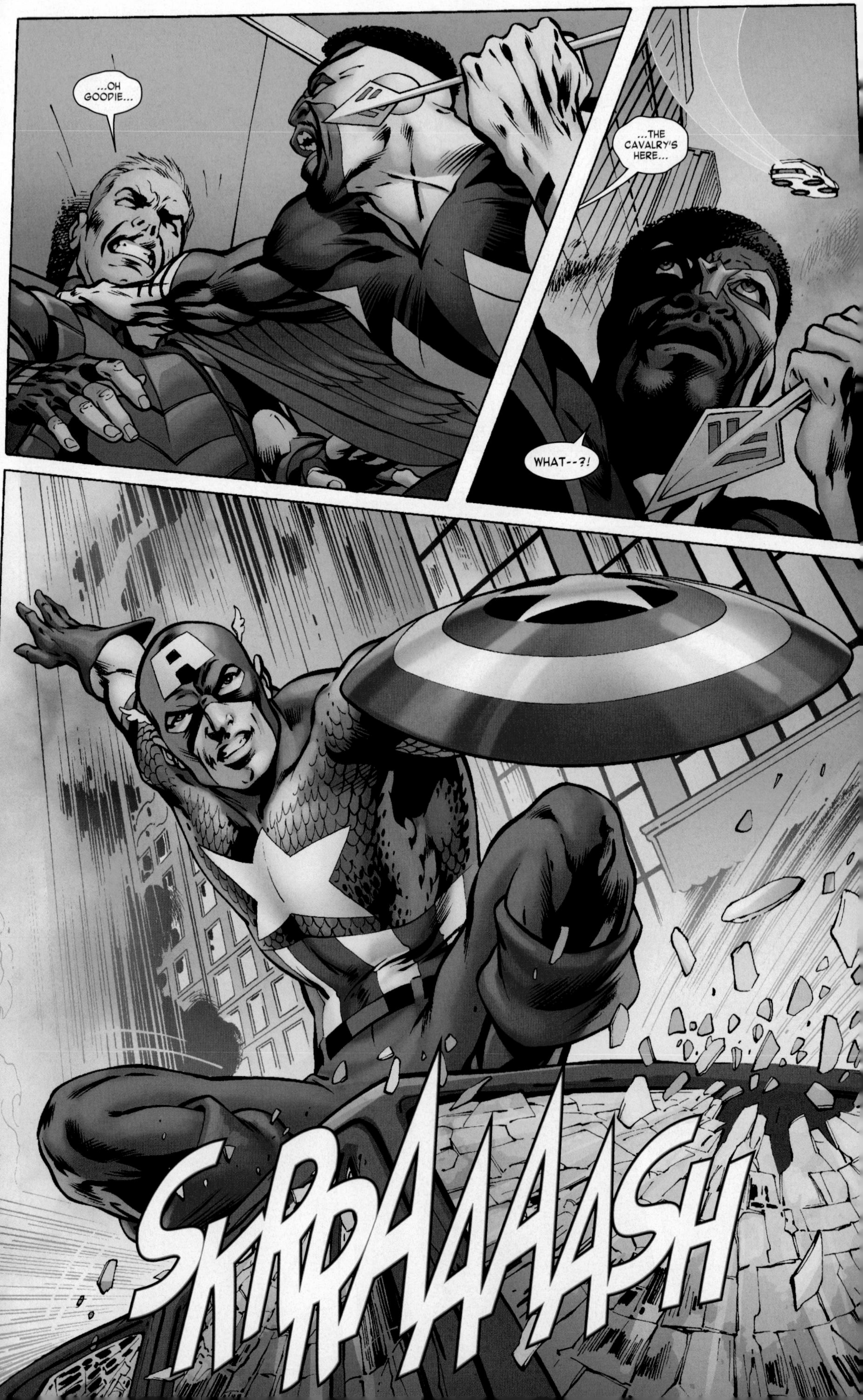
...OH GOODIE...
...THE CAVALRY'S HERE...
WHAT--?!
SKRRAAAAASH

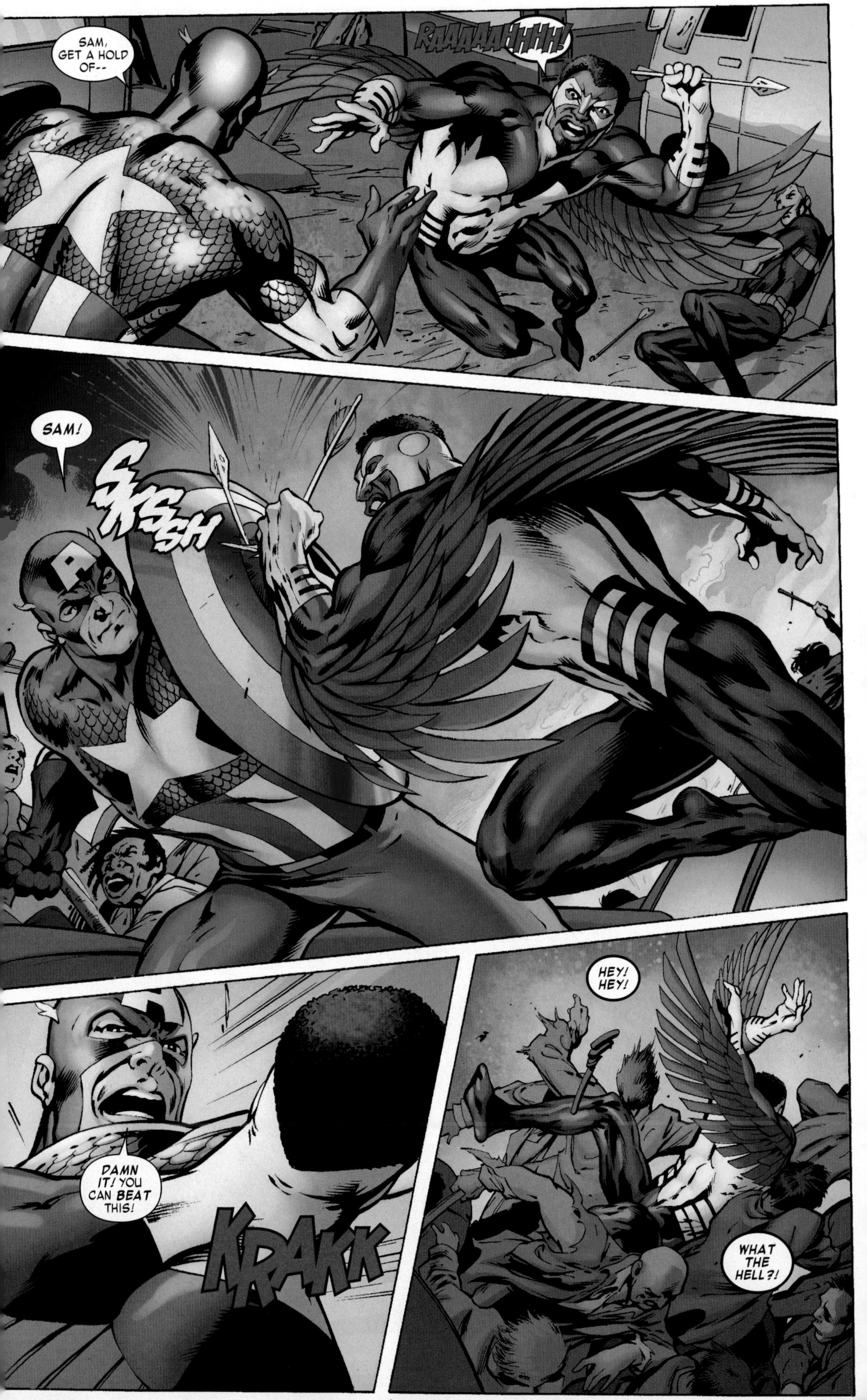
SAM, GET A HOLD OF--
RAAAAAHHHH!
SAM!
SKSSH
DAMN IT! YOU CAN BEAT THIS!
KRAKK
HEY! HEY!
WHAT THE HELL?!

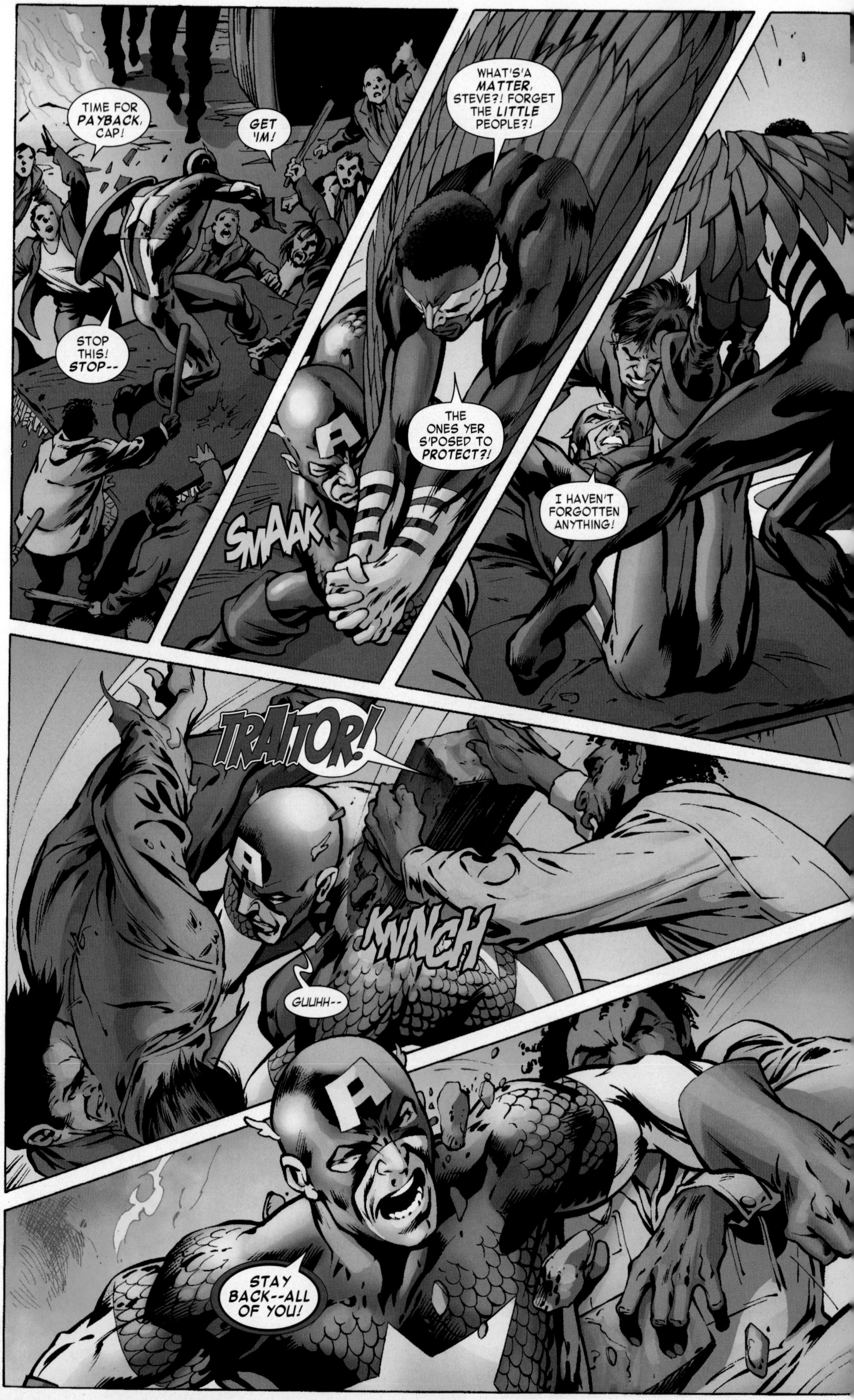
TIME FOR PAYBACK, CAP!
GET 'IM!
STOP THIS! STOP--
WHAT'S'A MATTER, STEVE?! FORGET THE LITTLE PEOPLE?!
THE ONES YER S'POSED TO PROTECT?!
SWAAK
I HAVEN'T FORGOTTEN ANYTHING!
TRAITOR!
KWNCH
GUUHH--
STAY BACK--ALL OF YOU!

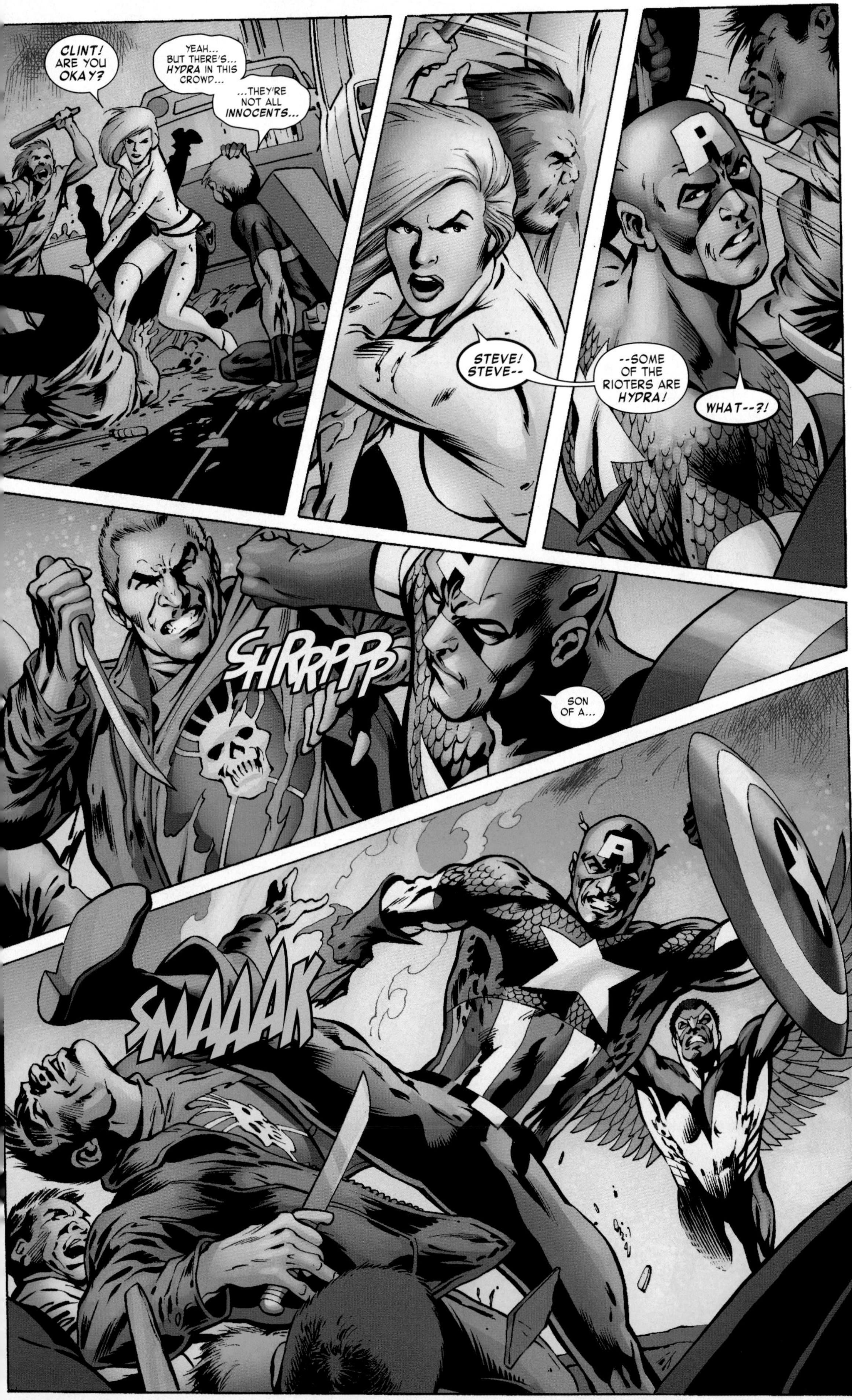
CLINT! ARE YOU OKAY?
YEAH... BUT THERE'S... HYDRA IN THIS CROWD...
...THEY'RE NOT ALL INNOCENTS...
STEVE! STEVE--
--SOME OF THE RIOTERS ARE HYDRA!
WHAT--?!
SHRRPPP
SON OF A...
SMAAAK

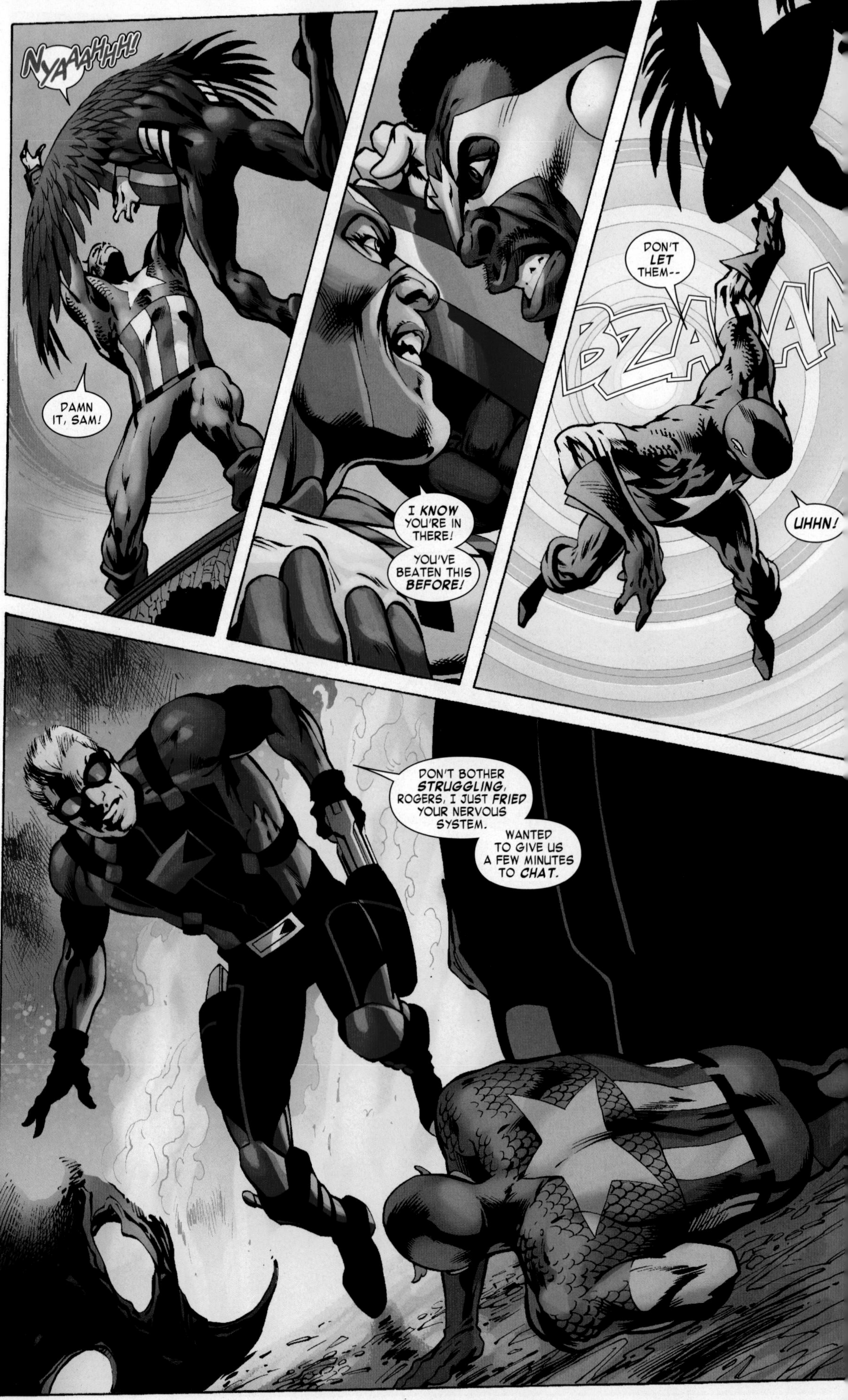
NYAAAHHH!
DAMN IT, SAM!
I KNOW YOU'RE IN THERE!
YOU'VE BEATEN THIS BEFORE!
DON'T LET THEM--
BZAAAM
UHHN!
DON'T BOTHER STRUGGLING, ROGERS, I JUST FRIED YOUR NERVOUS SYSTEM.
WANTED TO GIVE US A FEW MINUTES TO CHAT.

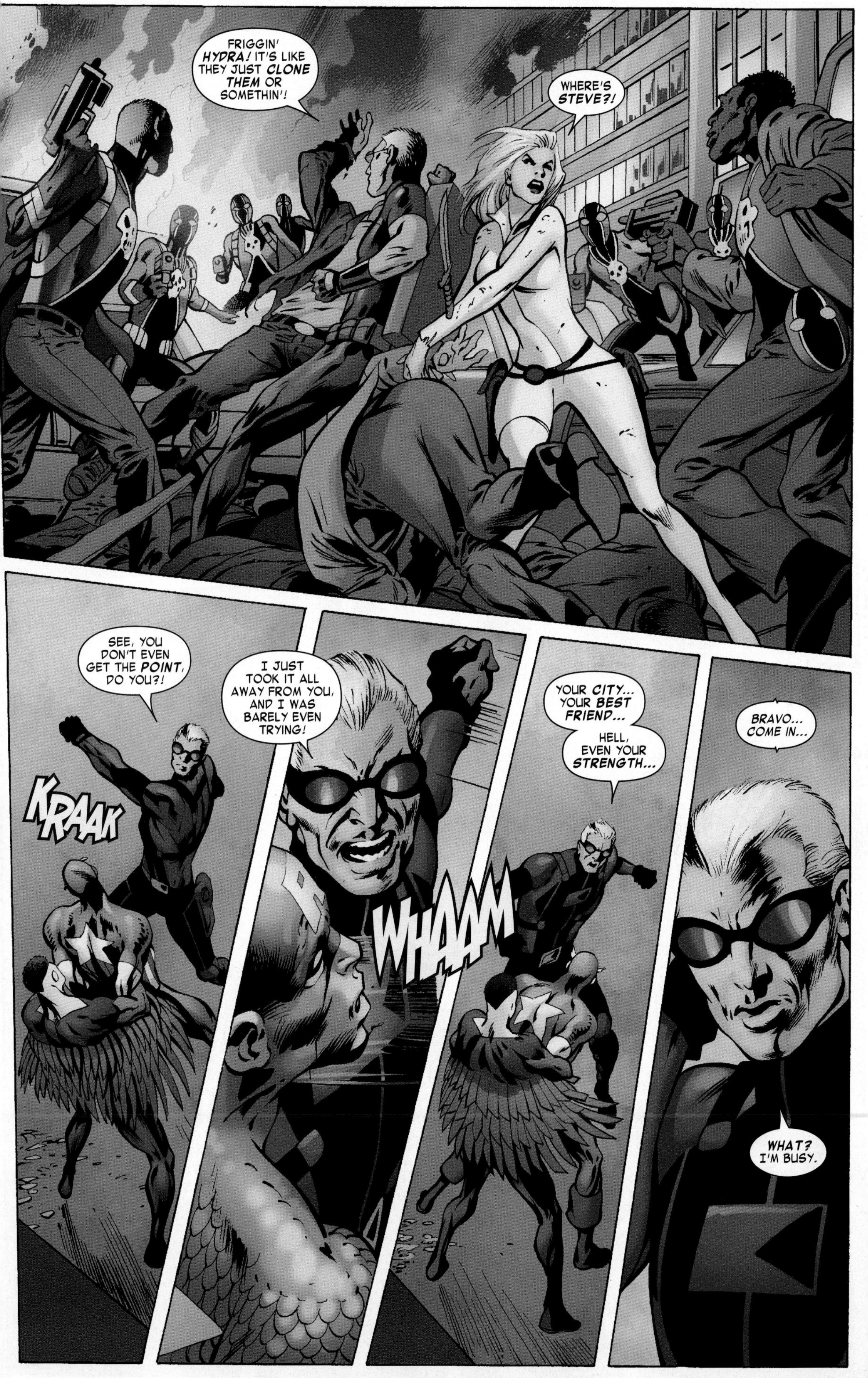
FRIGGIN' HYDRA! IT'S LIKE THEY JUST CLONE THEM OR SOMETHIN'!
WHERE'S STEVE?!
SEE, YOU DON'T EVEN GET THE POINT, DO YOU?!
KRAAK
I JUST TOOK IT ALL AWAY FROM YOU, AND I WAS BARELY EVEN TRYING!
WHAAM
YOUR CITY... YOUR BEST FRIEND...
HELL, EVEN YOUR STRENGTH...
BRAVO... COME IN...
WHAT? I'M BUSY.

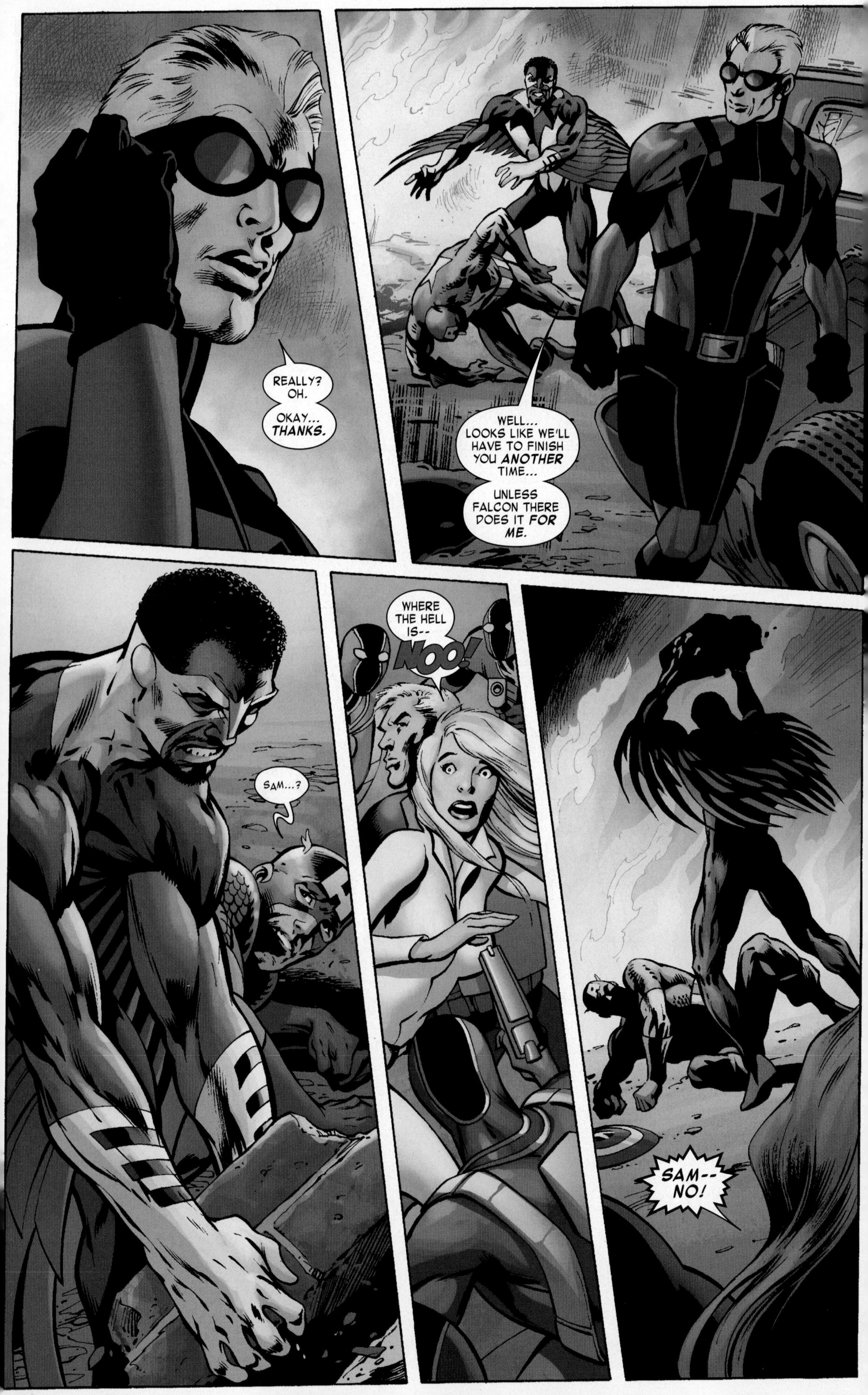
REALLY? OH.
OKAY... THANKS.
WELL... LOOKS LIKE WE'LL HAVE TO FINISH YOU ANOTHER TIME...
UNLESS FALCON THERE DOES IT FOR ME.
SAM...?
WHERE THE HELL IS--
NOO!
SAM-- NO!

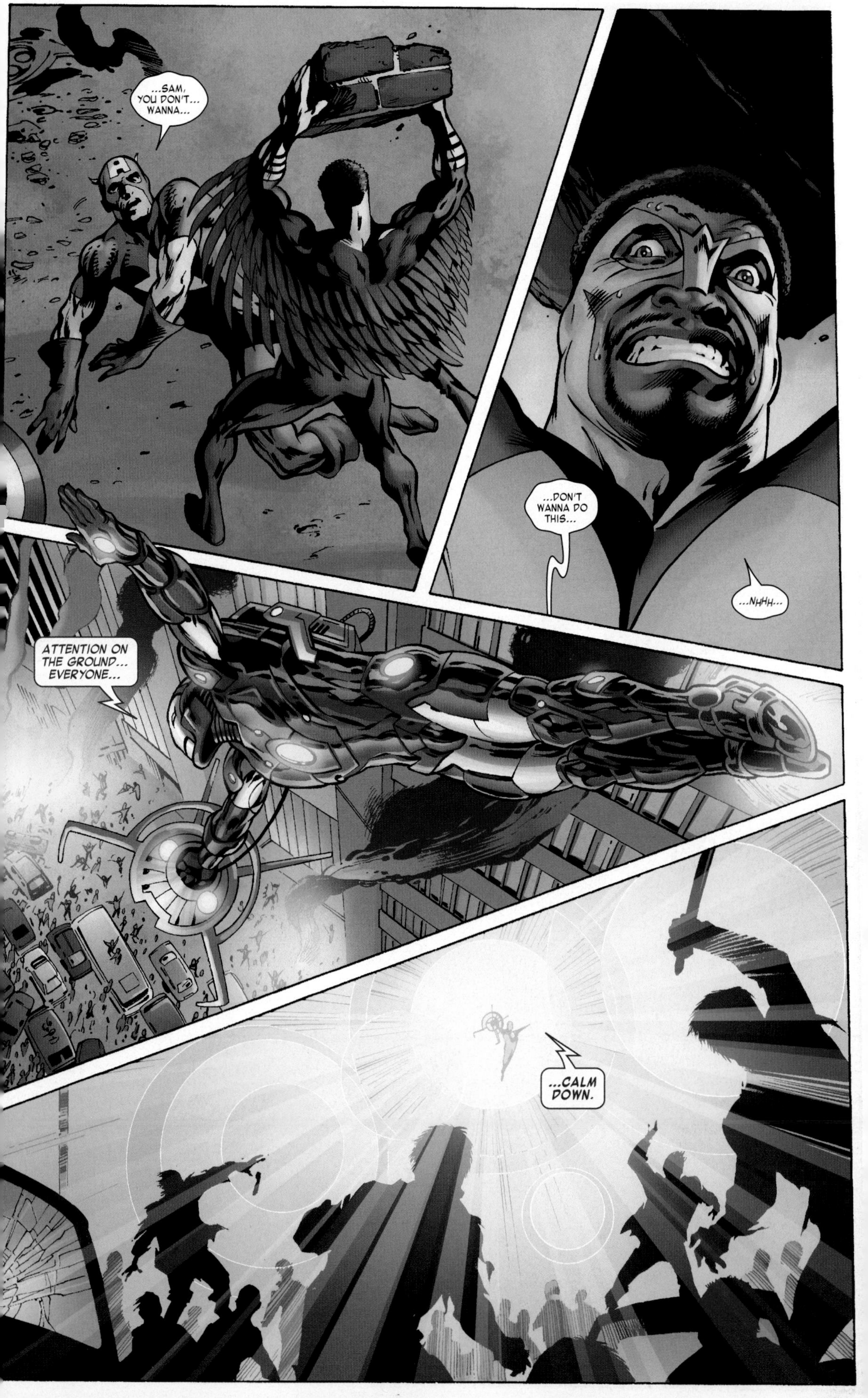
...SAM, YOU DON'T... WANNA...
...DON'T WANNA DO THIS...
...NHHH...
ATTENTION ON THE GROUND... EVERYONE...
...CALM DOWN.

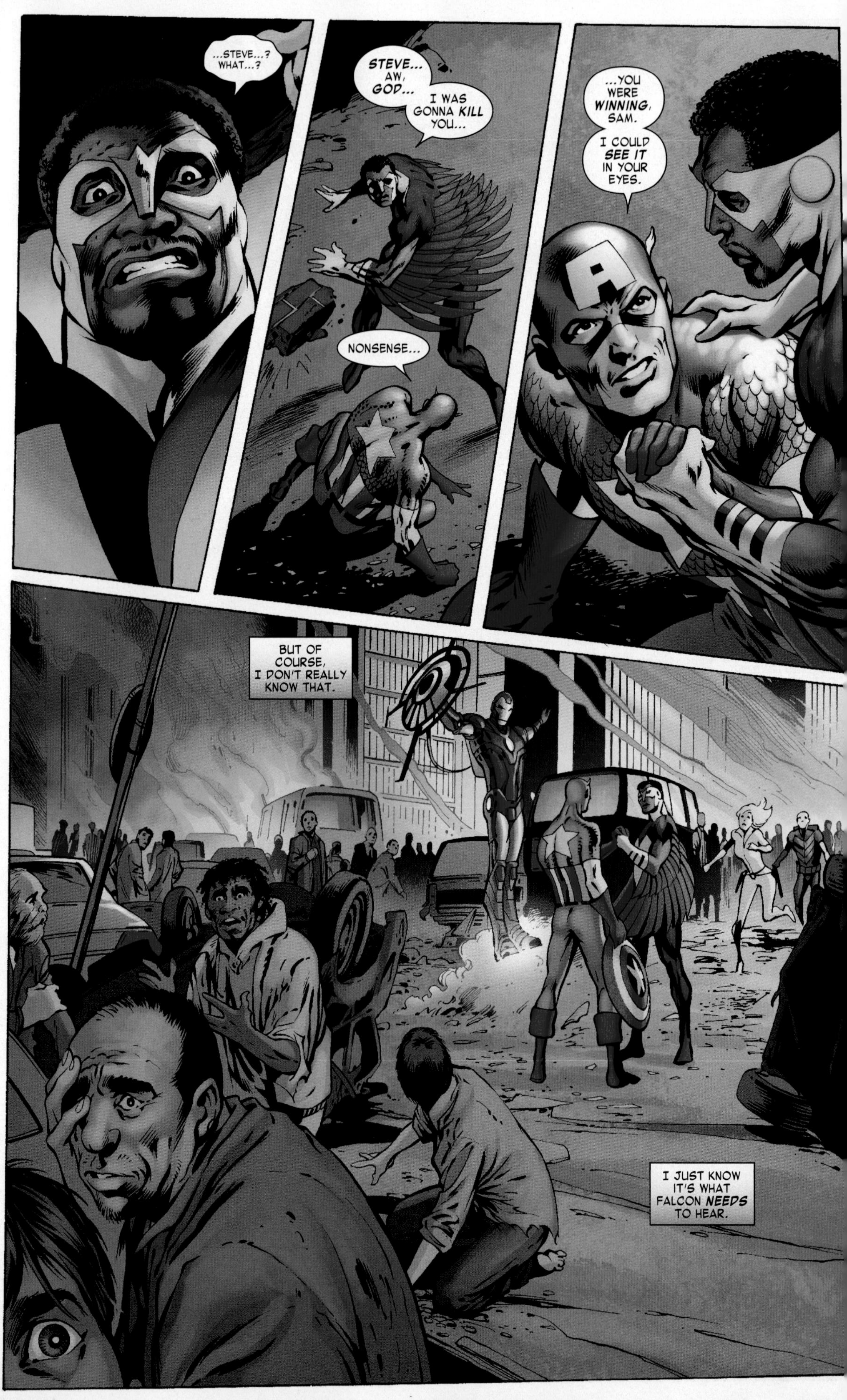
...STEVE...?
WHAT...?
STEVE... AW, GOD...
I WAS GONNA KILL YOU...
NONSENSE...
...YOU WERE WINNING, SAM.
I COULD SEE IT IN YOUR EYES.
BUT OF COURSE, I DON'T REALLY KNOW THAT.
I JUST KNOW IT'S WHAT FALCON NEEDS TO HEAR.

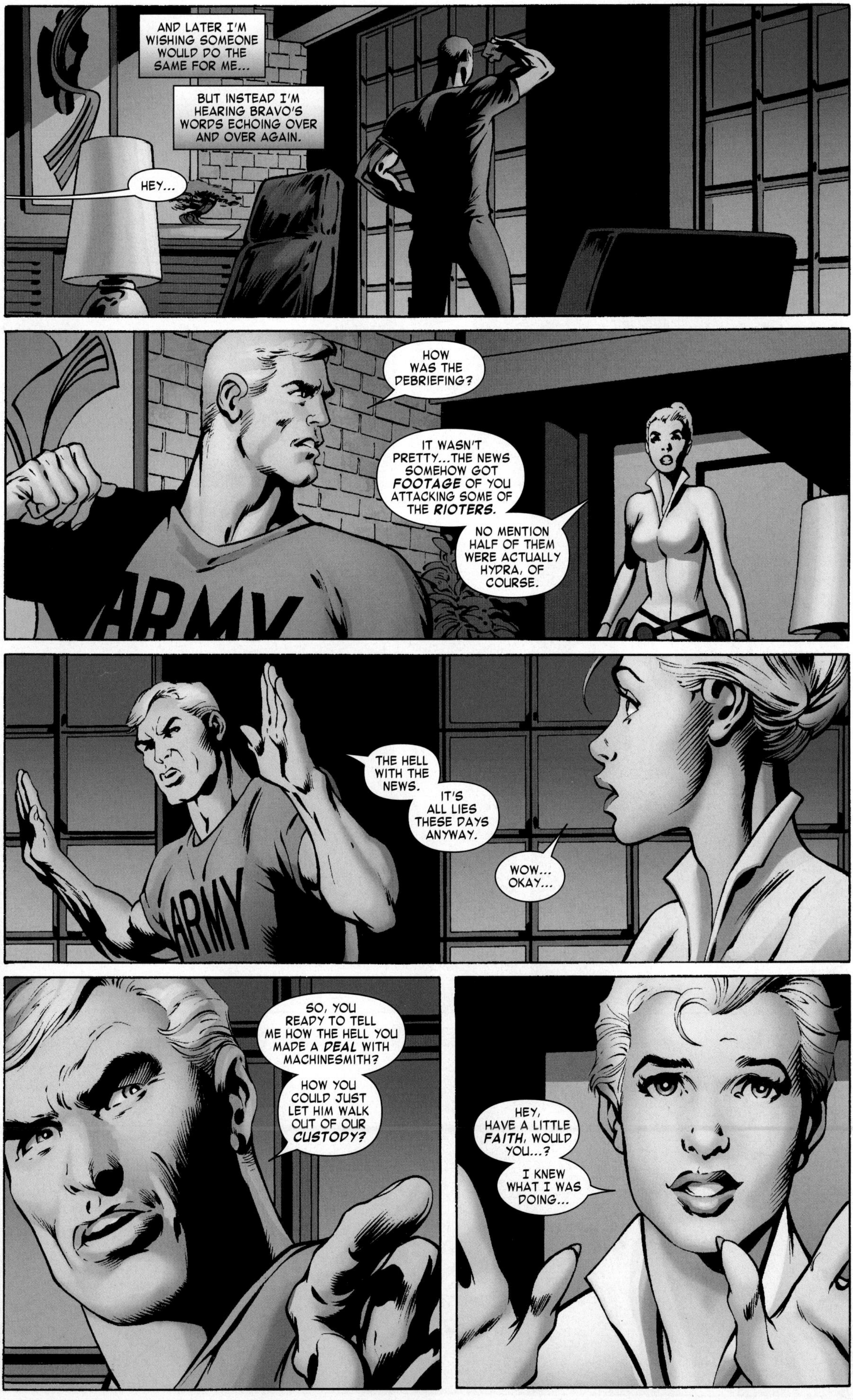
AND LATER I'M WISHING SOMEONE WOULD DO THE SAME FOR ME...
BUT INSTEAD I'M HEARING BRAVO'S WORDS ECHOING OVER AND OVER AGAIN.
HEY...
HOW WAS THE DEBRIEFING?
IT WASN'T PRETTY...THE NEWS SOMEHOW GOT FOOTAGE OF YOU ATTACKING SOME OF THE RIOTERS.
NO MENTION HALF OF THEM WERE ACTUALLY HYDRA, OF COURSE.
ARMY
THE HELL WITH THE NEWS.
IT'S ALL LIES THESE DAYS ANYWAY.
WOW... OKAY...
ARMY
SO, YOU READY TO TELL ME HOW THE HELL YOU MADE A DEAL WITH MACHINESMITH?
HOW YOU COULD JUST LET HIM WALK OUT OF OUR CUSTODY?
HEY, HAVE A LITTLE FAITH, WOULD YOU...?
I KNEW WHAT I WAS DOING...

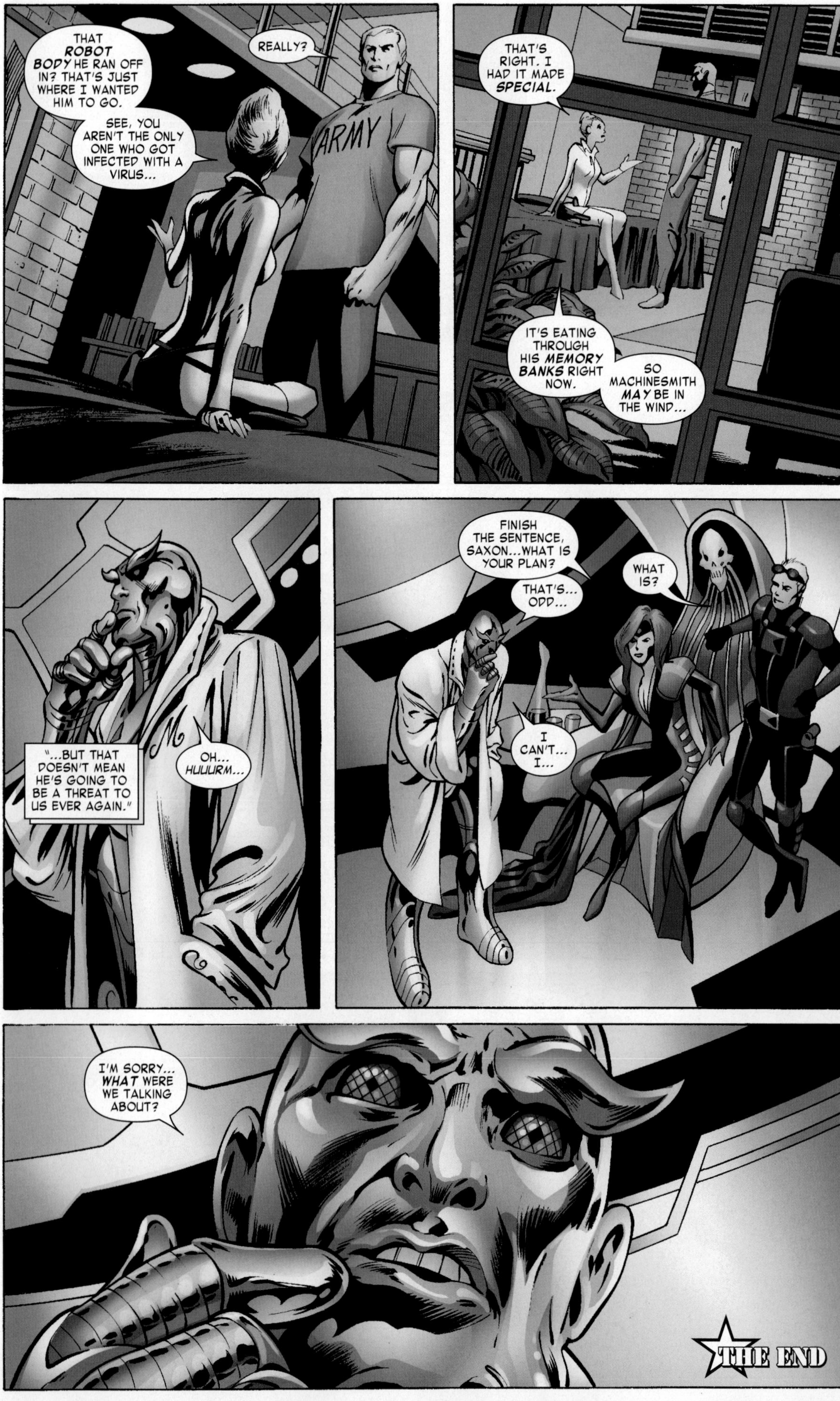

THAT ROBOT BODY HE RAN OFF IN? THAT'S JUST WHERE I WANTED HIM TO GO.
REALLY?
SEE, YOU AREN'T THE ONLY ONE WHO GOT INFECTED WITH A VIRUS...
THAT'S RIGHT. I HAD IT MADE SPECIAL.
IT'S EATING THROUGH HIS MEMORY BANKS RIGHT NOW.
SO MACHINESMITH MAY BE IN THE WIND...
"...BUT THAT DOESN'T MEAN HE'S GOING TO BE A THREAT TO US EVER AGAIN."
OH... HUUURM...
FINISH THE SENTENCE, SAXON...WHAT IS YOUR PLAN?
THAT'S... ODD...
WHAT IS?
I CAN'T... I...
I'M SORRY... WHAT WERE WE TALKING ABOUT?
THE END

#6 MARVEL 50TH ANNIVERSARY VARIANT BY GERALD PAREL

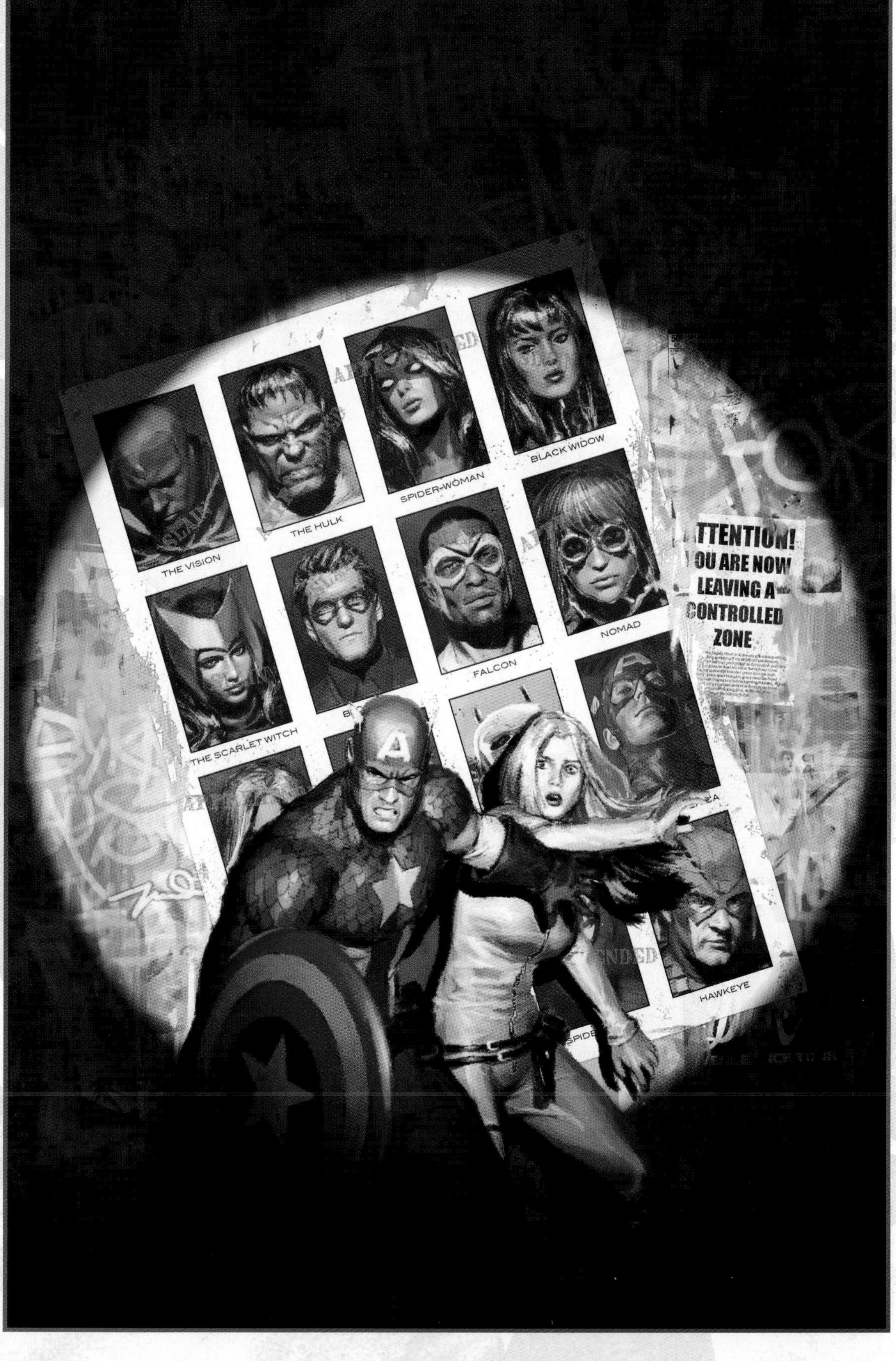
THE VISION
THE HULK
SPIDER-WOMAN
BLACK WIDOW
FALCON
NOMAD
THE SCARLET WITCH
HAWKEYE
ATTENTION!
YOU ARE NOW
LEAVING A
CONTROLLED
ZONE

#7 VENOM VARIANT BY MIKE PERKINS & JOHN RAUCH

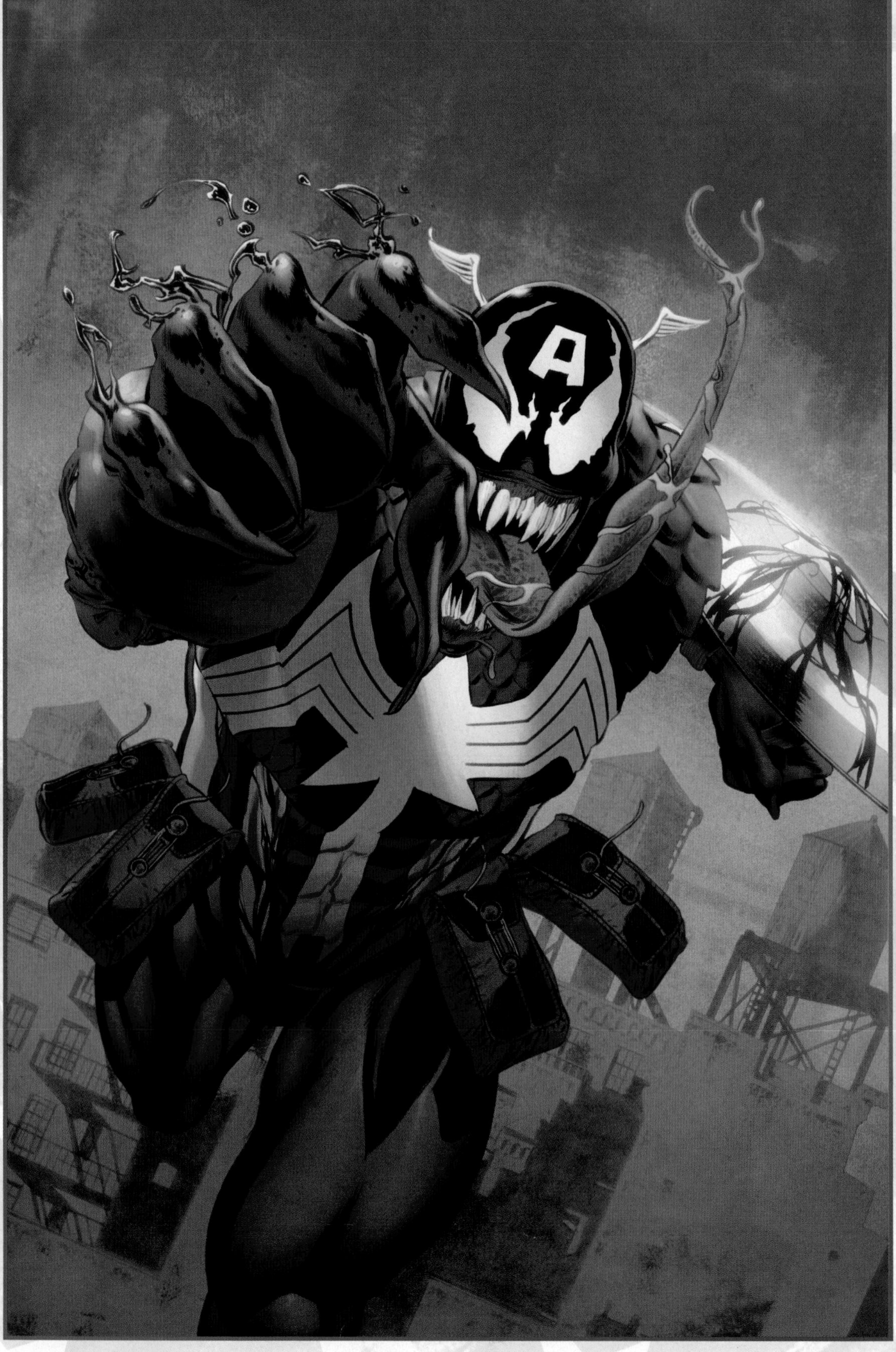

#10 AVENGERS ART APPRECIATION VARIANT BY GERALD PAREL

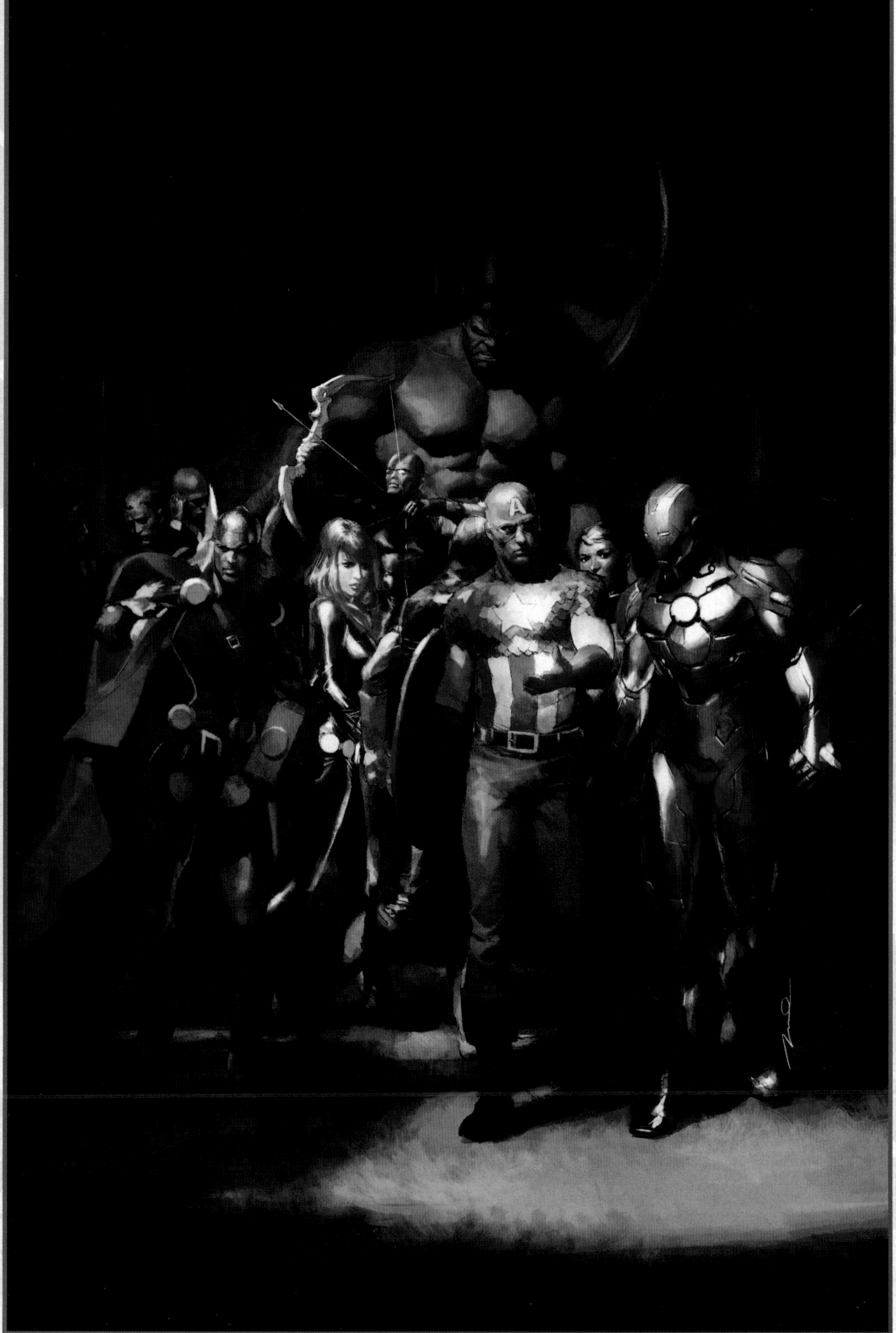